eality. Cogito ergo sum Ejosanai Friday, April 2, 1999 at 1:13 PM PST The simulated world which we are told we believe and which we cannot see beyond. I think, therefore I am programmed to think. JD Friday, April 2, 1999 at 1:13 PM PST What do you want it
LOL I mean it shows the deepest fear of all human kind... the reality of our everyday life, that we are not really free but slaves of our own minds... and it does it in a very interes... What the Matrix is? hehehe, it's what you want it
s the world of your perception. Control perception, and you control reality. kevin Friday, April 2, 1999 at 1:10 PM PST The Matrix is a construct - a simulacrum. A copy of a world tha... movie KIC
your screen. It will prompt you to enter "Code or Email". In this box, enter one of the following phrases and gain access to secret areas on this site): GEOF TRINITY DEJA VU SKROCE... day, Ap
y life josh Friday, April 2, 1999 at 1:07 PM PST If you care what we, the scattered mutant masses, eager to consume whatever you throw at us think... know that what I witnessed... speed
acle GREAT COMBO and GOOD TIMING!!!! g ulysse Friday, April 2, 1999 at 1:05 PM PST ...It's the smell! agent749220 Friday, April 2, 1999 at 1:02 PM PST Best Movie I've seen in... IZ Frida
see the true meaning of this. Like it states above. "What is the Matrix?" What is 'our' matrix? And how does this movie apply to our life and world? The plot was great. I just hope others can see it for what it really... mpress
ble purchase a poster...or any item pertaining to the matrix thanks lolly lolly Friday, April 2, 1999 at 12:55 PM PST The Matrix is another virtual world that corresponds with reality and computer basics as well. Brian "the Dragon" T Friday, April 2, 19
hey make it into a game. Don't you think that would be awesome? Able to jump building to building, hand to hand combat, and of course the awesome weapons! It would be cool if you could go through the entire city too. Stephen Friday, April 2, 1999
Guns, Trinity Neo Friday, April 2, 1999 at 12:48 PM PST I once had creole gator stew. It wasnt bad, but Gator tastes like chicken... Roo Dog Friday, April 2, 1999 at 12:47 PM PST Unfortunetly, nobody can be told what the matrix is. Xavier Friday, Ap
nly be able to wait. Is this world real? Or is it only Wonderland? Pinhead Friday, April 2, 1999 at 12:45 PM PST Is there a Matrix in which we can live peacefully?? Rob Friday, April 2, 1999 at 12:45 PM PST Oh My God this is the best movie i've se
REAT movie!! Fatima Friday, April 2, 1999 at 12:43 PM PST steak Funky Smell Friday, April 2, 1999 at 12:41 PM PST This movie was unbelievable! Not only does it have great fight and chase scenes, but it challenges your mind with its deep messag
T Even more beautiful than John Woo's, This Movie is a Piece Of Art. Not only for the visuals, but also for the excellent soundtrack, the good acting, and the complex story. A Piece Of Art I Tell You. Period. Funky Smell Friday, April 2, 1999 at 12:38 P
T I think it is the dimensional break between our world on earth and someone else's. David Friday, April 2, 1999 at 12:33 PM PST i thought it was the greatest movie i had ever seen. i loved the vfx it so was cool. i liked the panoramic video jobs. i ho
12:32 PM PST This is the coolest movie I have ever seen and I have already seen it 3 times. I am going again tonight. I want this movie to make special effects history. Tom G Friday, April 2, 1999 at 12:31 PM PST This movie was on ten!!!! I AM goi
es and Carrie-Ann Moss were wearing. They were sweeeet. Also, please tell me where I can find the shades that Carrie-Ann was wearing. I have to get a pair. Thanks. hunter Friday, April 2, 1999 at 12:30 PM PST rockin' movie rockin' web page Gh
he Matrix is such an excellent movie. Every now and then a movie comes along and it makes you analyze yourself and the world around you...what is real and what is not real? How can anyone define something as real? A.W Friday, April 2, 1999 at 12:2
y, April 2, 1999 at 12:23 PM PST I absolutely loved it. One of the best sci-fi movies ever! And of course I really really love Keanu Reeves. Cholinthia Friday, April 2, 1999 at 12:23 PM PST The matrix is a piecewise continuous function from zero to inf
onderland;epoc,switch,mouse;battery;phonecall operator; red, blue, tank, xion, zion. I can't think of any thing else Agggghhh!! Frost Friday, April 2, 1999 at 12:21 PM PST Need more Codes? Besides 'steak' ... hmmm? Passwords: morpheus trinity gu
jshamar Friday, April 2, 1999 at 12:14 PM PST The matrix is our reality. Or is it really reality. I think this is the best movie of the Year. Steve_069 Friday, April 2, 1999 at 12:10 PM PST The Matrix is a dream world made to cover our eyes from t
your movie. Brian Friday, April 2, 1999 at 12:10 PM PST See that little black box in the upper right? Click it and enter "steak." CrashOverride Friday, April 2, 1999 at 12:10 PM PST The matrix will take your mind to a new way of thinking... .So sit ba
t the troops. We literally are just a collection of atoms, reacting electrochemically to our environment..Who is to say what is real, and what is not? LOVED IT! Casey Friday, April 2, 1999 at 12:07 PM PST Reality is no longer Real Double Down Frid
ks ass babe! Glad I saw it and I'm gonna see it again. You guys did one helluva excellent job. One helluva movie I'll never forget. Keeps up the good work G-Theory Friday, April 2, 1999 at 12:05 PM PST Don't move...we have you covered Jer Friday, Ap
Reeves is too matrixy for words to describe. Jayde Friday, April 2, 1999 at 12:02 PM PST The Matrix is an energy field created by all living things which surrounds us and holds the universe together. Or is that the force? Either one ruled in more wa
ha, our Omega, it is our beginning, and it is our end. To realize the matrix is to become the exception, to become a virus and you will be expelled into the cold darkness that is truth, cast out of eden with no hope of return. If you know, you will feel it a
1999 at 11:56 AM PST The Matrix?...Unfortunately, no one can be told what the Matrix is. But you have seen it. You have lived it. The world you think you exist in...that is the Matrix. Sorry friend, your whole life is just a battery pack for A.I Your wh
AM PST The matrix is a highly trained and experienced group of beings that study and collect different people to experiment with. They are unknown to anyone except a select few. Deanna D Friday, April 2, 1999 at 11:51 AM PST the matrix is a co
Friday, April 2, 1999 at 11:50 AM PST This Web Page was done beautifully! Kelly Friday, April 2, 1999 at 11:50 AM PST The movie was incredible. I haven't seen a worthy sci-fi movie since Terminator 2. This movie is definitely on my most favorite li
at 11:49 AM PST UNFORTUNATELY, NO ONE CAN BE TOLD WHAT THE MATRIX IS...YOU HAVE TO SEE IT FOR YOURSELF THE MATRIX Friday, April 2, 1999 at 11:48 AM PST Too COOL for words!!!! Unicorn13 Friday, April 2, 1999 at 11:47 AM P
2, 1999 at 11:45 AM PST I AM WHAT I AM, I AM WHAT YOU SEE, AND THAT WILL NEVER CHANGE. THE MATRIX Friday, April 2, 1999 at 11:45 AM PST Take me back. I'm ready to join the forces of Zion. Definite Oscars for the talented a
HT! True to comic,scifi, and Anime fans! This is the way action movies should be made! I'll take the red pill any day! Alonzo Friday, April 2, 1999 at 11:43 AM PST The Matrix is the thin line betwen reality and fiction. The scary part is when you don't kn
blinds us from the truth. Unfortunately, no one can be told what the matrix is...you have to see it for yourself. Morpheus Friday, April 2, 1999 at 11:40 AM PST The Matrix is awesome. I am the " One " Robert Friday, April 2, 1999 at 11:37 AM PS
k brown Friday, April 2, 1999 at 11:35 AM PST I didn't see the movie yet. But I'm sure it kicks ass. Jason Friday, April 2, 1999 at 11:34 AM PST I'll let all of you know on Monday after I see it this weekend. Last night I saw the making of it on HBO t
erfectly, I can't wait for the sequels. In fact, I'm going back to the movie theater right now to see it again. Jonas K W Friday, April 2, 1999 at 11:31 AM PST One Word...RAW! AtlChip10 Friday, April 2, 1999 at 11:30 AM PST You guys KICK ASS!!! Th
nding bod to boot! Gloria Friday, April 2, 1999 at 11:29 AM PST We are all in the MATRIX now... MAX Friday, April 2, 1999 at 11:26 AM PST But this movie KICKS @SS. Love the fight scenes! I'm thinking of Keanu in a whole new light! Gcc Friday, Ap
y in where we live, but it is just a figment of our imagination. Ginger Friday, April 2, 1999 at 11:22 AM PST This is definitely one of the best movies that I have ever seen!! The entire movie kicked ass!! Cindra Friday, April 2, 1999 at 11:22 AM PST
now, if it were actually real. Our world would be the Matrix Michael G Friday, April 2, 1999 at 11:20 AM PST It is the reality of a single universe transposed over all three existing universes. Courtney K Friday, April 2, 1999 at 11:18 AM PST PERHA
eyes55 Friday, April 2, 1999 at 11:16 AM PST The Matrix is this thing. I'd describe it to you all but then I'd have to eliminate you. Pedro Friday, April 2, 1999 at 11:15 AM PST Simply, the best movie I've seen since 1977 - I was 12 years old then a
999 at 11:11 AM PST The Matrix is the reality of reality, the essence of life. A world where one receives so much pestilence and famine; the Matrix soon takes over. In such ignorance, we human beings do not realize that the Matrix has us. It has cap
at 11:09 AM PST As an avid viewer of Sci-fi film and cinema, I think I can safely say this will go into my collection with Dune, the Star Wars Trilogy, and Blade Runner. Wow...I'm speechless. Alex I Friday, April 2, 1999 at 11:08 AM PST May the trut
, April 2, 1999 at 11:00 AM PST Dear Matrix, All I can say is that this movie took me over. The Matrix has been out here for two days and I have already seen it twice. I plan to go see it again today. I just want to say thanks for the incredible image
AM PST DuDe! The MaTrIx is real! v2 Friday, April 2, 1999 at 10:56 AM PST Being conformed to the image and likeness of our flesh. While the truth is hidden in our spirit, but made real in the word. Holden Friday, April 2, 1999 at 10:56 AM PST I
9 at 10:51 AM PST I'm dying to get the sound clip of Trinity saying "Dodge this!" Can anyone help? Thanks. This movie ROCKED!! It's this kind of movie that makes people need to buy superior home theatre systems. Jason Friday, April 2, 1999 at 10:5
EHOLDER of THE MATRIX" Trish Friday, April 2, 1999 at 10:48 AM PST Great film! Robert Friday, April 2, 1999 at 10:47 AM PST thought the movie was gonna have cool special effects, and a lame plot, but it rocked, going to see it again tonight B
more than I expected and it blew me away. It has awesome special effects and a great, eerie story. I'm going to watch it again! Albert Lo Friday, April 2, 1999 at 10:45 AM PST A bad ass movie! JoeWG Friday, April 2, 1999 at 10:44 AM PST I wan
appenin' man. Its been out three days and i've seen it twice!! Pelumi D Friday, April 2, 1999 at 10:41 AM PST The Matrix, Perhaps the best action/sci-fi this year! Everything was well done and never a dull moment. This movie was highly outstanding a
Do you know where could I get a autograph of Carrie-Anne Moss? Tommy H Friday, April 2, 1999 at 10:38 AM PST What was it that Neo sold in the beginning of the flick? It reminded me of that movie Strange Days, is that what he was selling? all 'n
April 2, 1999 at 10:30 AM PST just saw the movie-was totally blown away! Best movie Reeves has ever done -intricate story-superior to the pablum moviegoers are usually force fed. Long live the matrix! L.ridge Friday, April 2, 1999 at 10:27 AM P
ovie is still running in my head after I've seen it 2 days ago. The best movie I've seen in my life. Now the matrix is in me!!! Gabit S. Friday, April 2, 1999 at 10:22 AM PST Cool movie, the off the world visual effects are awesome, and I can't wait fo
the best movie I've ever seen and I want to know when it comes out on dvd. Ive already seen it 4 times. 2x opening day, the day after and today Justin Friday, April 2, 1999 at 10:18 AM PST Doesn't that just ruin it for those who wanted to figure it o
M PST HERE'S HOW TO USE YOUR CODES (1.a) Go the front page, click on either the FLASH version or the regular version (doesn't matter). Click on the dirty keyboard at the bottom-right-hand corner of the image. - or - (1.b) click on the TINY wind
guilty pleasures Friday, April 2, 1999 at 10:15 AM PST Fantastic site and excellent flick. Loved having my Keanu moment. It left me wanting to see more. Have to see it again on screen. Medusa Friday, April 2, 1999 at 10:15 AM PST Cool movie...C
t last night and I think I'll go again this weekend... TNL Friday, April 2, 1999 at 8:35 AM PST x Friday, April 2, 1999 at 10:11 AM PST that was cool. thanx passwrd. Anymore? Zero Trust Friday, April 2, 1999 at 10:08 AM PST trinity also works fo
e don't know were we really are, but instead leaves us in a dream world. By understanding this dream we have the ability to manipulate The Matrix and do what ever we want. Asesino Friday, April 2, 1999 at 10:07 AM PST What is The Matrix? Aweso
2, 1999 at 10:06 AM PST This movie KIckED AsS!! never have I seen a movie that can compare to this one!! It was the best it also had a KiLLEr SouNdTrAcK!! Letty Friday, April 2, 1999 at 10:06 AM PST Do not unplug.0101 Friday, April 2, 1999
elp? Wouldn't he need someone to "plug him in" and keep an eye on him as per usual... hmm. Zach Friday, April 2, 1999 at 10:04 AM PST My favourite movie, gotta go beg for some cash so I can see it another couple of times Good job cast and cre
OW * Guns/GUNS/guns * Deja Vu/DEJAVU/DejaVu * STEAK/steak/Steak (this one is the extra Flash animation... gives a LOT of spoilers) I'll probably post this whole thingie up on a web site somewhere w/ pictures or something... really, it's dead eas
ssive machines that have taken over the planet. Kris Friday, April 2, 1999 at 10:01 AM PST A visual reality, accepted by the mind, created by the mind. Only the one will conquer ibiza Friday, April 2, 1999 at 10:01 AM PST Great film...if you like Sc
favorite!). Talk about in-depth content. Cool, cool, cool, SITE! Code=steak...Phillip Friday, April 2, 1999 at 9:56 AM PST what was the name of the old lady Neo visits to see if he was the "one"? Zero Trust Friday, April 2, 1999 at 9:55 AM PST ill tell y
Friday, April 2, 1999 at 9:55 AM PST THERE IS NO SPOON! BUT THERE MIGHT BE A FORK! DAVID S Friday, April 2, 1999 at 9:55 AM PST Keanu was GREAT. The movie ROCKED! I could not stop talking about it the next day. I am trying to get all t
laces, welcome 2 the brave new "real" world. SameNation Friday, April 2, 1999 at 9:54 AM PST The matrix is the world that has been pulled over our eyes. & The matrix may exist now. Archangel Friday, April 2, 1999 at 9:53 AM PST Great movie..
honorable Busta Rhymes"Gimme Some Mo'!" godzookie Friday, April 2, 1999 at 9:52 AM PST Oh yeah! The guns... like a holster for 10 of them! And Morpheus' shades! Hell yeha! I gotta find out where these guys shop...*chuckles* Coda Friday, April
here...in the present. The Matrix is ruled and controlled by "aliens" from another dimension, and when our time's up we get unplugged from the Matrix. Earth is just an illusion and WE need to WAKE UP! 0101 Friday, April 2, 1999 at 9:48 AM PST
ORPHEUS IS WEARING? THEY ARE KEWL!! ALSO KEWL IS NEO'S TRENCH-COAT!!! DAVID Friday, April 2, 1999 at 9:45 AM PST *sighs* What's the deal with steak here guys? Coda Friday, April 2, 1999 at 9:44 AM PST definitely one of the best fil
hile - SEE IT. pOOch Friday, April 2, 1999 at 9:44 AM PST Amazing Movie... Metro... Friday, April 2, 1999 at 9:41 AM PST This movie was "OFF DA HOOK!" And I'm glad that they gave Georgia Tech its props on their links page. RuffRyder Friday, Ap
movie is one of the best movies I have seen all year. The special f/x are unbelievable and the fight scenes are the coolest I have ever seen in a film. Amanda Friday, April 2, 1999 at 9:35 AM PST THE MATRIX IS DEEP: IT IS NOT LARGE IT IS NOT SMA
This is the best movie I have ever seen. schnick Friday, April 2, 1999 at 9:32 AM PST A great little exercise in style! One half compelling but murky sci-fi, the other half an homage to Hong Kong action! For some reason, it all comes together quite w
iday, April 2, 1999 at 9:30 AM PST steak fireman Friday, April 2, 1999 at 9:30 AM PST I think it's a strong possibility that the Matrix is real. Now the fun part is figuring out how to rebel...It's not so easy to find people who share your ideas and w
ow our brains to compute the idea. Travis K Friday, April 2, 1999 at 9:27 AM PST What is the Matrix? A new form of communication christopher J Friday, April 2, 1999 at 9:26 AM PST A whole new universe Corey B Friday, April 2, 1999 at 9:26 A
nation of... Martial arts, latex clothing, a brilliant plot, gripping cinematography, excellent acting, vivid special effects... Definitely a monumental movie!!! Just when you start to think there's no more NEW movie ideas out there... then there's THE MATR
2 AM PST Start to believe!! And go see this movie a million times!! Alix M Friday, April 2, 1999 at 9:22 AM PST THE QUESTION DRIVES US... THE ANSWER FINDS US... **THE RINGWRAITHS (AGENTS) ARE OUT IN BLACK...IN THE LAND OF MORD
ovie exciting. There was never a moment where I relaxed in my chair, because the movie was so intense, all the time. Excellent piece of work. Is there a way I can get a movie poster of The Matrix? Kyle Friday, April 2, 1999 at 9:19 AM PST The Mat
, April 2, 1999 at 9:15 AM PST All I can tell you is that there is no spoon. Swifty Friday, April 2, 1999 at 9:15 AM PST THERE IS NO SPOON... TC Friday, April 2, 1999 at 9:15 AM PST This movie is the greatest movie I have ever seen!!! See it
the matrix tells us what life is really like. Join The Rebellion. Lexicon Friday, April 2, 1999 at 9:08 AM PST A virtual fantasy used to enslave humanity Neo-9 Friday, April 2, 1999 at 9:07 AM PST AFTER THE MATRIX THE WORLD BENDS IN MY MI
way that they were set up and shot. I would definitely like to see a sequel, but only if the plot is good. I don't want to ruin the "goodness and quality" of the film at the expense trying to appease the public with a Matrix 2". Manny Friday, April 2,
999 at 9:04 AM PST Terminator meets Ghost in the Shell Great Movie jankster Friday, April 2, 1999 at 9:04 AM PST AMAZING!! I think old George Lucas MAY have to look over his shoulder on this one. I think I'll take the red pill...Skingraft Friday, Ap
, we wouldn't even know it. Gramadin Friday, April 2, 1999 at 9:01 AM PST Probably one of the best Sci-fi films i have seen. Nothing can compare to the story, visual effects and the believable characters. It was true to comic-sci-fi and anime and it w
days 8. total recall 7. the planet of the apes 6. blade runner 5. space oddyssey 2001 4. dark city 3. star wars trilogy 2. phantom menace 1. the Matrix!!!! Slave 0101 Friday, April 2, 1999 at 9:00 AM PST ACCESS TWO: STEAK Morpheus Friday, Ap
pleasures Friday, April 2, 1999 at 8:56 AM PST gonna see the movie tonight, it looks amazing! Blaise R Friday, April 2, 1999 at 8:52 AM PST I went out and bought the soundtrack last night, it has some Damn good songs on it! I am listening to it no
s well! If you see the movie wait and watch the credits-the music is great! Rage Against the Machine was an excellent choice for the soundtrack! BTW what is the password (steak) used for anyway? LOL I sure hope that there is a sequel! If anyone do
49 AM PST THe matrix is real... They made the movie so if it happened no one would believe it Neo Friday, April 2, 1999 at 8:48 AM PST tom anderson was ok, but neo was even better ;)) Friday, April 2, 1999 at 8:48 AM PST Best damn movie site
pril 2, 1999 at 8:42 AM PST Deep, Inspirational, action packed...Great to see action that doesn't sacrifice the true purpose of storytelling...Took me several hours to calm my thought process...talk about a neural workout... hope this sparks some sk
"humans taken over by artificial intelligence" story. But, I guess when you write a conspiracy story, you have to take things all the way - or go home. A masterpiece. skunkboy Friday, April 2, 1999 at 8:39 AM PST A computer that evolved into a god o
teak... enjoy! Great movie, BTW... I went to see it last night and I think I'll go again this weekend... TNL Friday, April 2, 1999 at 8:35 AM PST BOOTS!!! NEED I SAY MORE? Friday, April 2, 1999 at 8:31 AM PST Better than real! It will make you ? eve
MUST see!!! Special effects were off the hinges... Jinx Friday, April 2, 1999 at 8:21 AM PST I'm going to go watch the Matrix this Sunday and last night I went and bought the soundtrack which is FANTASTIC! I hope the movie is as good as the sour
Reality Czech Friday, April 2, 1999 at 8:19 AM PST I think just about everyone is going to see the movie again. So stop telling us. Flower Friday, April 2, 1999 at 8:16 AM PST I loved the movie! I'm going to see it again today! Elean00r Friday, April
nd the Ju jitsu. THE MATRIX Friday, April 2, 1999 at 8:09 AM PST What is the Matrix? One kick ass movie...great job... and you gotta love a movie that ends blasting old school Rage Against the Machine!! Steve Friday, April 2, 1999 at 8:09 AM F
il 2, 1999 at 8:03 AM PST what is the matrix Mike P Friday, April 2, 1999 at 8:01 AM PST illuminate..eyes watching...hidden prying..secrets...gift of fire...the reality you know is not real..the truth of this world will crash down soon..ashes to ashes
PST Ryan, have you even seen the movie? Reality Czech Friday, April 2, 1999 at 7:57 AM PST Carrie-Anne Moss is absolutely stunning. Good Golly. She kicks ass! Clee Friday, April 2, 1999 at 7:57 AM PST Very Very cool ass movie. If you haven't se
The Matrix was the matrix!!!! It was definitely one of the BEST and most entertaining movies that I have seen in a long time. I loved the special effects and the movie as a whole. Thanks for giving us 2 hrs to enjoy ourselves at the movies. Trans_4_n
urpassed any other movie I have ever witnessed in my entire life of quality movies. It was intelligent and stunning in visual graphics. The movie was mysterious hence It delivered great enjoyment for me. KEVIN Friday, April 2, 1999 at 7:50 AM PST
Friday, April 2, 1999 at 7:49 AM PST I'm not very content with reality...but, hey, this movie does raise some of my favorite questions! Reality Czech Friday, April 2, 1999 at 7:46 AM PST THE MATRIX IS ONE OF THE COOLEST MOVIES IVE SEEN IN
ltimatrix?) DIRK Friday, April 2, 1999 at 7:45 AM PST this movie was one of the best i have seen in a long time. Great job, loved the effects. jenny Friday, April 2, 1999 at 7:44 AM PST Reality is an illusion to keep humans content in a dream world
artificial, computer generated reality, but it is no less "real" than our own (which can be a scary line of questioning!). Reality Czech Friday, April 2, 1999 at 7:42 AM PST the world around us that isn't really real. d Friday, April 2, 1999 at 7:39 AM P
neasy doesn't it. so let's all go out and drive on the wrong side of the road, get my slide? Trapezious Otterbein Friday, April 2, 1999 at 7:33 AM PST What Clothing designer supplied the Suits that Keanu wore & what brand are the sunglasses they wo
nd click on that CPU. Enter steak as the code. You have to wait till the end of the credits to see the code usually but not now. josh Friday, April 2, 1999 at 7:29 AM PST The matrix cannot be precisely described. One could say that it is about the loss
ears being actualized, and moving beyond those fears anyway. aradia Friday, April 2, 1999 at 7:29 AM PST "What is the matrix?" is not the question you should be asking... Talon Friday, April 2, 1999 at 7:28 AM PST The movie was great but what w
l effects I've seen yet william Friday, April 2, 1999 at 7:21 AM PST sweet. jj Friday, April 2, 1999 at 7:20 AM PST strange, a movie that can be mind bending, slamming, but is any of this real anyway, maybe the movie is just a way to turn us away fr
moke of hell so that thy keen mind can see the matrix before me. Want to talk to the directors, if possible hook me up!! Lord Billiak Friday, April 2, 1999 at 7:15 AM PST i was really surprised. great movie. wonderfully thought out story with original ide
the sunglasses? (Morpheus' and the Smiths') Rae Friday, April 2, 1999 at 7:14 AM PST I think the matrix is a sub parallel world that crosses dreams or fantasies with reality, causing one awesome reality Sean Friday, April 2, 1999 at 7:14 AM PST T
Jet Pilot Friday, April 2, 1999 at 7:13 AM PST Sunglasses? Ray Friday, April 2, 1999 at 7:09 AM PST STEAK...nuff said? Neo Friday, April 2, 1999 at 7:09 AM PST I am infected with the MATRIX virus...if I dont see it again, i'll die!!!!!.. P.S KEANU
morning and life was different...well this movie sometimes makes you wonder. Cyberknight Friday, April 2, 1999 at 7:04 AM PST the matrix is the world around us that has been pulled over our eyes to prevent us from seeing the truth... Frederick Frid
1999 at 7:00 AM PST steak Frank Friday, April 2, 1999 at 6:57 AM PST Definitely the best movie of this century! Critic Friday, April 2, 1999 at 6:56 AM PST steak Killprocs Friday, April 2, 1999 at 6:54 AM PST skroce darrow Randolph Friday, April
has to be the single best movie I've seen in ages.. Superb everything- special effects, action, and a spectacular plot.. It was cyberpunk to the core!! So many intricate connections, from biblical references to the very beginning, when Neo was getting
nk about is far more. What if it is true? What if that's real? What if? This web site is amazing and is definitely the best I've ever seen. CrooksFriday, April 2, 1999 at 6:40 AM PST man, the Matrix was amazing, cerebral, philosophical premise and jo
lot of the things in the movie. If you want to know what the Matrix is then see the movie yourself. Ian Friday, April 2, 1999 at 6:38 AM PST I saw the movie last night. It totally ROCKED!!! steevin Friday, April 2, 1999 at 6:37 AM PST I loved the mo
itely going to this one again. Gramadin Friday, April 2, 1999 at 6:30 AM PST Is anyone else wondering if there was a chemical released in the air ducts during the film that intoxicated our minds? I have never been affected by a film this deeply, obsess
1999 at 6:28 AM PST I loved the movie!! PANDORA Friday, April 2, 1999 at 6:27 AM PST One word and only one word describes this movie---WOH---It is freaking amazing, from a complex and deep story, to incredible effects, and excellent acting
best sci-fi movies I have ever seen. The special effects are like nothing you have ever seen before. Be prepared for the movie experience of your life. I told someone its the best movie I have seen this year...lets make it this DECADE!! I intend to se

THE ART OF THE

MATRIX

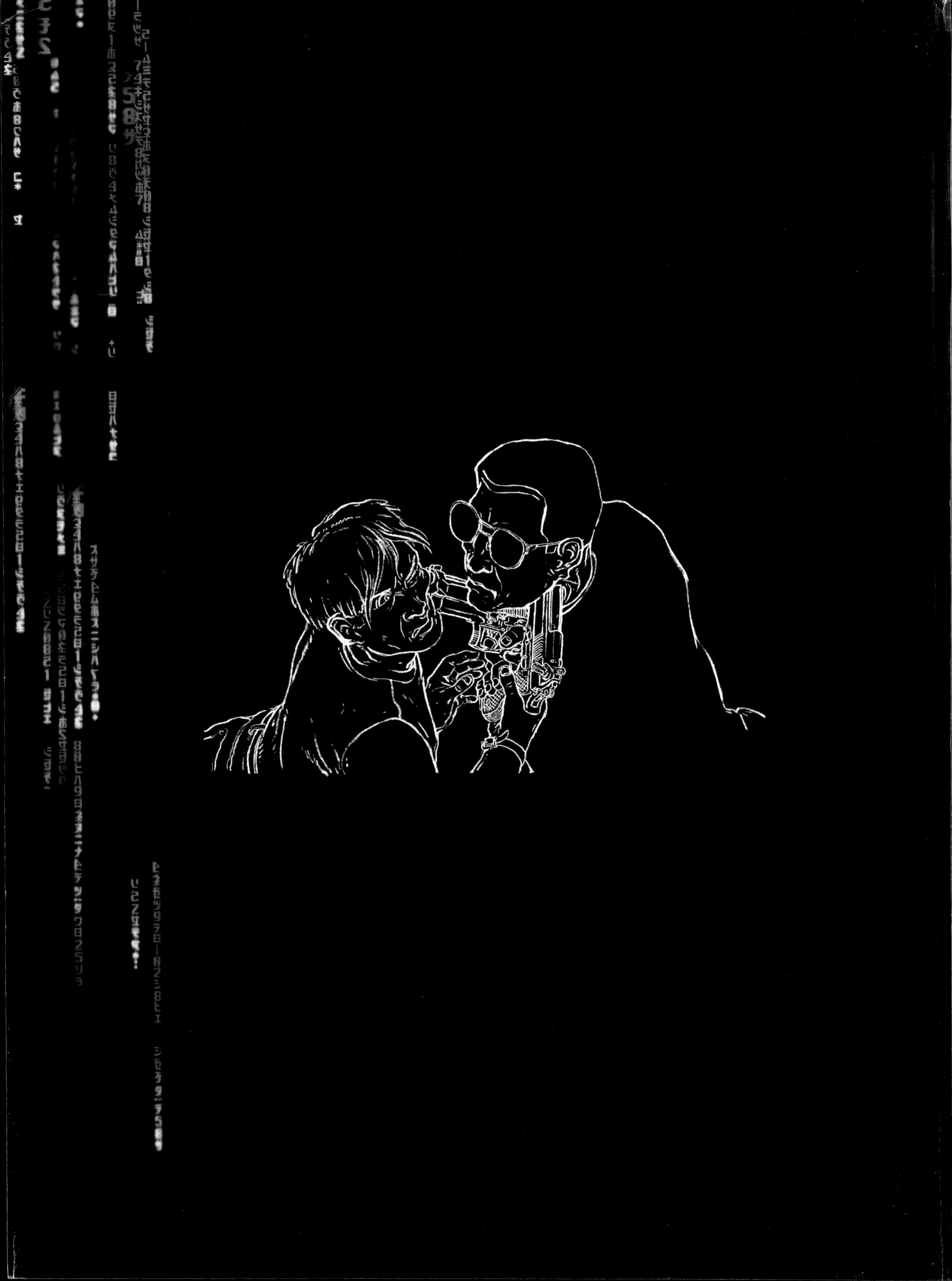

THE ART OF THE
MATRIX

SCREENPLAY
Larry & Andy Wachowski

PRINCIPAL STORYBOARD ART
Steve Skroce (Black and White)
Tani Kunitake (Color)

CONCEPTUAL ART
Geof Darrow

ADDITIONAL ART
Warren Manser
Collin Grant
Larry and Andy Wachowski

INTRODUCTION
Zach Staenberg

BOOK EDITOR
Spencer Lamm

AFTERWORD
William Gibson

SCENE NOTES
Phil Oosterhouse

Newmarket Press
New York

WB Worldwide
Publishing

This book is published simultaneously in the United States of America and Canada.

Printed in Belgium

ISBN: 1-55704-405-8 Hardcover

Library of Congress Cataloging-in-Publication data is available upon request.

Quantity Purchases
Companies, professional groups, clubs, and other organizations may qualify for special
terms when ordering quantities of this title. For information, write to Special Sales,
Newmarket Press, 18 East 48th Street, New York, NY 10017; call (212) 832-3575 or fax (212) 832-3629.
mailbox@newmarketpress.com   http://www.newmarketpress.com

Produced by Newmarket Productions, a division of Newmarket Publishing & Communications
Company: Esther Margolis, Director; Frank DeMaio, Production Manager

Warner Bros. Worldwide Publishing book project staff:
Paula Allen, Director of Sales; Skye Van Raalte-Herzog, Manager of Book Production

Compilation, Text and Design by Redpill Productions:

Spencer Lamm: Design/Interviews; Sharon Bray: Production/Design Assistant

http://www.redpill.com

Acknowledgments: this book began production in mid-1999. Many people have shared their time
and input. Thanks go to Steve, Geof, Tani, Warren, Zach, Collin, Phil and, of course, Larry and
Andy Wachowski. Additional thanks go to Pat Basile, Kevin Bricklin, Dan Cracchiolo, Lorenzo Di
Bonaventura, John Eakin, John Gaeta, Olga Gardner, William Gibson, Diana Giorgiutti, Chris
Grau, Peter Grossman, Michael Harkavy, Keith Hollaman, Charles LoBello, Lukasz Lysakowski,
Laurence Mattis, Nicole McSorley, Noah Mizrahi, Steve Nebesni, Melanie O'Brien, David Peterson,
Victor Russo, Tim Shaner, Joel Silver, Rob Simpson, Tony Syslo, Kevin Tinsley and Jason Williford.

—Esther Margolis, Publisher & Spencer Lamm, Editor

WARNER BROS. PRESENTS
IN ASSOCIATION WITH VILLAGE ROADSHOW PICTURES · GROUCHO II FILM PARTNERSHIP
A SILVER PICTURES PRODUCTION KEANU REEVES LAURENCE FISHBURNE "THE MATRIX" CARRIE-ANNE MOSS HUGO WEAVING AND JOE PANTOLIANO MUSIC BY DON DAVIS
CO-PRODUCER DAN CRACCHIOLO EXECUTIVE PRODUCERS BARRIE OSBORNE ANDREW MASON ANDY WACHOWSKI LARRY WACHOWSKI ERWIN STOFF AND BRUCE BERMAN PRODUCED BY JOEL SILVER

   R RESTRICTED UNDER 17 REQUIRES ACCOMPANYING PARENT OR ADULT GUARDIAN WRITTEN AND DIRECTED BY THE WACHOWSKI BROTHERS SOUNDTRACK ALBUM ON MAVERICK RECORDS
VILLAGE ROADSHOW PICTURES SILVER PICTURES WARNER BROS. A TIME WARNER ENTERTAINMENT COMPANY ©1999 Warner Bros. All Rights Reserved

www·whatisthematrix·com

SOUNDTRACK ALBUM FEATURING RECORDINGS BY MARILYN MANSON · PRODIGY · ROB ZOMBIE · RAGE AGAINST THE MACHINE · RAMMSTEIN · DEFTONES

First Edition

2000   2001   02   03   10   9   8   7   6   5   4   3   2   1

THE ART OF THE
MATRIX

INTRODUCTION

Zach Staenberg • Film Editor

THE MATRIX was a very special experience for me, so I want to say right from the start: I am not objective. I love this movie and it is really gratifying that so many others seem to feel the same way. I first met Larry and Andy in February of 1995, after reading their script for BOUND. It just popped right out and grabbed me. The writing was very visual, and I never had any doubt that these two young guys who had never made a movie could make a great one, so I went in to interview with them for the position of film editor, and I would have been very disappointed if I hadn't been hired. There was just something about that script and those guys...

Looking back over my working experience with the brothers as the film editor on BOUND and then THE MATRIX, it's pretty easy to see what that something was. They are natural collaborators, allowing the people around them to thrive. But on the other hand, their vision of the film is singular. I can't say how many times I've been working with one of them in the editing room and later the other would walk in and his comments would feel like déjà vu. Sometimes it's funny, sometimes it's aggravating, and sometimes it's just plain weird. And they know what they want. Dino DeLaurentis was on the BOUND set while the scene where Ceasar trashes Johnny's apartment was shot. The coverage was unusual, in a way that I now recognize as being consistent with the Wachowskis' unique point of view, but a little unnerving for an experienced producer dealing with first-time directors. Dino finally threw up his hands, saying, "They know what they want!" Deep down, he trusted them. Larry and Andy understand how a film needs to work, and how to elicit their vision from the hundreds of people involved in the production of a film. It's a very clear, strong vision.

This "sense of the movie" was communicated to me on BOUND simply by the script, along with our many conversations. Though BOUND was storyboarded, Larry and Andy's drawings were indecipherable hieroglyphics and stick figures, and were used chiefly as their own personal guide. But THE MATRIX script demanded a far more elaborate production, with a need to communicate more intricate ideas—complicated ideas that were hard to grasp—quickly to a large crew. At its height, the movie employed around 450 people, and to many of those people the storyboards became their bible.

It didn't hurt that Geof Darrow and Steve Skroce are both established and celebrated comic-book artists, and that Larry and Andy were formerly comic-book writers and are major afficionados of the best of comics and graphic novels. From this background they developed an understanding of how images convey meaning and how story can be expressed visually. I think they found some kindred spirits in Geof and Steve. In collaboration with them, and all the other artists who drew storyboards, the brothers were able to see that vision drawn before they made the movie. The results of their collaboration are illustrations with a great deal of detail and the actual visual language of the movie.

Obviously, different directors have their own styles. What we've seen from the Wachowskis, in BOUND and THE MATRIX, is not naturalistic, but stylized and often extremely graphic. They're not simply recording something beautiful, but using the camera and the technology behind the camera to create something beautiful. Much like painters or sculptors, they're combining elements in a controlled environment, making something new, using the camera to create art. In THE MATRIX, the storyboards and the way they were used were an integral part of this inventive process. There are many places in the movie where you can just look at the frames, and you're looking at pages from a graphic novel. The images have tremendous power.

The first thing the storyboards did for me was to get me excited beyond all belief. They are extremely compelling. When you look at them you feel as if you can see an exciting movie. I felt, damn, I want to see this footage—I want to see this movie. I would leaf through them and start pacing around. I couldn't contain myself. I had spent a lot of time sitting around talking about the movie with Andy and Larry. It became clear to me from those conversations that the "spoon boy" scene is a crucial turning point in the story. This is the moment when Neo looks beyond the surface and begins to feel the whole.

From this point the impossible starts to become possible for Neo. The creation of the storyboards was a turning point in the physical development of the movie. Upon their completion, the studio was able to begin to see the whole, and THE MATRIX was green-lit. The impossible became possible.

And then, jumping ahead to when the movie was being shot in Sydney, I was often struck by how many key shots from the storyboards were on film. Certain shots and sequences feel like the storyboards come to life. It must be very thrilling for the artists to see that, to see their illustrations realized so beautifully.

It's not surprising to see this strong correlation between the footage and the storyboards. There was very little wasted filming, and that's because they did so much preliminary planning in the storybords, working out ideas and visual concepts before the filming began. Many times, on set and in visual effects meetings, I heard someone say, "Just look at the boards." On set this allowed them to focus on the details, those things that turn a shot from mere coverage into something special. The boards were of paramount importance for the visual effects people. Nearly 20 percent of this film went through the digital domain. This meant much of the footage had to be aligned with images that would be added later. The number of variables this creates are too numerous to get into here. But again, Larry and Andy proved to have chosen the right players. Everyone involved came through at a higher level than anyone could have hoped for.

Ultimately, film has a peculiar dynamic all its own. When the actual locations are established, when the props are built, when the actors are on set, and all the pieces are finally together for filming, things work in ways that cannot be predetermined. You never know how things are going to go on any given day of filming. So sometimes, the footage is not exact to the storyboards, and there are not storyboards for every scene. But the storyboards provided me with a great point of reference, always allowing me to see what the scene should feel like. I'm sure this was also true for the cinematographer, Bill Pope, the production designer, Owen Paterson, and our visual effects supervisor, John Gaeta, as well as the hundreds of other talented individuals who contributed mightily to this movie. The storyboards provided us with a window into that organic sense and vision held so deeply by Larry and Andy. Even though there was a lot of pressure and innumerable elements to juggle on this production, we were way ahead of the curve compared to people working on other films where there isn't as cohesive a vision.

The careful planning of THE MATRIX resulted in a film which met and exceeded the obstacles. It was a difficult movie to produce. But we followed the Wachowskis' lead, along with their script and story-boards, and had a great time making the movie. What we couldn't have known back then was how THE MATRIX would tap into the collective fears and curiosities of its audience. All you've got to do is go to any of the myriad web sites dedicated to THE MATRIX or the official site, WhatIsTheMatrix.com, to find people talking about it. There's a palpable buzz. Ultimately THE MATRIX was and continues to be about the nature of intellectual freedom, the ability to make things happen because you believe it is possible to do so. It's a thrill and an honor to be part of a film that has so much to say on so many levels.

As to the future, I'm very, very excited about working on THE MATRIX 2 & 3. Larry and Andy envisioned all three of them from the onset, and that is why the backdrop of THE MATRIX is so vast. Unlike most sequels which take the characters and the motivations and simply move them to another environment—setting up the same people in a parallel situation—the new MATRIX films will form a true trilogy with story and character arcs going across all three movies. Ultimately, we'll be able to watch all three as one long movie. It is daunting to make a sequel to a popular movie, but in this case I think it can be done. These are collectively the most talented people I've ever had the pleasure to work with. Larry and Andy are working on the scripts as I type this. Steve and Geof are already preparing to get back to work on the next sets of storyboards. Many of the other principal players, both before and behind the camera, will be back.

I don't know everything that will happen in THE MATRIX 2 & 3. But the corner has been turned, where the impossible becomes possible.

"There is no spoon."
I think that says it all.

Zach Staenberg
April, 2000

FOREWORD

With a film as visually rich and complex as THE MATRIX, there is a massive amount of preproduction. Details on details, all done before a single frame of film is shot. For THE MATRIX, this included elaborately orchestrated fight sequences, extensive stunts, and a high number of scenes shot against green screen for later computer manipulation. The result was an unusually high amount of preproduction art. So, by design, this is a large book. Our problem: what not to include, because we had to limit the page count to some degree. The average screenplay book is roughly two hundred pages. Sometimes these books show a few of the storyboards. We wanted to show all the storyboards. All the conceptual illustrations. Would 300 pages be enough? 400? We ended up clocking in at almost 500 pages, still wanting to show more. We maxed it out, including far more pages than is normally used for such a project. For the most part, it's all here. The principal storyboards by Steve Skroce, the principal color storyboards by Tani Kunitake, conceptuals by Geof Darrow, and the film's foundation, the script by Larry and Andy Wachowski. Our goal in presenting this material is to express some sense of the massive planning that went into the film, focusing on the initial material, the first leg of MATRIX production work. All told, with art produced by the various visual effects houses, set designers, and props departments, there's more material than can fill a thousand pages. While this book does give insight into the production of THE MATRIX, the focus here is not on the filming, but on what set the stage.

Preproduction started in 1997, with Larry and Andy Wachowski enlisting the talents of two leading illustrators from the world of comics, Steve Skroce (CABLE, SPIDER-MAN, WOLVERINE) and Geof Darrow (HARD BOILED, BIG GUY AND RUSTY THE BOY ROBOT), to prepare storyboards and conceptual drawings in the hopes of showing Warner Bros. what they had in mind. This was before the film was green-lit. THE MATRIX was a larger story than their first film, BOUND, and they needed to express it clearly. In close collaboration with Steve and Geof, Larry and Andy worked hard to visualize the image-rich screenplay, and as work continued, other artists were brought in where needed, to continue zeroing in on the visuals they wanted to realize. Looking back, with the film firmly sitting in over three million homes on DVD, it might seem odd that THE MATRIX was such a hard sell, but back then, the studio was wary. Steve Skroce, the principal storyboard artist, in the end flew to Los Angeles three times over a span of fourteen months, producing over 600 hundred storyboard images.

Combining all this initial art, the brothers were able to walk people, especially the studio, through the script, producing essentially, a 400-page comic book. This book showcases the bulk of that work, presenting what was shown to the studio so many months ago. This art was used both as a tool to sell the picture and then as a detailed map for production. With this in mind, we've done more than just print the boards used in final cut. Over the course of the fourteen months, changes occurred to the script. This book gives insight into the evolution of the film by leaving intact some of the originally conceived moments that didn't make it into the final film. Some of these moments are peppered through the core storyboards and are those that came closest to being filmed, as when Trinity uses a bolo in the Government Lobby scene. Others are in the back of the book, scenes that were cut or changed before filming even began. Taking a heads-up from the DVD medium, we have running commentaries with the artists to help point out some of the differences to the final film, and to add insight into the whole production process.

Without question, what's found here is only the beginning, the starting point for many more months of work. By the time THE MATRIX began filming on March 14, 1998, the list of artists who had worked on the project was massive, including teams working under not one but three visual effects companies (Manex, Animal Logic, and Dfilm), producing everything from the computer-generated DocBot, Sentinels, and Fetus Harvesters, to matte paintings detailing locations as elaborate as the Fetus Fields, to the Matrix code itself. The hope is, of course, with adequate interest, to produce a compendium volume, showing the work produced during this second wave of production. But without getting ahead of ourselves, this book is about the beginning, from the earliest script excerpts to the sketches by Larry and Andy themselves, through the first wave of art produced for THE MATRIX.

It's been a pleasure putting this book together. Enjoy the details.

Spencer Lamm
June, 2000

"YOUR MEN ARE ALREADY DEAD."

Trinity Chase

Scenes 2, 4, 7, 8, 9, 10, A10, 11

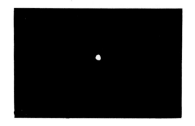  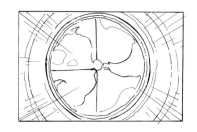

Steve Skroce: I met Larry and Andy [Wachowski] way back when they were writing at Marvel comics. Even though Larry got sole writing credit on this book, a title called ECTOKID, this was really both Larry and Andy (though up until now, not even Marvel knew that). We did about nine issues of the book together. From there we got to know each other and kept in touch. That was roughly seven years ago.

About three, three and a half years ago, and before THE MATRIX was green-lit, Larry and Andy convinced some people at Warner Bros. to fly me out to Los Angeles from Vancouver for a couple of weeks to work on a few action sequences. They needed to show the scale of the whole thing—the proportion of it. This helped the studio see what Larry and Andy were talking about and the type of film they were planning to make.

Skroce: Back in the beginning, there weren't too many people involved. As to artists, it was me and Geof Darrow [the conceptual design artist]. Geof came out to meet Larry and Andy and then went back to France to design the Power Plant and the first few creatures. About five or six months later they got more money and Warner Bros. flew me and Geof back out, hiring more artists, an art director and a line producer. The film wasn't a sure thing at this point, but it was closer. For a couple of months we were essentially drawing the movie into a giant comic book, myself, Geof, Collin Grant, and Tani Kunitake. When that was finished, they showed it to the heads of Warner Bros.—a comic book they could go through showing exactly what the movie was about. There were so many ideas that needed to be digested in this movie, it was very hard for anyone to get how they were going to tell this story until they actually saw it. They needed to be shown how the images and narrative would work together to explain the complicated ideas.

Skroce: Early on, Warner Bros. were really excited about the script. They knew it was something cool, but a lot of the ideas—the instantaneous technology and Hollywood actors doing crazy kung fu—had never been heard of before. They were interested in this, but they still had to be really convinced what this movie was going to be before they would throw more money at it. I guess any time you do something new, it's a crapshoot, no matter how good it is, so they wanted to be pretty sure.

Skroce: A funny aside: many of the characters took on nicknames, like the cop here getting smashed in the face. He was Officer O'Malley. He didn't do too well against Trinity, as you can see in the drawings.

Skroce: Everything was in Larry and Andy's heads from the beginning. They had specific ideas about what Trinity would do, like super-kicking the cop across the room, and running on the wall when the cop is trying to put the handcuffs on her. This was all well thought out before I drew a thing.

Skroce: It was really easy to work with Larry and Andy. I read all of the script revisions as they were building them, so I knew the story well. Besides that, and often beyond the script, they had very specific ideas for the images they wanted to create, which meant very little wasted effort. Larry and Andy drew thumbnails that they'd show me, and from them I would do quick sketches. They'd say, "Hmmm, maybe frame this one a little more like this." So I tweaked my sketches until the brothers were happy, and from there I drew the actual finished boards. We would do that, keeping me busy for a few days, then start on the next sequence and do it all over again.

Skroce: The first time I went out to Los Angeles, they wanted to show the big money stuff, to really impress Warner Bros. with the level of action they were going for. One of the first things I worked on was Trinity running on the rooftops, the Agents chasing her. The second time, we fleshed out this early material. By then, Larry and Andy knew roughly the kind of budget they were getting, so it was easier to figure out what was actually going to be filmed.

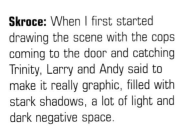

Skroce: When I first started drawing the scene with the cops coming to the door and catching Trinity, Larry and Andy said to make it really graphic, filled with stark shadows, a lot of light and dark negative space.

Skroce: In the end, I went to Los Angeles three times. After the second trip, the movie was green-lit, so I came out one last time to make adjustments to the boards based on script changes. Originally, the movie had so much impossible big action, they couldn't get a budget that big. Having seen THE MATRIX, you can get an idea—with the epic scope it has, imagine if it had been a $120 million movie.

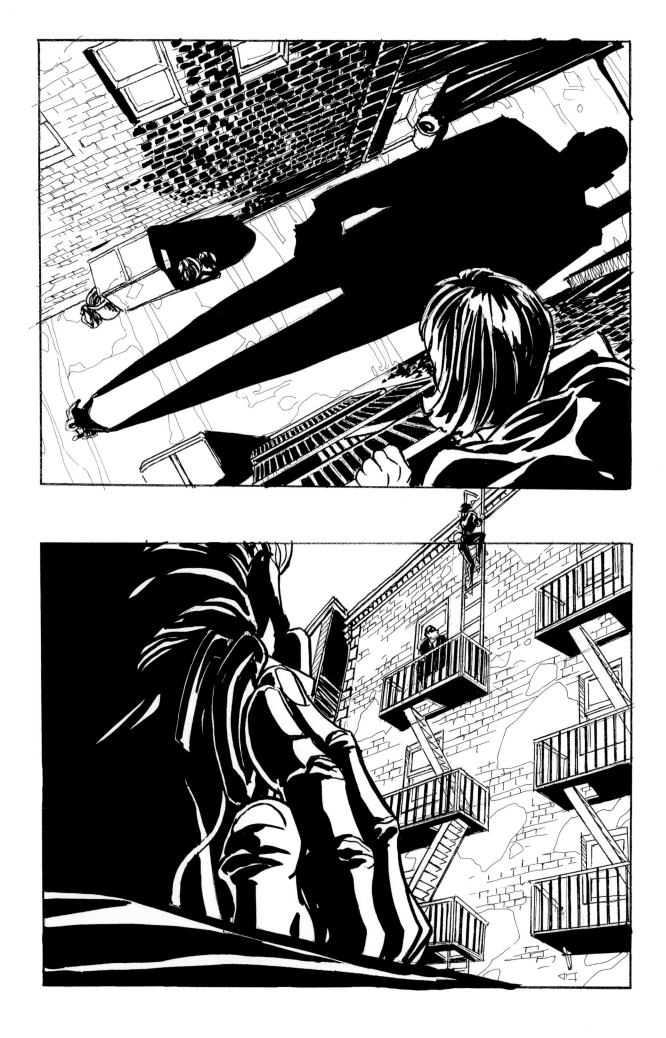

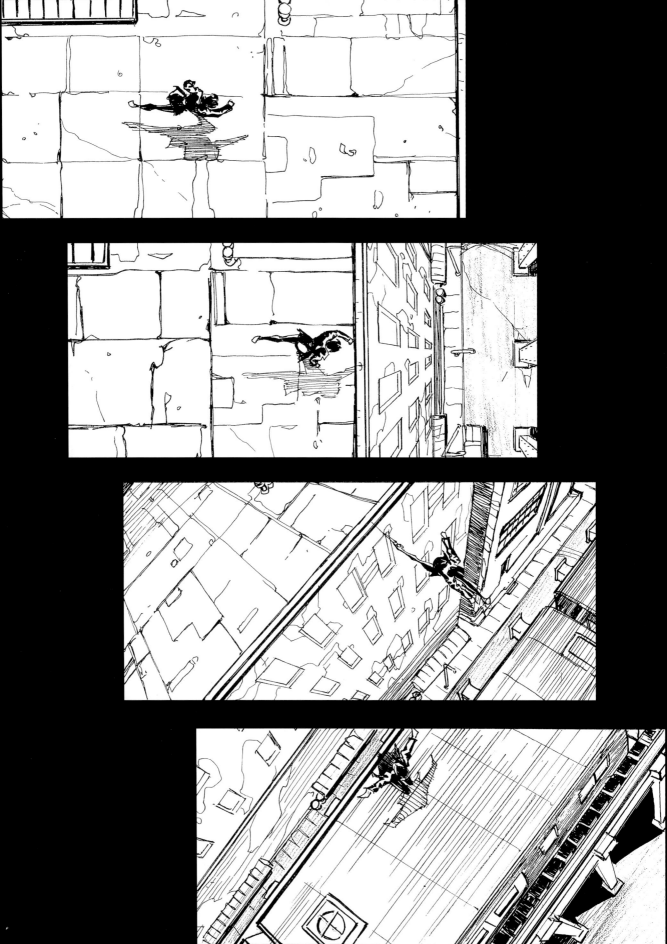

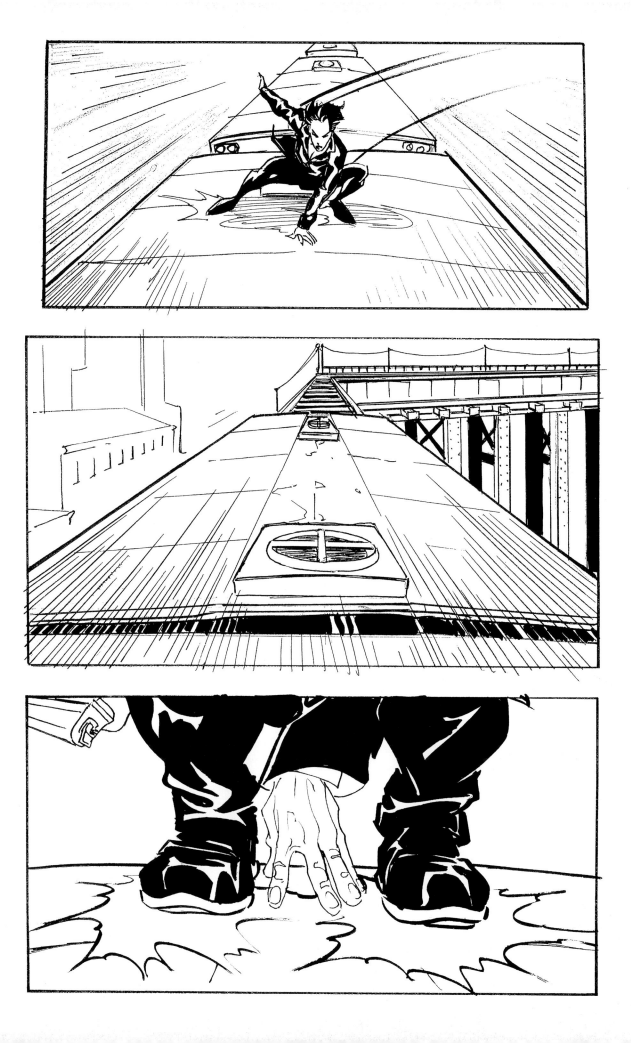

Skroce: Some shots were dropped completely or changed, like this one where Trinity is on the train. This whole scene was changed to rooftops. The impossible jump is, however, as it was originally drawn.

Skroce: Originally, Larry and Andy wanted to shoot this scene on the El train in Chicago, their hometown, which is why it's drawn with an elevated train, but the scene changed after the film was green-lit and the location moved to Sydney. The leap where she aims herself at the little yellow window in the building was all boarded the first time I went to Los Angeles, and is in the film, but originally she was jumping from a moving train. From the beginning, they wanted this one specific shot, the one where she's flying through the air towards the window. They described where the camera would be, starting on her right side, and then as she spins, so would the camera [see insert, left]. To get this, they had to first shoot her in a flying pose against a green screen, then use computer-generated imaging to paint in the background that would also move, following her spin. In the movie it happens lightning-fast, but it took a lot of work to pull this off. In the first shot, the camera is side-on as she dives off the train towards the window, then the camera moves above her, so it is moving around her body from her right to her left. Now we are over the top of her and the camera comes down the other side, so she looks upside-down as her fingers are just about to penetrate the window. Then she comes smashing through and crumbles down those stairs, coming up with her guns.

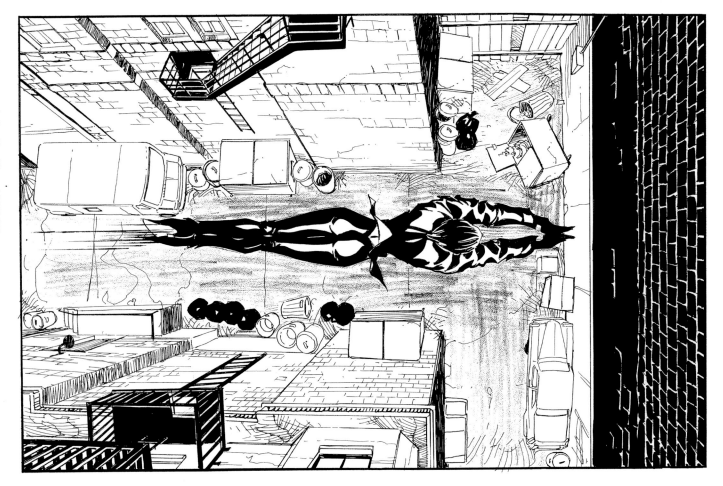

Trinity . Chase

38

Skroce: This illustration [below] was going to be a shot of the Agent on the elevated train zipping past, being taken away. When the scene moved to a rooftop, the Agent wouldn't just stand on the roof looking at Trinity, he would have been in the window right after her. In the movie, the Agents know where she's going—the phone booth—so they go there first.

Skroce: One thing Larry and Andy were really interested in was to make these boards as dynamic as possible. A lot of storyboards for film have arrows pointing to things, but Larry and Andy are not into that at all, we went for a real comic-book storytelling style. Most of these boards were done on comic-book illustration Bristol board; if you go through it, it reads like a comic. Rather than just having arrows pointing to this speeding truck heading to the phone booth, they wanted me to use speed lines and comic book techniques to indicate things. They wanted the boards themselves to be an entertaining experience to go through, rather than just a basic static visualization of the script. Being from the comic-book world, when I started I felt, now that I am an official movie storyboard artist, I should draw official movie storyboard-type arrows. Larry and Andy didn't like that very much, they were like, "Why'd you draw that arrow?" But they forgave me. Here's my first and just about last experience with storyboard arrows [below].

Skroce: Often, Larry and Andy had specific ideas about page layout because they needed the boards to read with little explanation. The story itself is hard enough to get a grasp on, so they used the illustrations to get people through the action, allowing them to get closer to the story.

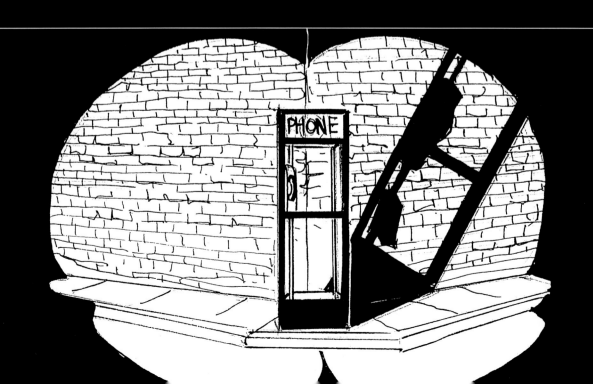

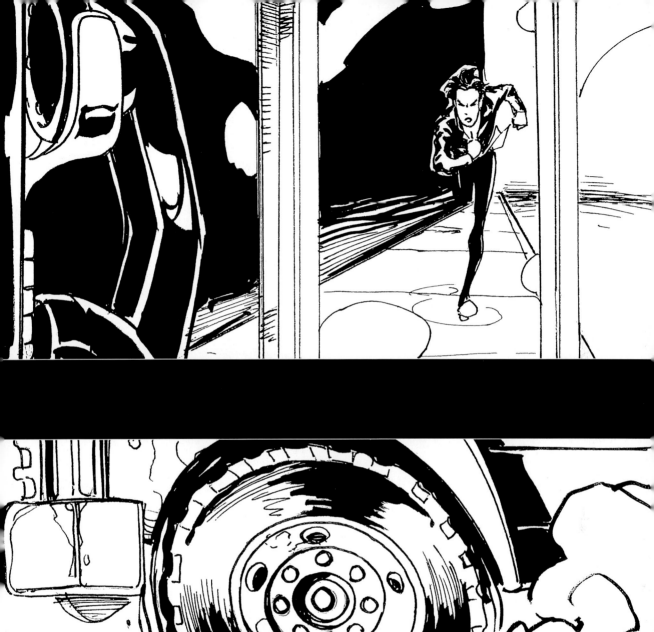

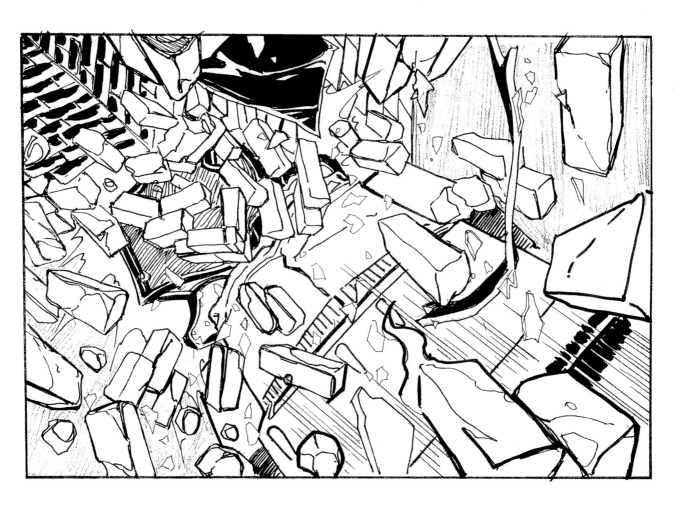

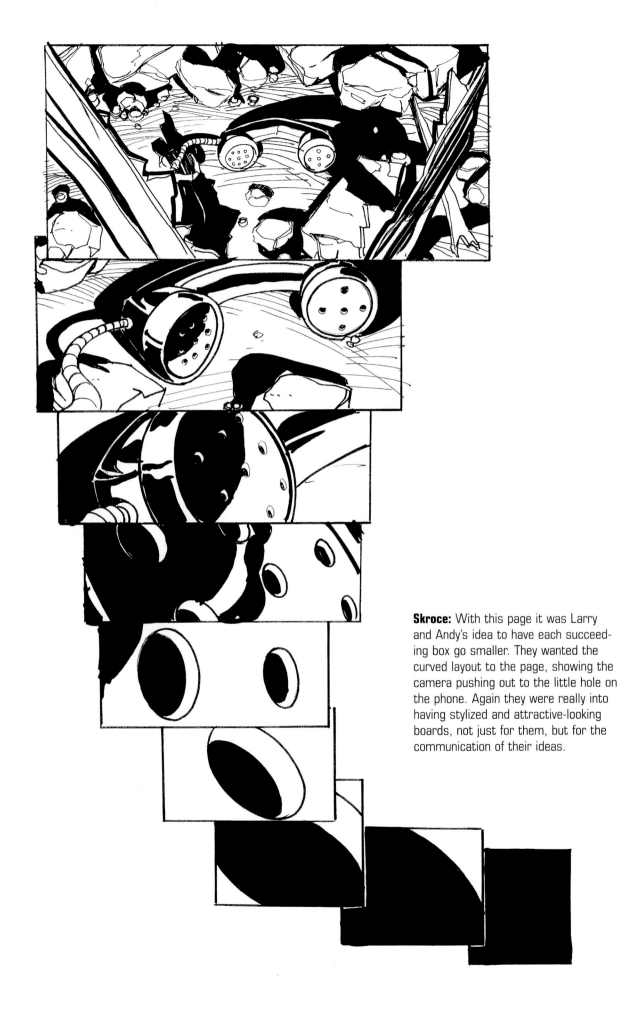

Skroce: With this page it was Larry and Andy's idea to have each succeeding box go smaller. They wanted the curved layout to the page, showing the camera pushing out to the little hole on the phone. Again they were really into having stylized and attractive-looking boards, not just for them, but for the communication of their ideas.

"WHAT GOOD IS A PHONE CALL IF
YOU ARE UNABLE TO SPEAK?"

Interrogation Room

Scene 20

Steve Skroce: As you go through the storyboards, you'll notice stylistic changes in the artwork. Some art is older than other pages, not necessarily in sequence. This was among the first I drew, made obvious by Neo's long hair.

Skroce: One thing Larry and Andy were really worried about was how scary this scene was going to be and whether Warner Bros. would go for it. And the scene only gets creepier as it goes on. Again, they had really specific thoughts on this. By the time I got my hands on it, the bug was already designed by Geof, so I was looking at his drawings. They wanted the bug to start out as a conventional wire-and-metal bugging device, and then grow into this very techno-organic thing. It needed a life-like look, to be some sort of biomechanical creature.

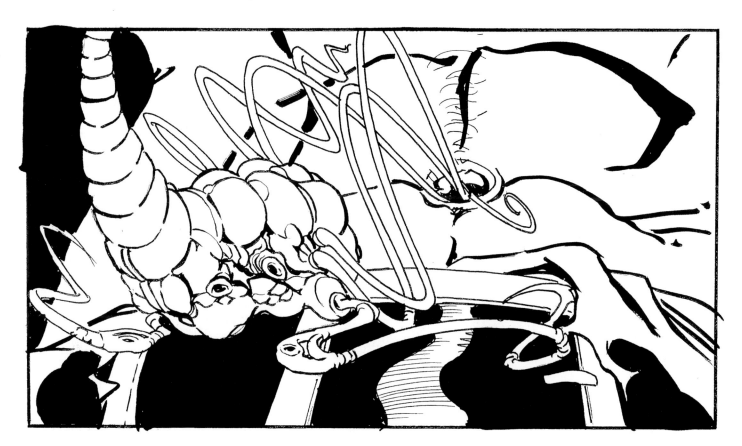

53

Skroce: Larry and Andy wanted this creature going into Neo's body, with tentacles moving around underneath the skin, to be as nightmarish as possible.

"WE THINK YOU'RE BUGGED."

Bug Extraction

Scene 24, 25

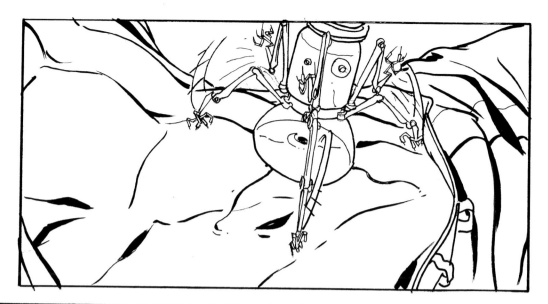

Steve Skroce: Here's a rack focus panel [second down] starting on Neo's abdomen and then pulling back to the monitor showing what this writhing creature looks like under his skin. We're pulling focus to see the bug wrapped around his intestines on the screen. They wanted to have a close-up of the bug as it starts to get anxious about being caught.

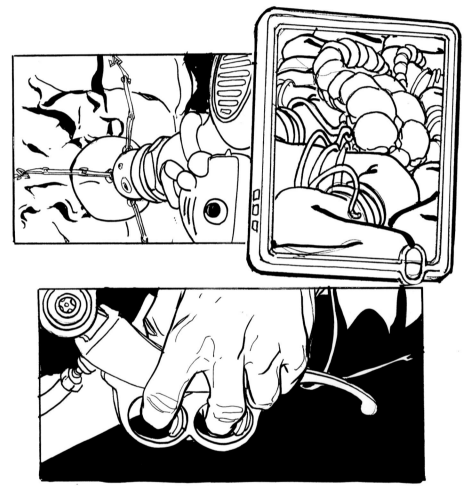

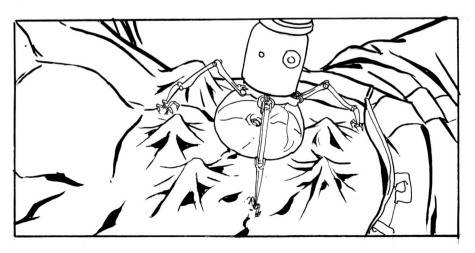

[At the bottom] is a close-up of his abdomen with the front of the bug extractor, showing the little tentacles coming out and the bug going crazy under the skin. Then the electricity hits, which was cut from the film. Originally there was a big flash when Trinity shorts out the bug and then it was to go black. In the film, this was turned into one shot where the cup from the extractor shows the bug starting to get sucked up into it, then we see the receptacle where the bug goes. You can see a little bit of bloody gore around the belly button. Most of this sequence is in the film, but cut up because it wasn't convenient to have the camera where it would have had to be to show it this way. The scene ends very accurately, where the bug is dropped out of the car and turns back into the ordinary wire-and-metal listening device.

Skroce: The Bug Extraction scene was, incidentally, the last thing I drew. Geof had already designed the bug extractor with Larry and Andy when I got to it. They tried to think through in pseudoscience how the bug extractor works, what it is doing to Neo and his body, and how it is supposed to get the bug out. One hand steers the camera to where the bug is and the electrical field shorts out the bug. Trinity's right hand is the trigger hand where, once the bug is in her sight, she hits the trigger and sucks it up.

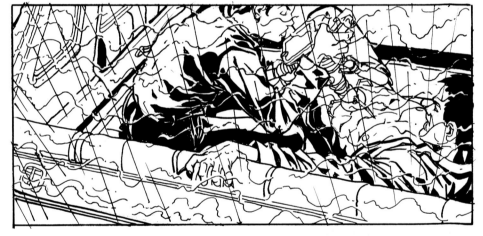

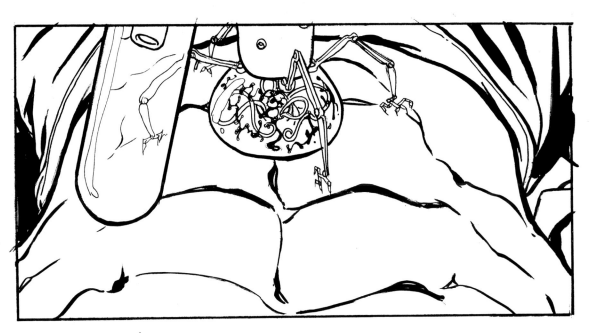

"...ALL I AM OFFERING IS THE TRUTH."

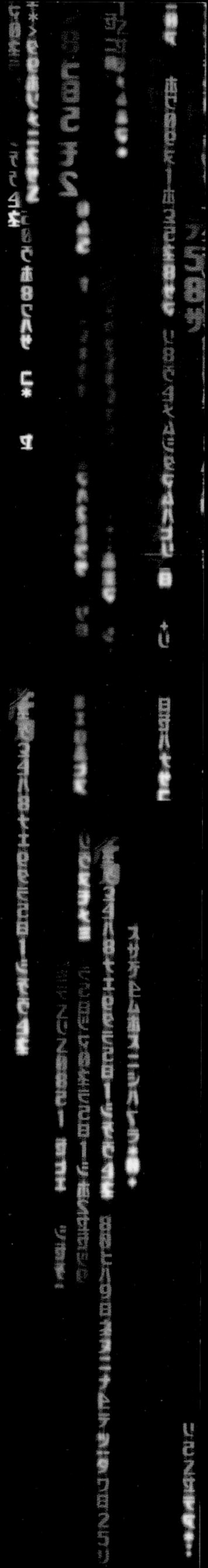

Lafayette Pills

Scene 28

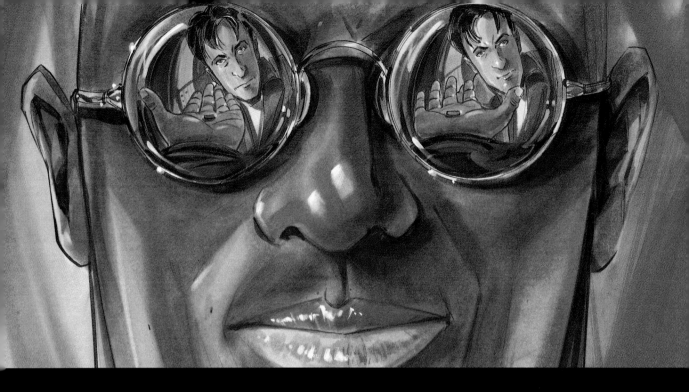

Editor: Any scene that included an optical effect needed to be boarded. Collin Grant illustrated this shot because the reflection of Neo in Morpheus's glasses was digitally added in postproduction. The glasses Laurence Fishburne wore during filming were masked with green to allow the needed shots to be dropped in.

"HAVE YOU EVER HAD A DREAM, NEO,
THAT YOU WERE SO SURE WAS REAL?"

Lafayette Mirror

Scene 29

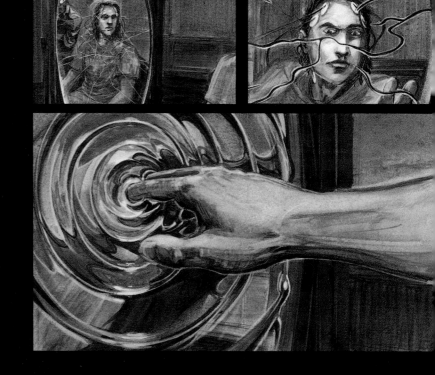

Tani Kunitake: I was contacted initially by one of the film's producers and right away went to have an interview with Larry and Andy. First off, they asked a bit about my film history and the projects I'd worked on. At that point, I'd done some conceptual illustrations for ARMAGEDDON and some other films, including the conceptual designs on BATMAN AND ROBIN for Warner Bros., so I guess that's where the contact was made. They looked over my portfolio and seemed to like it, asking what I felt about THE MATRIX, the story. I was very interested in the project, it was a really well-written script. Being fresh off BATMAN AND ROBIN I also liked the idea of getting into something a little more serious. THE MATRIX was the kind of science fiction story I always wanted to work on, having been polluted in my youth by seeing ALIEN. I left hoping I'd said the right things and, it seems I did, they hired me. I was shown the previous artwork by Steve Skroce and Geof Darrow and really liked the work they'd been doing. I knew Geof's work from comics like HARD BOILED, so it was really exciting to be working from his conceptuals. Back then, it was a really small crew—there were only the producers, Larry, Andy, and the other artists. Larry and Andy have a very non-Hollywood style and approach. As an artist, I'm usually screened by a production designer who deals with the director. Unless there is a special case during production, I usually have very little interaction with the director. With THE MATRIX, we were working with Larry and Andy directly. They would come into the room after meetings with the studio and update us—even on casting choices they were looking into. It felt like we were a large part of the production, at least in the conceptual stages.

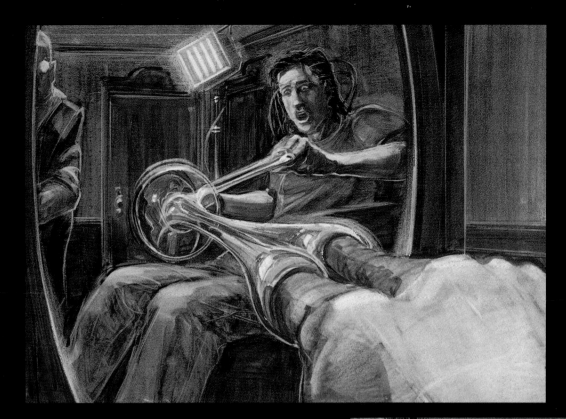

Kunitake: Before we got into the Lafayette Mirror scene, Larry and Andy showed me a great deal of M. C. Escher's work. What they wanted was a lot of reflection, pathways, doorways through the reflections, which is all in the script. I really enjoyed this scene because I particularly enjoyed this part of the script, it's one of my favorite scenes. The large withdraw from the mirror after Neo has touched it is a scene where they especially wanted to have hyper-real reflections. They wanted to see reflections grow for the principal characters. It happens very fast in the film and I guess it can only be seen in still frame, but it is there.

Kunitake: For reflections, there were five or six pieces of reflective material I used as reference; they were like mirrored balls. Larry and Andy wanted to distinctly get away from the "Terminator look," and that would be to have the reflection evolve with all the shapes/forms. They wanted mirrors within mirrors, reality and reflections compounding into infinity. With the open hand, we have more of a madhouse, everything has been distorted in Mr. Anderson's life. He sees himself as mad and distorted, and then it totally overtakes him.

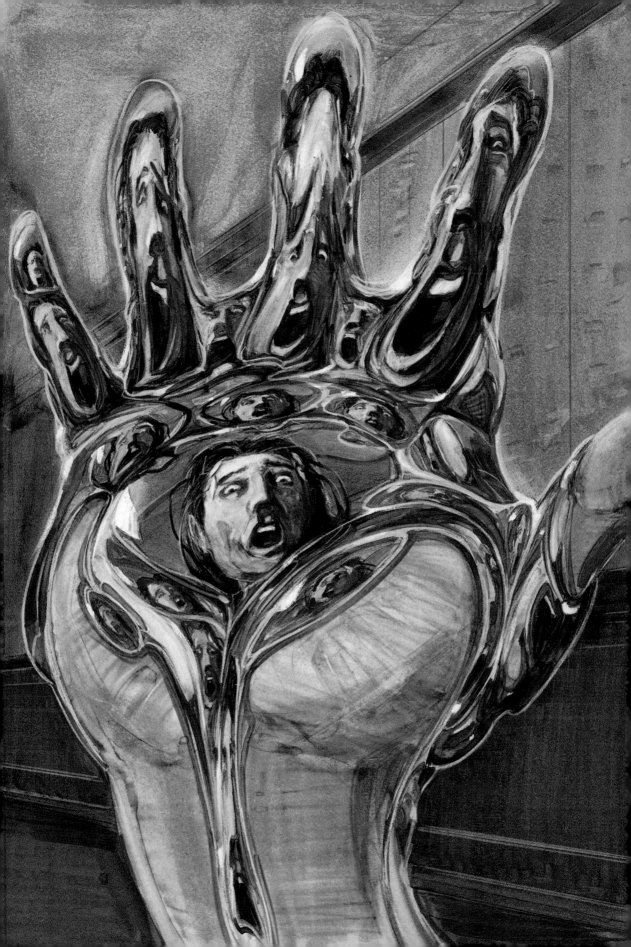

Kunitake: I would work with Larry and Andy doing thumbnails, blocking out the scenes with them. They would move about the room acting it out or use action figures to show the framing through a little viewfinder. After the thumbnails were done, I'd go ahead and execute the illustrations.

The medium I used was ink marker and color pencils on vellum, which is like a tracing paper. This allowed me to scrub it off at any time with alcohol. If Larry and Andy didn't like part of the frame, wanted part of it altered, even a color change, I was able to rapidly make the modification.

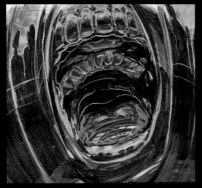

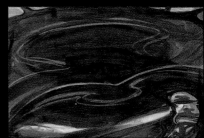

"WELCOME TO THE REAL WORLD."

Power Plant

Scenes 30, 31, 32

Tani Kunitake: The Power Plant was a fun one, the awakening scene. Again, Larry and Andy were pretty specific with the action blocking, but it was fun illustrating what they wanted.

Here, they wanted Neo to awaken in the pod and have the audience see what it was like through his eyes. So we went from inside his body, when the mirror flushes down through his throat, to him awakening in the pod, giving a really nice transition to the next scene, looking out through Neo's eyes. You've gone inside him in the previous scene and now come bursting out into the real world.

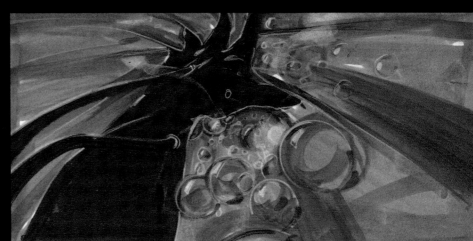

This is before I got the orders about not using arrows. On seeing them, the brothers immediately said, "No arrows!"

Here we have Neo stretching through the membrane [right]; birth is always painful. We've got him attached to breathing tubes and the like to stop him from suffocating. All of this is straight from Geof's conceptual designs. Getting handed Geof's designs, complex beautiful pieces, and having to replicate them, you end up silhouetting a lot; he puts an amazing amount of detail in his drawings. Basically, what I was doing, besides blocking out action, was emphasizing the environment, the way the environment would feel, what color and light it was going to have. Each of the boards have a dramatic color palette. The Power Plant is very red throughout, compared to the sickly artificial green of the Matrix.

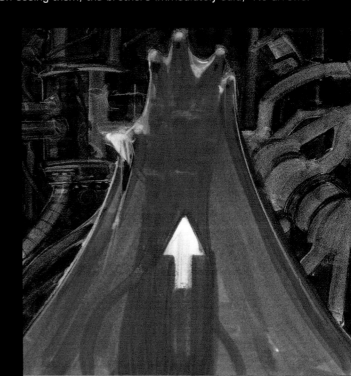

Kunitake: Here's Neo suffocating. He's just yanked the tubes
out of his mouth, discovering
he's plugged in everywhere,
not really believing anything
that is happening around him.
There were going to be little
machines running around, little
RepairBots, like spiders, which
would scurry and scamper
around the pods; they can be
seen in Geof's conceptuals
[see page 257].

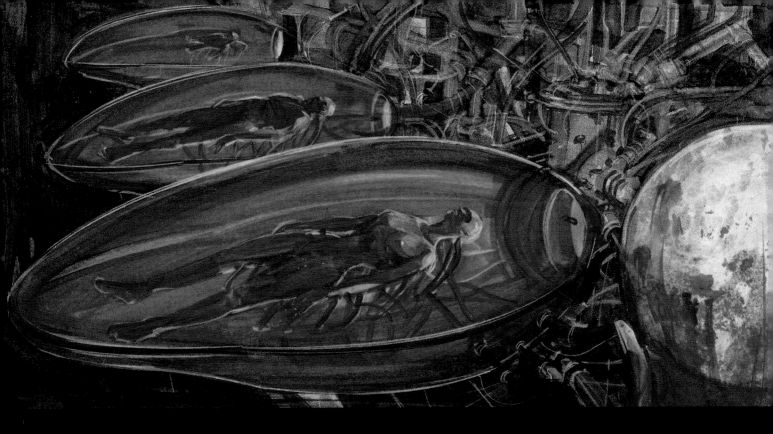

Kunitake: Inside the pods, Larry and Andy wanted a thick red gel. For the initial boards in this sequence, it's pretty much black and white, adding red. Then, when he breaks out of the pod, we add more of the other colors, getting to an establishing shot of the total environment. It was basically a transition from black, white, and red to a full-color environment.

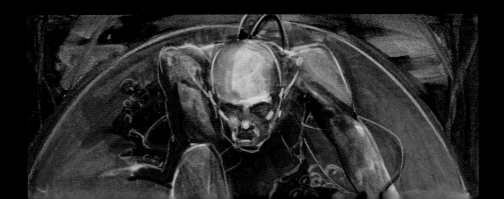

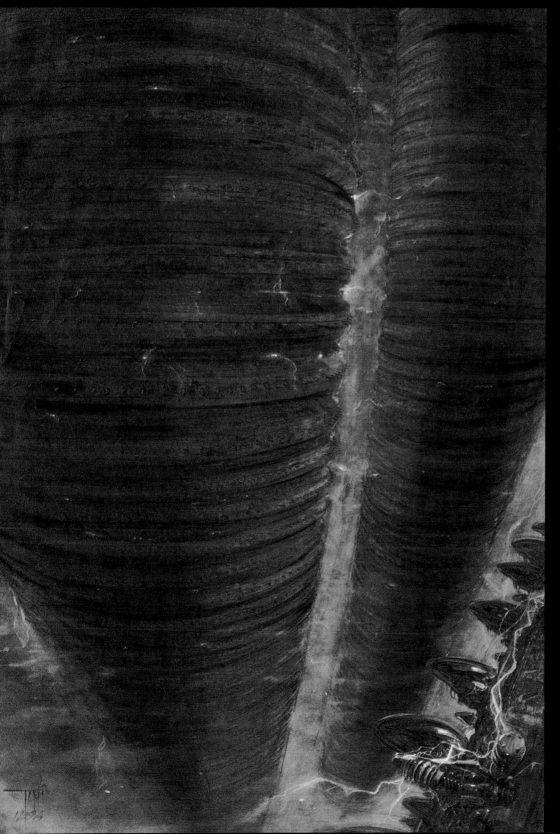

Kunitake: This [below] is one of the very first I did. It's interesting because it started off as an environmental conceptual mainly to find the color palette, the scale of the towers Geof had drawn, and to try to get everything from the light flashes to the mounting smoke to the feel of infinity. Initially, I was hired as a conceptual illustrator for the environments, to create illustrations based on Geof's designs, adding lighting and the sweeping camera movements. It was after this illustration that Larry and Andy asked me to continue in a more storyboard/storytelling direction. We started with this shot and got the environment set with the color palette and then went through the sequence shot by shot. They were very specific what moments they wanted to see in color.

Kunitake: One thing that was really nice in the film, something that wasn't in the storyboards, was the reflection Neo sees of himself on the face of the DocBot. I thought that was a really cool evolution from the boards, tying in to his whole path. When this robot comes down, very threatening, Larry and Andy wanted a bit of a shock, so it reaches out and grabs his throat. As an audience, you're thinking it's going to twist his head off, but it actually disengages. They'd talk about how the DocBot is reading Neo as a dead body, a dead battery, and disengages him so it can flush him from the pod. Even in the script, they wanted it to be very graphic, very shocking. I was trying hard to get that sensibility.

Kunitake: The direction and feedback Larry and Andy gave was better than good. It was like they had this psychic link. I'd ask if I was going in the right direction, and they'd turn to each other and one would start a sentence and the other would finish it. We'd be back and forth, I'd sketch a bit, then they'd sketch a bit. The sound effects were particularly fun. Larry and Andy made sound effects as they described things, making what they wanted even clearer.

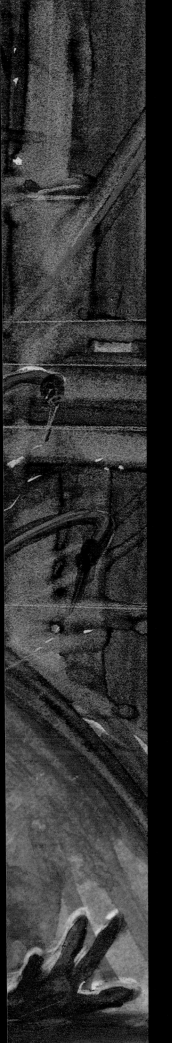

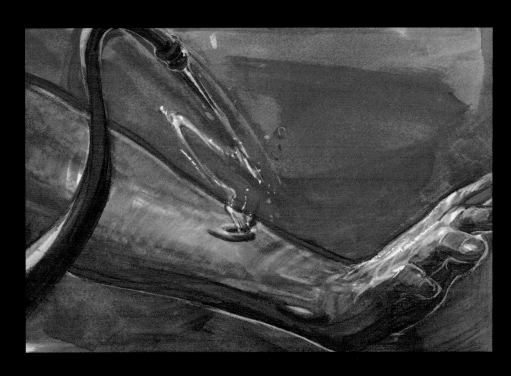

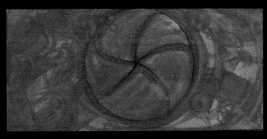

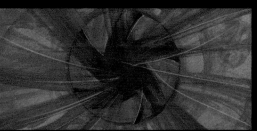

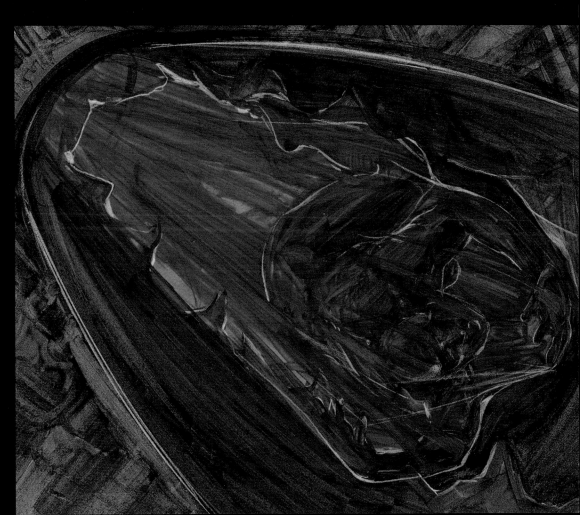

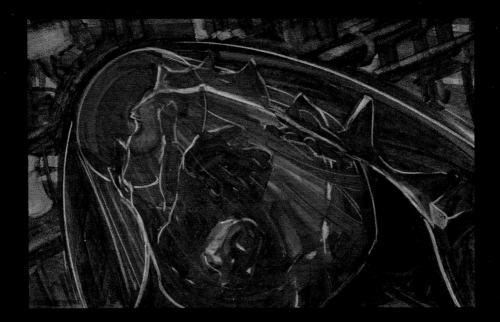

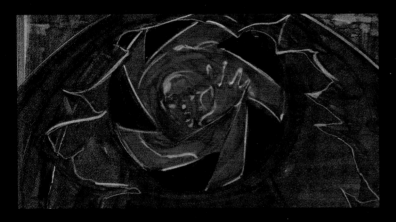

Kunitake: Here we see Neo being aborted, flushed down the toilet. I like the way they handled it in the film a lot better. The main difference is the color. Here Neo seems to hold onto the crimson until he gets immersed in the sewage. The way they filmed it feels a lot more visceral in comparison. They went into high contrast with the nightmarish flashes as he shot down the tube.

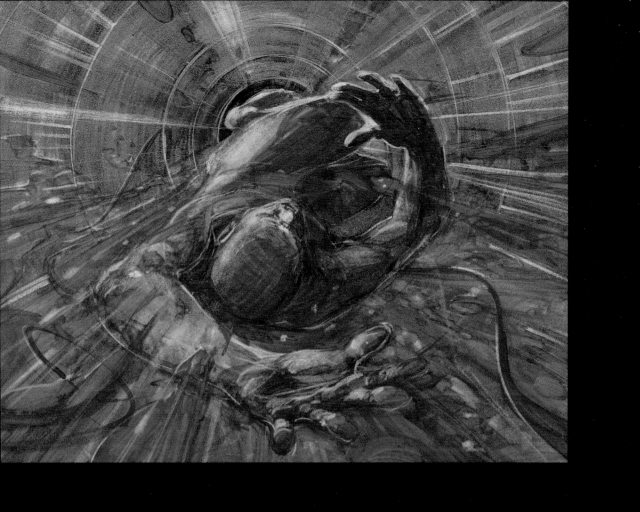

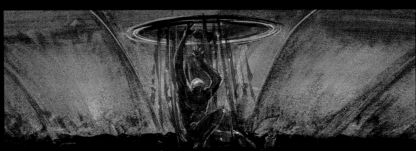

Kunitake: One of the earlier concepts we talked about was a membrane wrapped around Neo, a kind of birthing sac, which would have traveled down the pipes with him, breaking away. That's why the scene in the boards seems a little longer—and he is so full of crimson—because there was a shedding process going on.

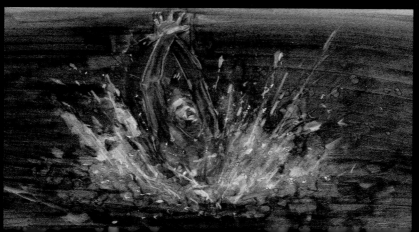

83

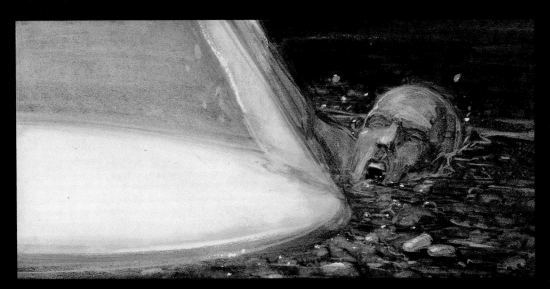

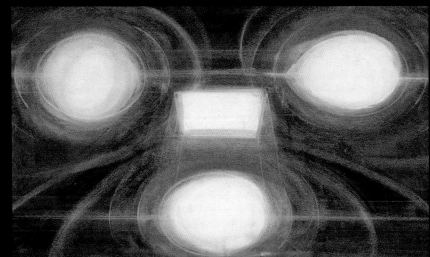

Kunitake: It was great working with Larry and Andy. For one thing, the script was strong, you could get a visual understanding just by reading it. What's more, they were able to describe the shots with a specific graphic request for each image, even telling me what they wanted to feel in the scene, making my job all the easier.

Kunitake: The first time I saw this sequence on film, I was surprised at how close it was to what we boarded. It felt good. I'm glad the studio approved all of the images we conceptualized. Usually, that's not the fact in film. Often, things get dumped out because of budgetary constraints and time. These shots are a really nice thing to see on film because in the earlier stages of conceptualizing, your expectations are very high. When you see the translation to film, it doesn't usually meet your expectations; with this film it did, and in fact actually improved—the shots went to a higher level.

THE MATRIX was not just another job for me, it's the best thing I've ever worked on. It was disheartening when they killed THE MATRIX for a little bit during preproduction, but I felt strongly about this project and was hoping it would get turned around, which it thankfully did. THE MATRIX was a difficult concept to sell, but what Larry and Andy did was excellent, holding the studio's hand with these very visual storyboards and conceptuals, walking execs through the understanding of the film.

Kunitake: Unlike a lot of films where we are restricted in our illustrations to the limitations of an aspect ratio, Larry and Andy wanted these boards to tell a story and not be typical framing. It was very interesting that they did not want action arrows or blocking directions with each frame. They wanted a solid piece of art, like a snapshot of what they wanted to see on film. This is from their comic background, no doubt. It was nice working with people from this industry, a rewarding experience. I think with this approach, having a loose frame, Larry and Andy were able to take the image and develop it even further. They weren't boxed in by a predetermined camera setup. With the boards, they wanted to capture the feelings of the shots as well as illustrate the images.

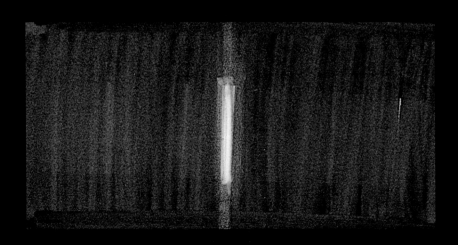

"THE DESERT OF THE REAL."

History Program

Scenes 39, 40, A40, 41

Editor: The History Program was split between two of the artists, Collin Grant and Steve Skroce. Collin starts the sequence with Morpheus filling Neo in on the "Real World." Steve enters with the feeding of the jacked-in baby.

Editor: Virtually none of the shots in this scene were traditionally realized. The entire sequence, including the transition shown here moving through Morpheus's glasses and into the Fetus Fields, needed to be meticulously planned to allow for the months of production ahead for visual effects.

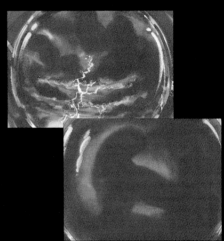

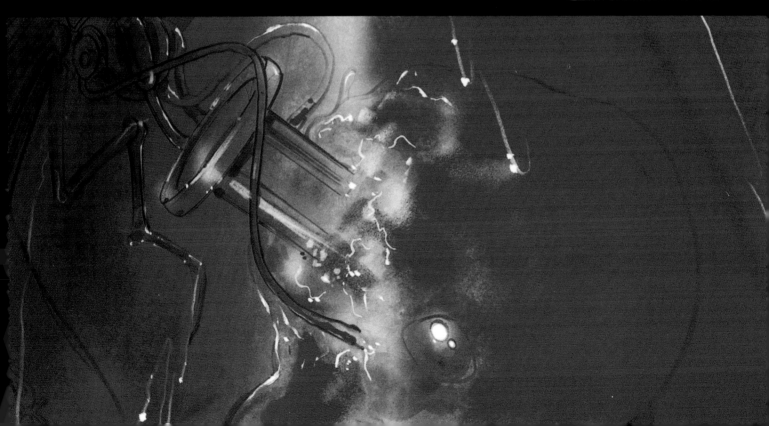

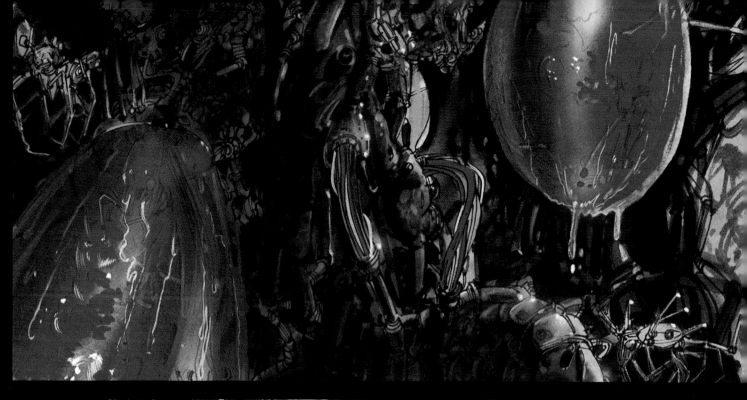
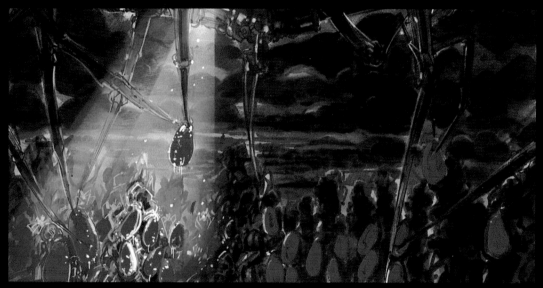

Steve Skroce: Here [below] we pull back from the hole pouring out the pureed people. I know Larry and Andy were a little fingers-crossed with the baby because they were afraid people would be freaked out by the image. I didn't work from Collin's boards, as I just did the one camera move pulling back from the hole to the reveal of the baby and the people in the pod, which is a different place from what he drew. I worked from Geof's drawings and, of course, Larry and Andy's input.

Even though I was working in black and white, they wanted red to be the focal point, a high contrast point to the dark slime and metal. That was my experience with the colored boards—a red Sharpie.

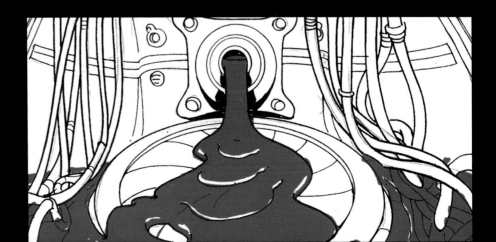

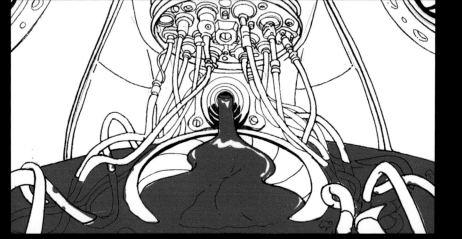

Skroce: For the baby, Larry and Andy said to take the image of Neo, Geof's image with all the cables coming out of his spinal cord and every other orifice [see gatefolds—page 257], and make it a baby instead. It was clear what to draw there because I was working from Geof's drawing. I will say that doing boards in the real world are a serious pain in the butt because Geof would spend a week or so on one of those impossibly detailed drawings and I had to bust these out in a few hours.

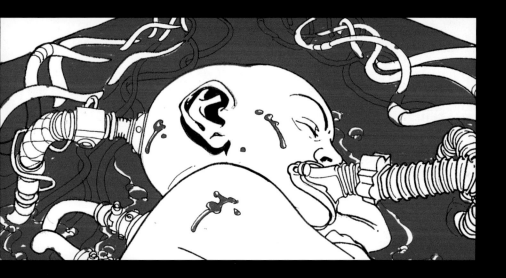

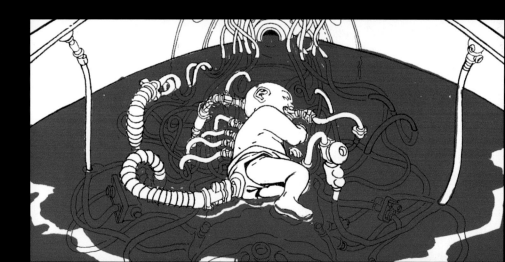

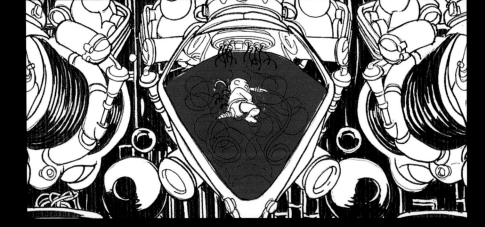

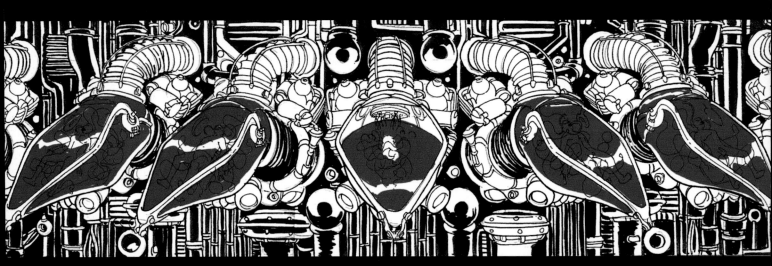

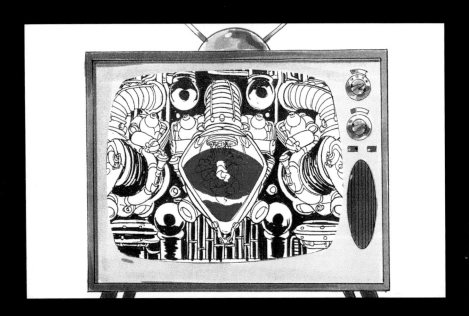

Editor: This sequence ends with a combination of two illustrations, the only time in the storyboards where boards by two of the artists are combined. The interior of the TV to the left is by Steve, while the exterior is by Collin.

"DO YOU BELIEVE THAT'S AIR
YOU ARE BREATHING NOW?"

Steve Skroce: To get the Dojo scene exactly as Larry and Andy saw it in their heads, we choreographed it all. They'd get up and act their ideas out, or we would do it with action figures. I was like the camera, and they put me where they wanted me. I'd look through the director's viewfinder at the action figures and they'd set the shot. The image framed in the viewfinder was the one I used. From there I did a sketch, a thumbnail, and they'd look at it and go, "Yes, that's the one," or tell me how they wanted it tweaked.

However, we started working on the Dojo sequence before Wo Ping [stunt choreographer] got involved, using a pretty simplistic room to illustrate. Wo Ping kept some of the key frames, some of the basic ideas, but with his experience working fights, he changed much of it. The details created by him are far more than what we originally drew in these boards.

Skroce: While working on the Dojo sequence, we rented Hong Kong kung fu movies and watched them endlessly.

Skroce: We watched everything, MEALS ON WHEELS, IRON MONKEY, THE TAI CHI MASTER, FIST OF LEGEND—all the classics. Larry and Andy are big fans of these movies. They introduced me to them around four years ago.

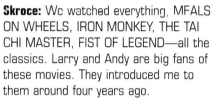

Skroce: This shot [right] was in the film as an overhead shot where Morpheus sweeps Neo's feet and Neo does a flip over him. In the movie, they both right-kick each other's head and block at the same time. So Wo Ping moved the players around, but key frames are there.

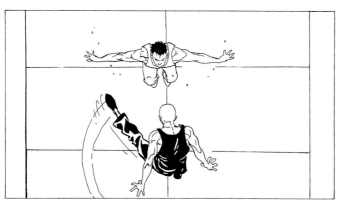
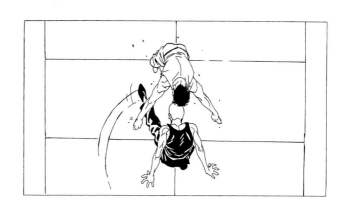

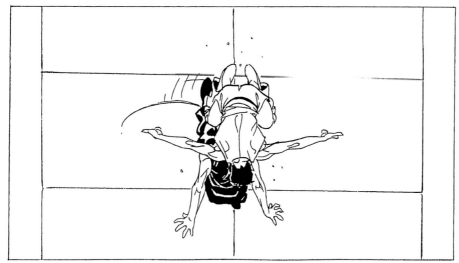

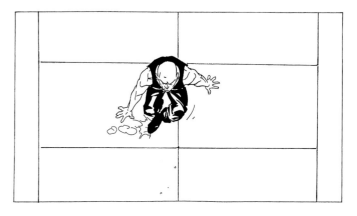

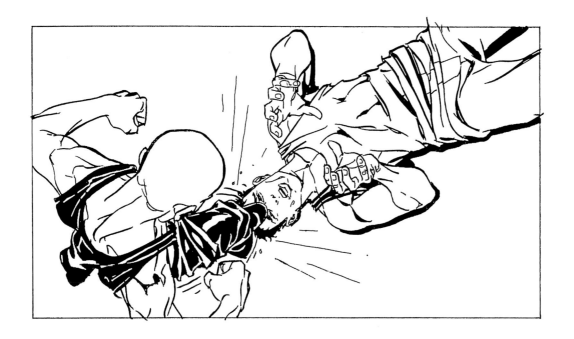

Skroce: While Wo Ping changed a lot of this, we do have the big knee smash after Morpheus does the giant leap across the room.

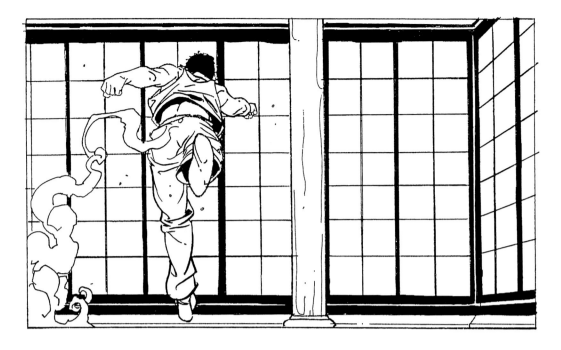

Skroce: Here's where Neo runs away from Morpheus and heads up one of the poles. Neo jumps off and does the big backflip [opposite, bottom]. In the movie he leaps over Morpheus and lands beside him rather than in front of him.

Skroce: Essentially, this [below] is the same shot in the film where Morpheus does the cool move of a side-kick into the guts, sending Neo smashing into the wooden pillar. Again, they wanted a stylish comic-book feel and gave me a bit more time to add the extra polish they needed.

"THERE IS NO SPOON."

Spoon Boy

Scene 79

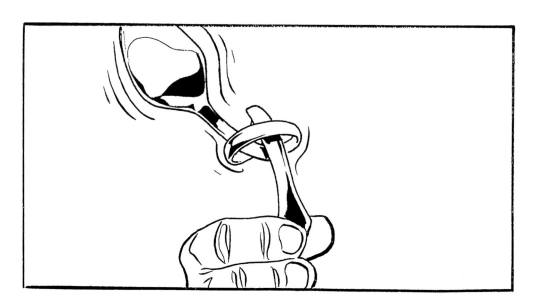

Steve Skroce: As with the rest of the locations, Larry and Andy had specific ideas about what the Oracle's place would look like. They wanted a regular apartment, but to have in the drawing what looked like little Shaolin monk kids. In the end, Spoon Boy looks the same in the film as he does in the boards. I had redrawn him a couple of times because initially I made him look a little bit more angry than he was supposed to look, which didn't convey the tone they wanted [see title page—opposite].

Skroce: For this scene, we got spoons out and looked at them to see what your reflection would do if you twisted them around, looking at the ways they warp the reflection. Discussion was given to the shot of a concave spoon and what it does to a reflection. The fear was it might confuse people, the way it reverses the image out [below], but it does do this, and is the way it's done in the film.

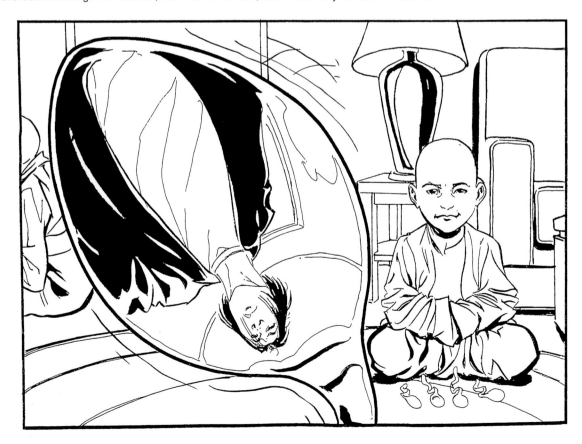

"IT'S A TRAP."

Lafayette Trap

Scenes 91, 96, 97, 99, 101, 107, 108, 110, 115, 117

Steve Skroce: For the Lafayette Trap scene Larry and Andy wanted a building that had a big central atrium, one with overlooking balconies. They sent a scout out to find a location like this and take photos for reference, which is what I worked from. This first illustration [left] was cut; there's no helicopter in that scene. The next drawing [center] is basically the same as in the film, except it doesn't look like Mouse. A lot of the characters in the boards don't look like they do in the movie because at that point they weren't designed, and had not yet even been cast.

Skroce: Larry and Andy didn't limit their imaginations whatsoever at this early stage for fear of budget limitations. They crammed the script full of whatever they could think of on the first run-through, no matter if it seemed impossible. This illustration shows the shadows of the cops coming up and Morpheus looking down. Because they didn't use the original location, which was in Chicago, this shot is slightly different in the film; there isn't a spiral staircase, it's just a regular stairway. But the composition is basically the same, with Morpheus in the foreground and the shadows of the cops. One thing the brothers don't like to do is board any of the talking heads, only the specific shots they need extra time to set up for, which is why we cut from here to the crew in the wet wall.

Skroce: This is not in the movie, their climbing into the wet wall. But the idea of them going into the wet wall was retained.

Skroce: Originally, Cypher got stuck in the wall and made a bulge, knocking tiles off the wall. In the film, they just had him sneeze. This saved setting up this wall where they would have to rig tiles to fall off. It was easier to shoot with the sneeze and it did the same thing.

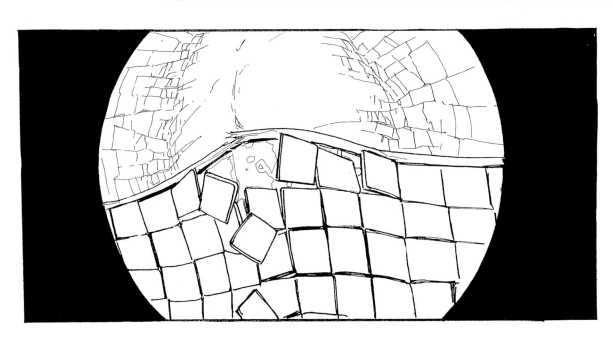

Skroce: This was changed [right]. A main sewer pipe running up through all the toilets was going to be shot up and spew sewage onto Cypher.

In this illustration [above], Neo has his back facing us, which isn't the way it happens in the film. On screen, he's turned around the other way because they wanted Neo to shoot back straight away, as he does in this [bottom] shot, but without having to turn.

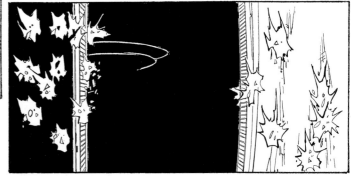

Skroce: These bottom two shots aren't in the movie. They were replaced with close-ups where you don't actually see Morpheus looking down. To get the inside of the wet wall, which I'd never seen, Larry and Andy described it as slats of wood with plaster in between each piece, drawing on their carpentry skill, no doubt.

Skroce: This sequence is the same as in the film, right up to where the fight between Morpheus and Agent Smith cuts in. As far as the choreography in the bathroom, the fight itself, that's all Wo Ping. There was no point storyboarding all of it. I showed the head-butts, which are in the film, but most of it got worked through with Larry, Andy, and Wo Ping's stunt crew. They decided later how they wanted to cover it.

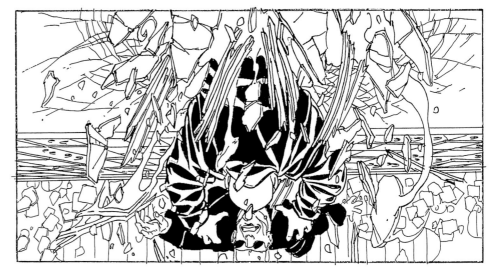

Lafayette Trap

129

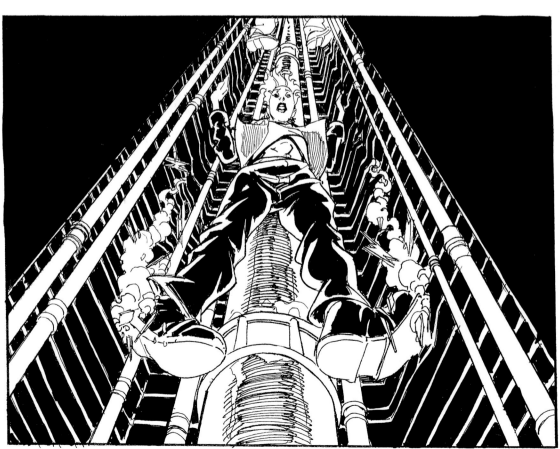

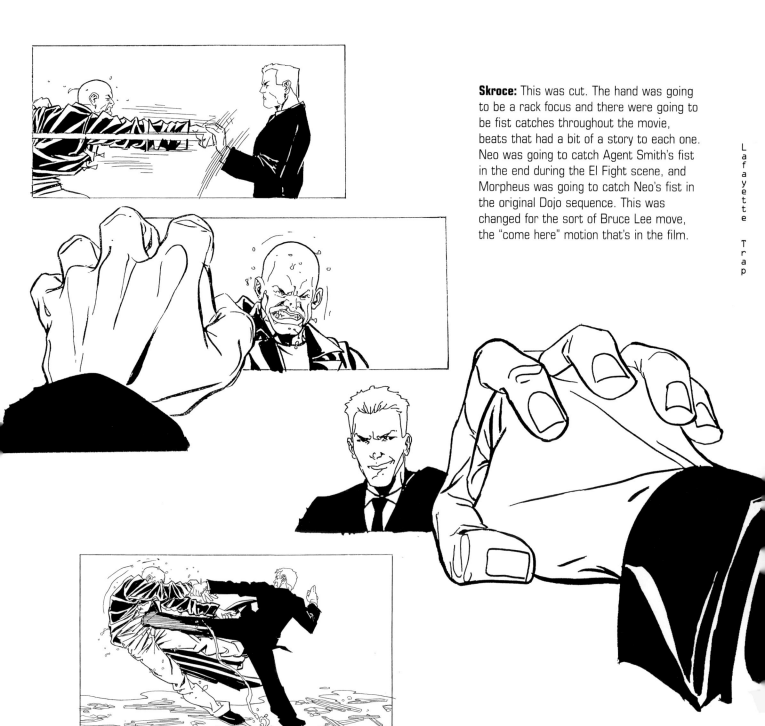

Skroce: This was cut. The hand was going to be a rack focus and there were going to be fist catches throughout the movie, beats that had a bit of a story to each one. Neo was going to catch Agent Smith's fist in the end during the El Fight scene, and Morpheus was going to catch Neo's fist in the original Dojo sequence. This was changed for the sort of Bruce Lee move, the "come here" motion that's in the film.

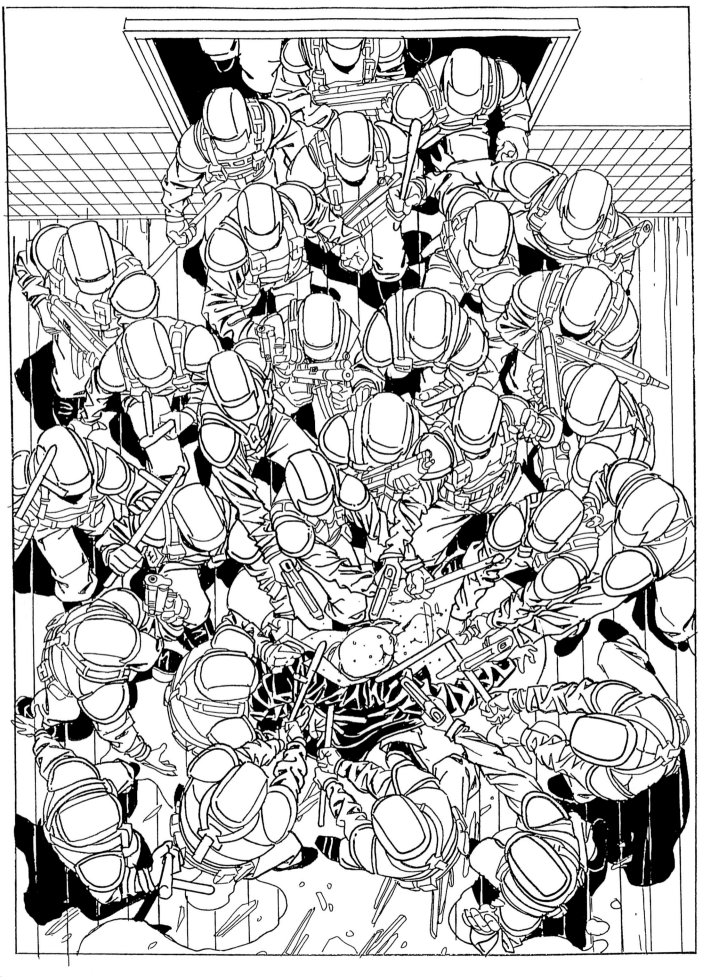

DARK GLASSES, GAME FACES.

Steve Skroce: These first illustrations are pretty much the way it is in the movie, Neo walking in and giving the guy a punch to the chest, sending him flying. Originally, I wanted to have the little change cup go shooting out of the guy's hand [top left], like when you go through a metal detector and have to take your change out of your pocket and give it to the guy. But they didn't put that in the movie. I heard Wo Ping thought it was funny, though.

This sequence was changed pretty dramatically from when it was first storyboarded [see page 429]. Originally, the Government Lobby was going to be a hotel. Morpheus was still being held, so the story was the same, but he was being held in a hotel room. When Neo and Trinity walk into the hotel lobby, they do have a shoot-out, but not before sending the people screaming out of the hotel. I think it was going to be less of a shoot 'em up. Then Larry and Andy came up with the Government Lobby idea and you get the biggest shoot-up in the movie.

Skroce: The Government Lobby is a fairly accurate sequence of shots to the storyboards, but this one [below] is not in the film, no one gets a shot off.

Skroce: Here we have Trinity throwing a couple of knives at the guard. In the film, she just shoots him.

Initially, Larry and Andy were going to have super guns made for this scene, but it didn't work out. They used regular M16s, which did the job. In the first version, they also had Trinity doing more hand-to-hand combat, rather than using guns, but by the time they got down to filming, it just didn't flow right.

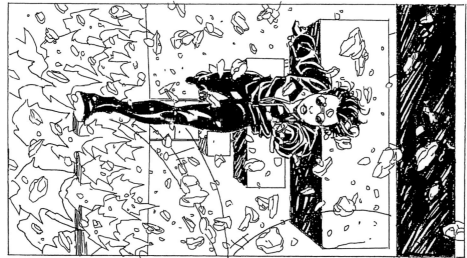

Skroce: Originally, where Trinity runs on the wall and flips off, the camera was going to be one fluid shot. Here in the boards, as soon as she starts running on the wall, until she jumps off behind a pillar, it's pretty much the camera following her and then just panning a little bit as she lands. In the movie that's not how it's cut. She's running on the wall and as she jumps off, it cuts to a shot of her upside down and you see her head and shoulders turning in slow motion as she's landing.

Skroce: Trinity was always a PVC chick. In the storyboards, Neo was a bit more army fatigues; he's definitely got more fashion sense in the film, looks cooler. The trench coats and sunglasses were always Larry and Andy's idea. Especially in this scene, the glasses were there to look cool, but also as a safety consideration for the actors in the midst of all this debris.

Skroce: The Government Lobby scene is where Neo first starts to discover his powers as The One, what he can actually do. That's the reason he starts doing all this nutty stuff. It's the most fantastic thing we've seen him do up to this point, and then, to top it off, he does a flip while firing upside down, doing a handstand.

143

Skroce: The last panel [bottom], where Neo lands, doesn't really indicate he has landed behind the far wall (after he does the one-handed handstand and comes upright). I drew this crazy thing—which is kind of ridiculous now that I think about it—where he's moving so fast that by the time he lands, the shells that were ejecting out of frame left in the previous panel are still mid-air, whizzing past him. He's moving faster than the shells can land.

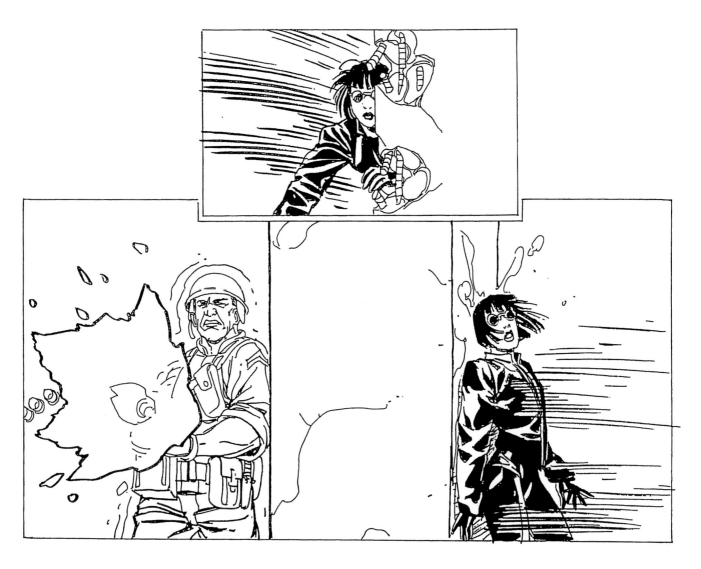

Skroce: Here's Trinity sneaking up on a soldier, out of sight on one side of a pillar. She's about to do a little bolo trick, but it got cut. I guess it slowed things down a bit.

Skroce: In the boards, while the bolo trick is happening, on the opposite side of the room a soldier is shooting at Neo. While the bolo got cut, this does happen, just not in the order shown here.

Skroce: These shots didn't happen [top to bottom], although they lead to a sequence that does [over].

Skroce: Here's Prince Charles, as we called him. Andy took one look, said the name, and it stuck.

Skroce: Here, Neo comes up and kicks Prince Charles hard with his right leg, swinging him around fast. When Neo finally lands and stops, the coat sort of wraps around him like a cape. Unfortunately, this was not worth going to the lengths needed to shoot, all the mumbo jumbo you'd have to go through to do it— physics played into that.

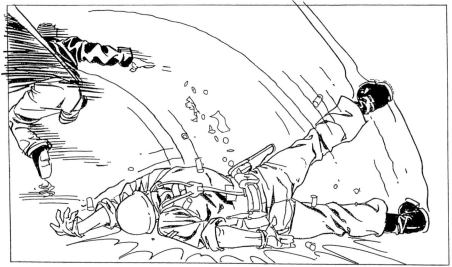

It would have been cool though, and in keeping with the hero Neo is becoming. In the movie, he does have somewhat super human strength, which we were underscoring with the coat.

Government Lobby

Skroce: For the end of the Government Lobby scene, Larry and Andy kept saying they wanted this to be a living animation—an impossible amount of debris coming off the pillars—and, as I was drawing, they kept saying, "More." The pillars were supposed to look like chewed-up apple cores by the end of it.

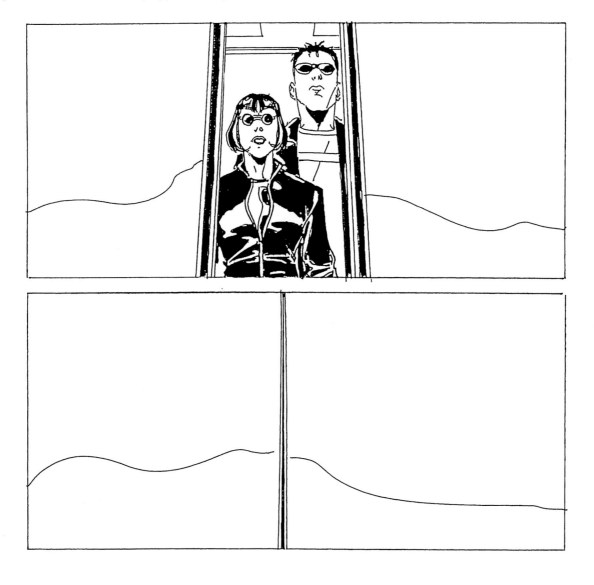

"I THINK THEY'RE TRYING TO SAVE HIM."

Elevator Shaft

Scenes 154, 155

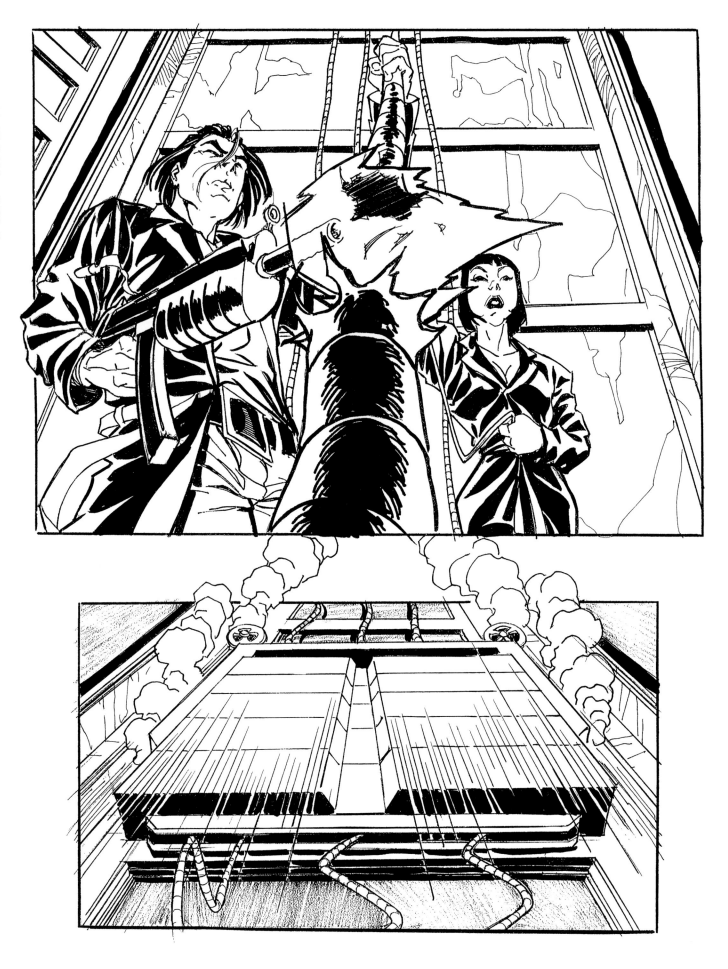

Steve Skroce: Here's where "There is no spoon" is said. It's one of the earlier sequences I worked on. I drew it before I drew the revised Government Lobby scene. They have more guns in the boards and Neo's hair is different, although Trinity looks the same. In the film, the big gun Neo is holding turns into a handgun.

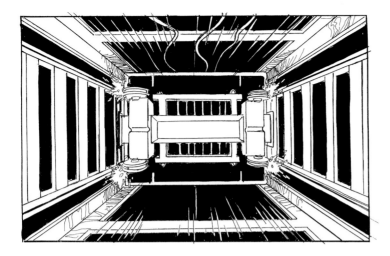

Skroce: I can't wait to draw boards for the sequels because I'll have costume references and a better idea of what the movie looks like. The film is now a thing you can reference. The Matrix exists.

"DODGE THIS!"

Government Roof

Scene 157

Steve Skroce: The Government Roof scene is interesting because it takes illustrations from my original two weeks, my second period of working and my last time out. So some of these drawings were done months apart, but they appear right next to each other.

Skroce: Here's a series that doesn't make it in the film [center through next three pages]. There was a lot more time spent killing these guys on the boards.

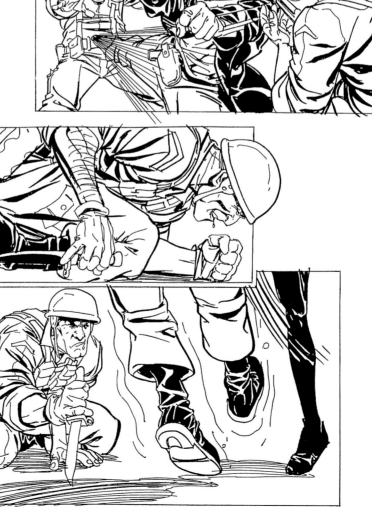

Skroce: These shots would have been cool if the sequence had been in the film. What Larry and Andy wanted to do was have Trinity break the guy's arm and send the knife flying up into the air. We would see the compass at the end of the knife by a rack focus, and see the needle point north; it would then fall with Neo catching it and, in one motion, take out the guy with the gun, who was seen earlier about to shoot Trinity.

Skroce: This is Neo's Bullet Time sequence which is completely accurate. Larry and Andy showed me the moves they wanted with the director's viewfinder and we used the action figures again. Larry actually got up and did the motions of Neo as he was dodging the bullets and Andy would catch him as he fell back. We moved the coffee table in my hotel room, and Larry got up and closed his eyes imagining what it would be like in his mind. He'd do the motions so I could get an idea of what his body was doing, then I'd sketch him while he did that a couple of times. From there we would move to the action figures and decide on the angles we wanted.

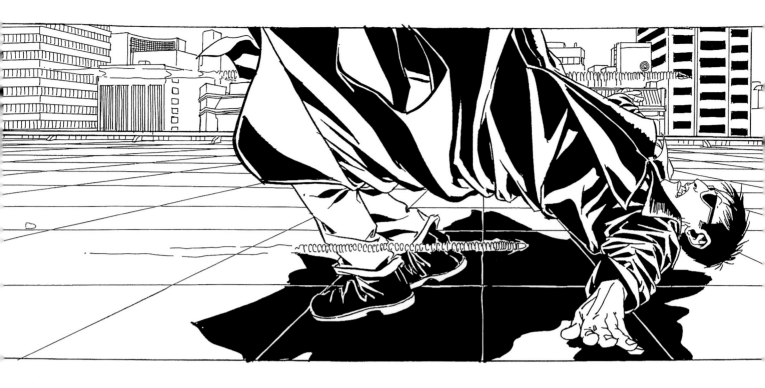

Skroce: Getting these ripples took a long time to figure out. The ripples of the bullets were described to me as being like dropping a pebble into a pond, so I just imagined that effect, but over and over again, dropping through layer after layer.

Keanu Reeves was on wires during this scene, with a fan blowing on him to make his jacket move like a cape. In the boards, we show him as just fast enough to get out of the way of those bullets, just dodging them. This is Larry and Andy thinking the action out, making it look more realistic, trying to figure out exactly what movement you would make when you're moving this fast. You'd see one bullet coming and you'd fling your arm up this way, if you could move that fast, trying to twist your body out of the way of all these things coming at you super fast.

Skroce: And then, we're out of
Bullet Time with Neo taking a bullet.

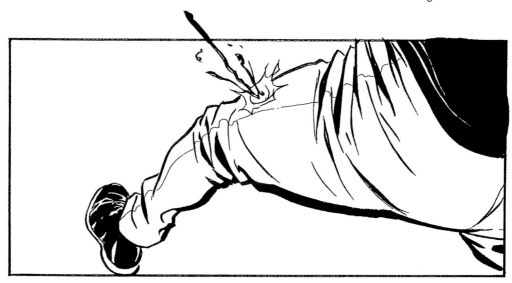

Skroce:
"Dodge this"
is in the film
pretty much
as I drew it.

When we were doing the sketches, Larry and Andy said,
"The gun is as big as she is, with a wide angle lens."

"HE IS THE ONE."

Helicopter Rescue

Scenes 161, 163, 164

Steve Skroce: You can tell most of this sequence was drawn in the first two weeks by the way I'm drawing and the notes, which are by Larry and Andy. In these early days they put notes on the boards.

This one [below] is kind of special, as it's actually the first drawing I ever did for THE MATRIX. It was a tough drawing to do, one which didn't make it into the movie. It would have been impossible to put a camera where it needed to be to get this reflection so it would've been a special effects shot, which wasn't worth it.

Pull Jones into room; reflection in puddling water.

Agents react to sound of descending helicopter.

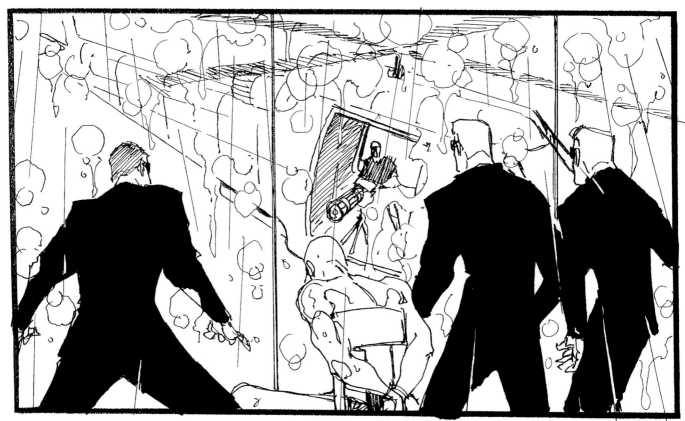

Boom up as helicopter drops down, Neo seen through curtain of water rippling down window.

Outside as Neo arms.

KA-CHIK

The window is shiny black, opaque. As bullets shatter it we see more of the room inside, like an eggshell cracking open. Hundreds of casings spin in slo-motion.

Skroce: This shot [above] is in the film, but Neo's foot is on the landing bar of the helicopter instead of in the copter as I drew it. [Below] is the room getting chewed up; the idea is retained but it's not the way Larry and Andy actually shot it.

Half-circle dolly as the room is chewed to bits. Chaos erupts all around Morpheus.

Skroce: Here it's just chaos, the Agents running from Neo as he fires. The Agents all get hit, but in the film you can't really see any of the squibs [blood packs] going off like you see them here in the boards.

Jones dives for door opening.

Track with bullet trail as Jones is hit, door reduced to toothpicks.

Smith rolls up firing.

Smith floats backwards amidst an eruption of soft cottony bed guts.

Dolly in as...

Skroce: Because this scene was originally set in a hotel room, there's a bed getting all chewed up and, as Smith lands on the bed, he turns back into the cop. This was drawn when we were still working out the idea of how the transformation would look. The idea was, as the cop dissolves, the Agent would come up and out of him like coming up through water.

...white flash, electric static, Smith sinks...

...disappearing into a cop.

Skroce: This shot [above] is dead-on, an impossible amount of shells coming down. This [below] is the first time I drew Larry and Andy's version of a rack focus, which they wanted illustrated by an image breaking its box.

WHIZZZ, gun stops spinning, smoke pours out of barrels, rack focus...

Quiet hiss of sprinklers.

Skroce: [Below and over top] are from later drawings. By my third time in Los Angeles, we had reference for the buildings in Australia, so most of the helicopter shots needed to be redone.

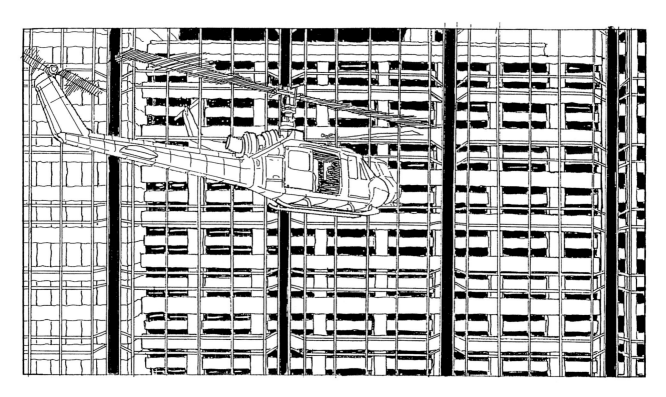

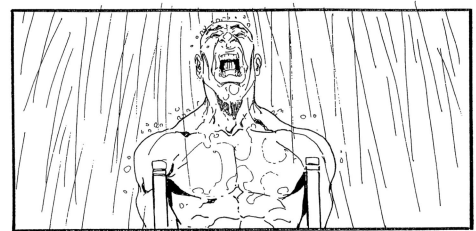

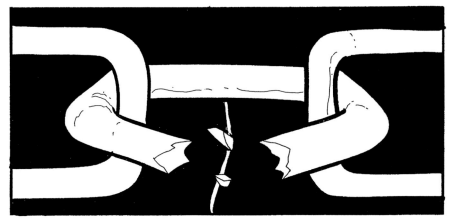

In hallway, marines become agents. Sunglasses push through
face, eyes flat on glasses.

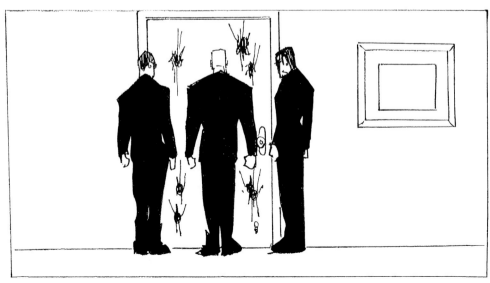

Agents in hall.

Smith sees Morpheus running for the window.

Shoots line of bullets through wall.

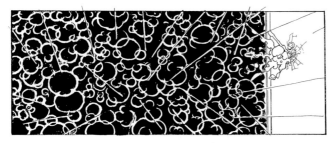

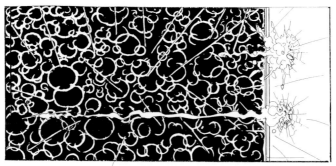

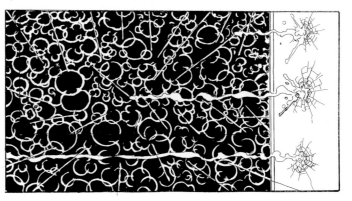

Skroce: This is the Bullet Time sequence with Morpheus. Larry and Andy described the bullet as a burning-hot ember coming at Morpheus and hitting his leg, then sizzling past.

Bullet time; low angle track in at Morpheus moving in the super slo-mo, bullets sizzling past us, as we pass through the chalky jet trails.

Skroce: The shot of Neo fastening the safety line (right) is cut in the film; when we get there, it's already attached. They didn't need a shot of him doing this, it slowed everything down.

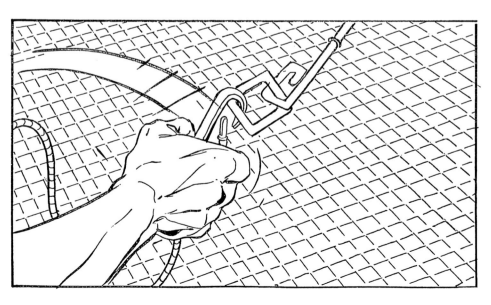

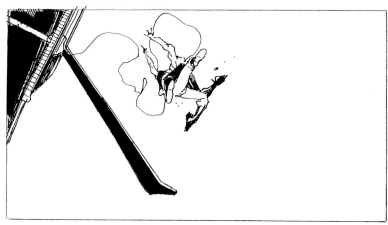

Skroce: This illustration [facing page, bottom] was the "I love you, man" drawing, as we called it. It's pretty much how it appears in the film.

They fall straight at us, under-crank, blades flashing black above them.

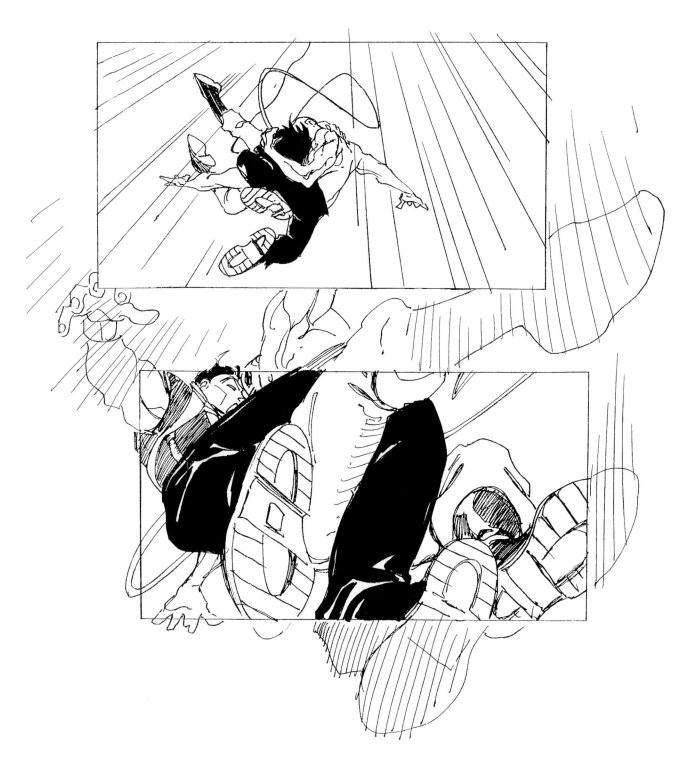

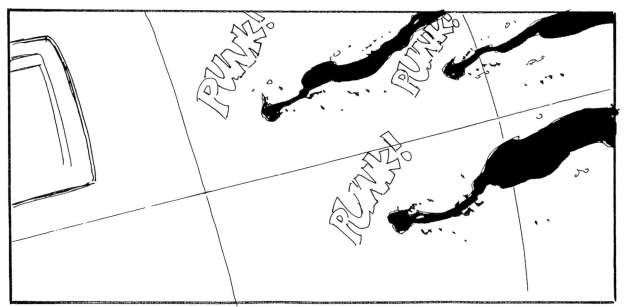

Black oil blood begins pouring out of the helicopter.

The helicopter dies.

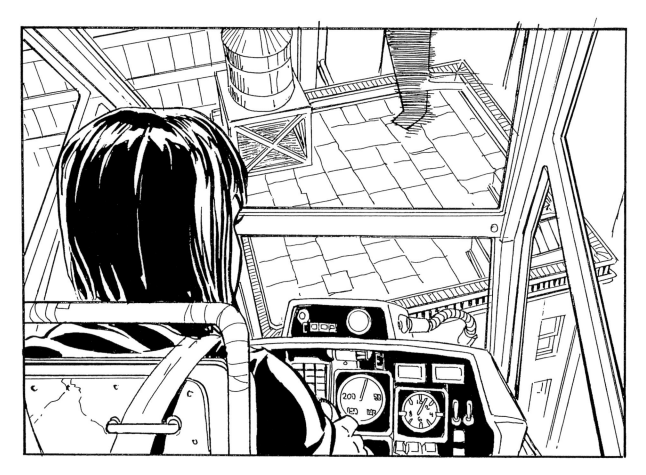

Skroce: There was a time where Larry and Andy thought the helicopter shot wasn't going to happen. Warner Bros. wanted to have it cut because they thought it would be too expensive, but the brothers convinced them otherwise, with help from these boards.

Skroce: This was another place we used action figures and a director's viewfinder to set up what Larry and Andy wanted to have happen. They had very specific ideas of where they wanted characters to land and move. For the Helicopter Rescue scene we actually bought a model helicopter and built a scale four-story building out of a cardboard box, adding a little Agent Smith. This was just Larry and Andy with a couple of rulers and some scissors. We would use the director's viewfinder to see how big the helicopter would be in relation to the building, and how big a distance it would be with the spinning helicopter blades.

Neo struggles to unhook the rope.

Skroce: With all the illustrations, there was extensive communication on every image. I never second-guessed what Larry and Andy had spoken to me about. We had completely agreed on what each image was going to look like before I did a finish for any sequence. They are truly amazing to work with.

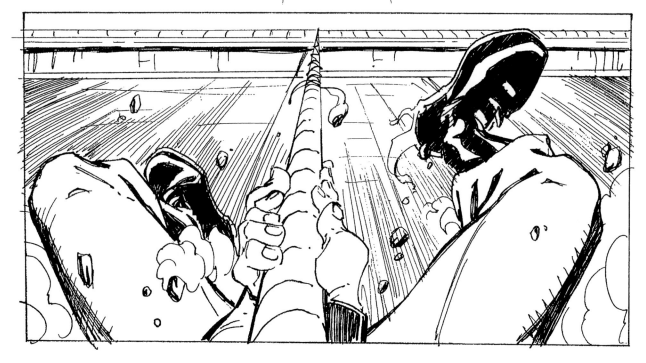

Skroce: Here's where Trinity shoots the cable and uses it to swing out of the helicopter.

Skroce: The idea of Neo at the edge of a building holding onto Trinity while the helicopter crashes does happen in the film, and would seem an impossible shot. To get this, they used models, real people, and CGI, all working together seamlessly.

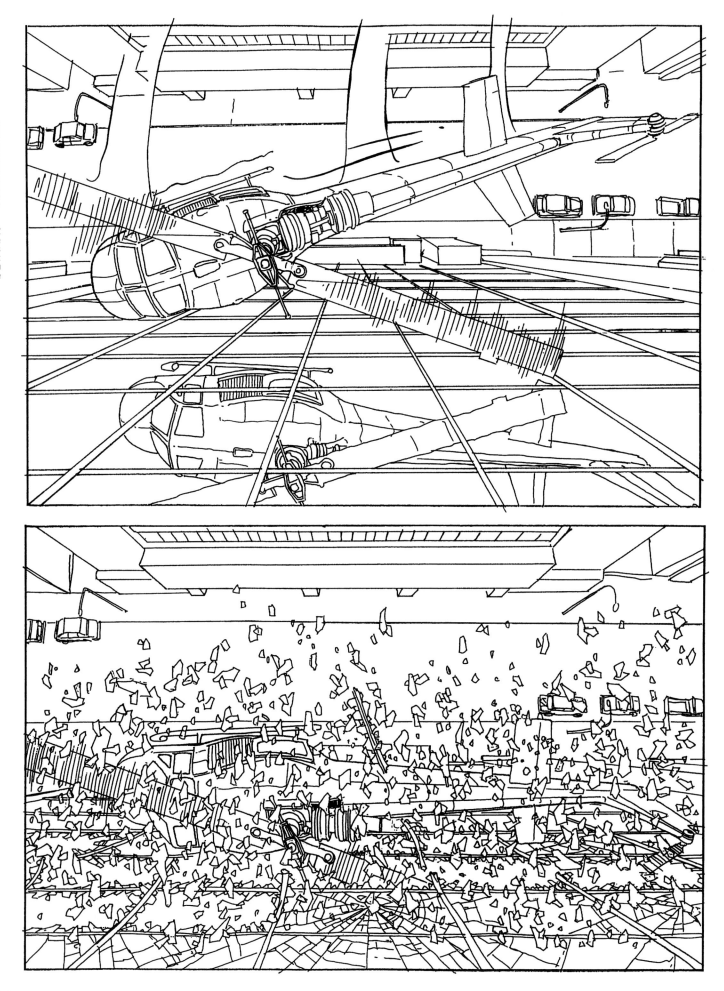

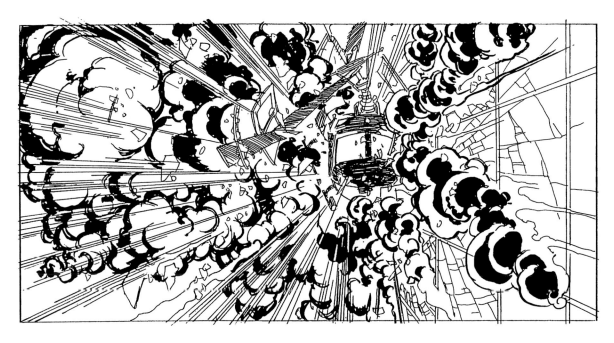

Skroce: This shot of the helicopter exploding [above] is not in the film. There were no close-ups of this. We cut from the helicopter as it starts to go off. I worked 24 hours straight on this sequence.

The explosion hurls her at the building across street, the building that Neo is standing on.

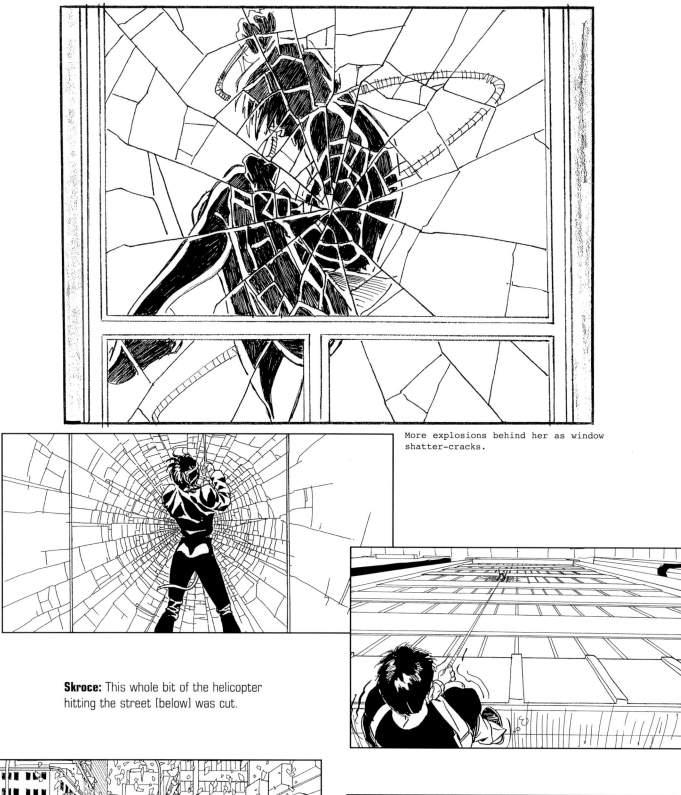

More explosions behind her as window shatter-cracks.

Skroce: This whole bit of the helicopter hitting the street [below] was cut.

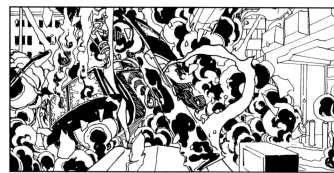

"MY NAME IS NEO."

El Fight

Scenes 172, 174, 176, 178, 180

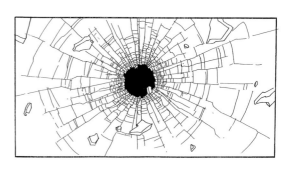

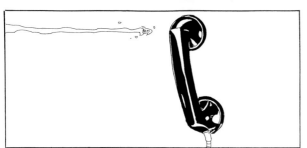

Steve Skroce: Here's a scene where Geof Darrow [see Conceptual Designs—page 257] drew a series of storyboards. Mine go up to the phone exploding, with a few illustrations towards the middle.

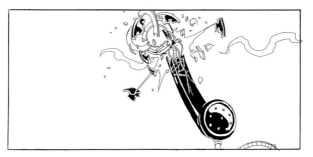

Geof Darrow: After drawing all the conceptuals, I really wanted to give storyboards a shot. I got tired of drawing the machines. I never had to draw so much so fast.

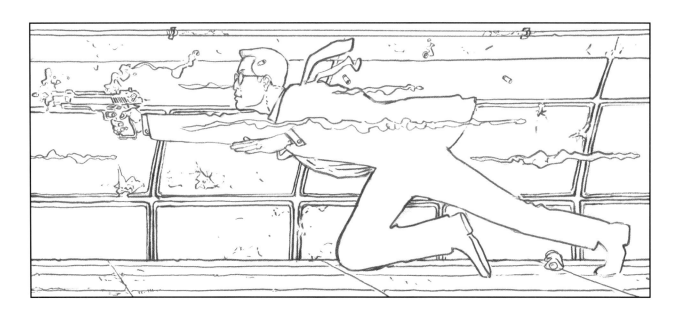

Darrow: For reference on some of this scene I took pictures of Steve [Skroce]. For the fist, I drew my own hand, using a mirror. Larry and Andy were laughing because I've the classic stars dancing around Neo's head, getting across the fact he's hurting.

In this scene, Larry and Andy wanted there to be girders because, originally, it was the Chicago subway. To have Neo hit metal and concrete looks better because you have all that shit flying off. But these were all drawn before Australia was the location, or even before Wo Ping got involved. After we did these illustrations, it looked like the film was going to be made, but it was up and down. All through the time we were working on these storyboards, it was never a sure thing.

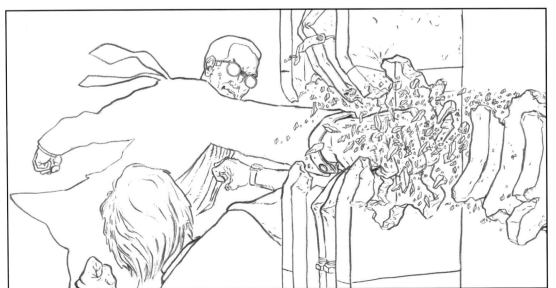

Skroce: The big idea with these four illustrations [above and right], which were dropped, was to have this recurring fist catch action running through the film. It was replaced with the "come here" hand motion first used in the Dojo sequence. Neo does get thrown back by Agent Smith in this scene, but is thrown into a derelict newsagent, not a wall.

Darrow: We [the illustrators] worked very closely with Larry and Andy on each shot. Tani Kunitake, who worked on a bunch of movies before THE MATRIX, would even say he had never had that much access to a director; usually the drawings are just dropped off and the art director picks them up. But with Larry and Andy we would show the work to the directors ourselves and have feedback directly from them.

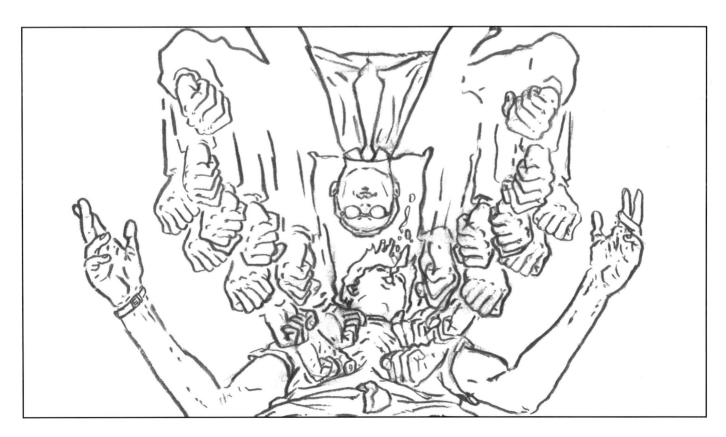

Darrow: Typical storyboards aren't nearly as complex as what's been done for THE MATRIX, but at the same time, they don't have to be. In Larry and Andy's case, it helped a lot, because the studio wouldn't have gotten the scope of it if they'd been normal storyboards.

Editor: The below image is not upside down. The board is exploring a unique camera angle which did not get used in the final film.

Darrow: Most movies are so straightforward, they just need the camera placement, it doesn't matter if the drawings are finished or not—you've arrows pointing things out. But if it's drawn right you don't need them, you know the guy is running in that particular direction. I did a couple of storyboards that were nothing but arrows, just for a laugh; there were arrows going in all sorts of directions, from different perspectives.

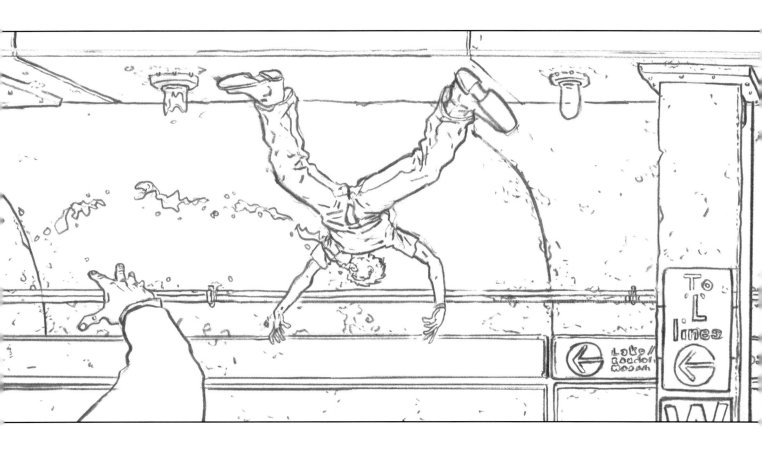

Darrow: Larry and Andy were there, telling me shot-for-shot what they wanted for these boards, so there wasn't too much guesswork on things. They would use action figures to show the scene, or sketch it. For instance, they did a rough drawing for the chair in the Neb. Their drawings are basic, but as long as you get somebody who can understand what they're driving at, it works [see Preliminary Thumbnails—page 407].

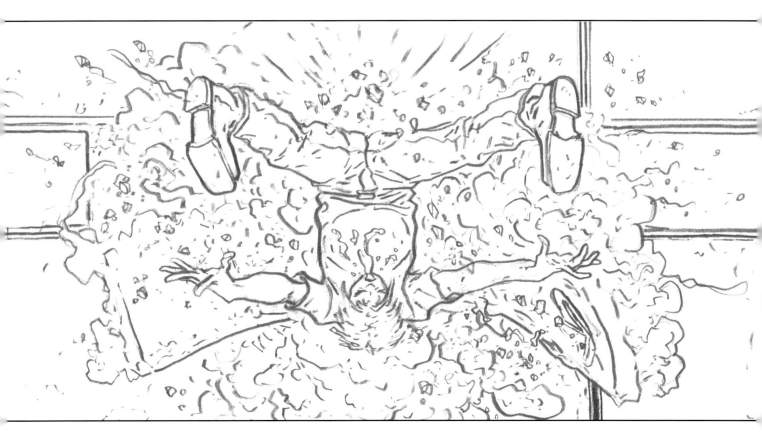

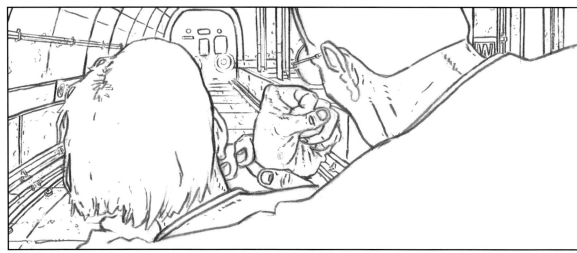

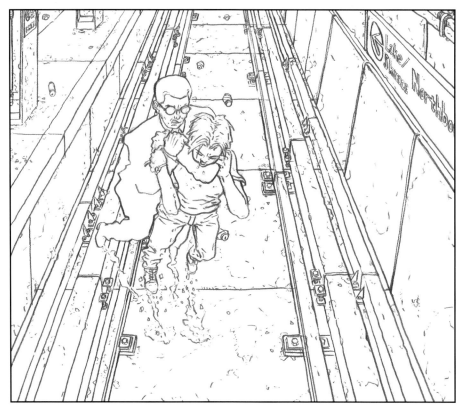

"GOOD-BYE, MR. ANDERSON."

Chase Finale

Scenes 203, 205, 211, 212, 213

  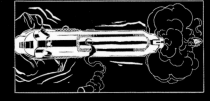

Steve Skroce: Originally, in these boards [above and right], the gun fires and the camera moves around Neo, but we don't see he's been hit, can't see the splatter of blood yet.

The camera moves from right to left, frame-right to frame-left, around him, and you see the big blood splatter, which was changed to his chest, and him looking down.

Tani Kunitake: When Larry and Andy were first talking about this scene, they wanted to give subtle visual cues to where we are, masking the Matrix with a very slight green tint, and outside in the real world, with a slight blue tint. To heighten this, in these illustrations I painted the backside of the vellum green, giving me this natural green tint that would permeate through whatever I put on top. Then, as I needed any color besides green, I just built up the opacity for that color, giving everything a built-in green tint.

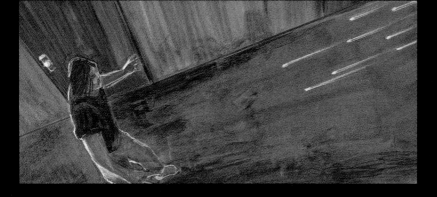

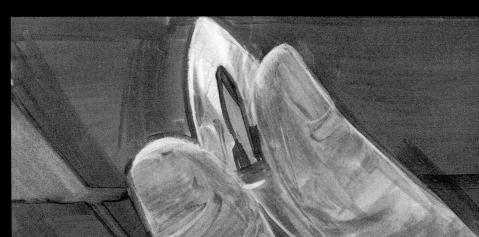

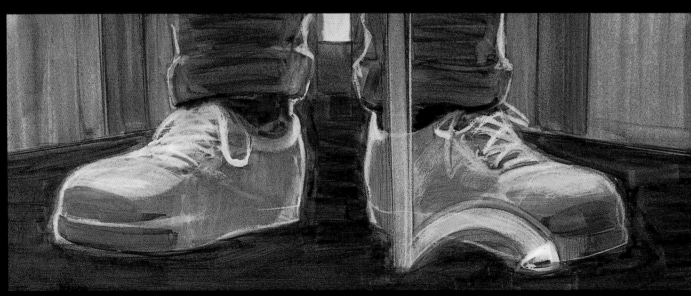

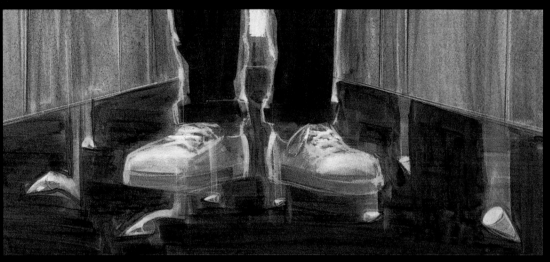

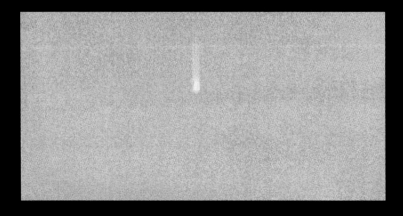

Kunitake: The code wasn't fully developed
when I did these boards, but the ideas are
the same. The reason for going in and out
of the Matrix was to show the crew reacting
to the code going nuts. It wasn't that the
code was moving progressively in any way,
it's bulleting, speeding, spinning, rushing,
impossible for anyone to read. That's the
moment when Neo sees in code.

Kunitake: Larry and Andy wanted Neo's dive into Agent Smith to be pretty clean, like a big disappearing act.

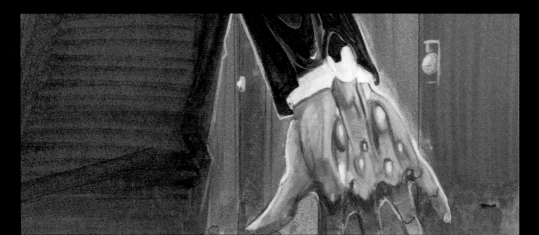

Kunitake: For this sequence, with the Agent Smith explosion, we did quite a few passes. We were looking at a lot of anime, wanting to capture the feeling of this in the exploding body. The first pass on this scene was really fleshy, but didn't feel right, it felt more comical. The Agent didn't explode like a shell, as he does in these boards, it was more like he was all flesh. This one I drew on the second pass. They wanted more of a slow build-up, where he would kind of boil up and percolate, reaching the threshold, cracking some, and finally shattering, revealing Neo underneath.

“SENTINELS.”

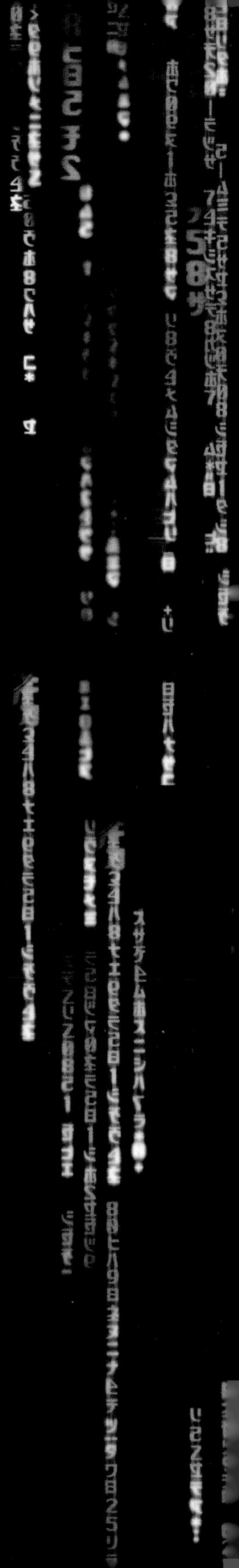

Sentinel Attack

Scenes 199, 200, 202, 204, 206, 208, 210, 214, 216, 217

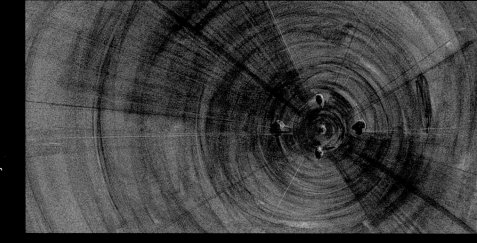

Tani Kunitake: At this point, Geof had already done his conceptual designs (see page 257), so we knew how the Sentinels looked, but we didn't know exactly how these things were going to move. Working with Larry and Andy, I made the Sentinels look like they move fast, like speed-bikes, down this circular corridor. The tentacles were a problem, it felt as if they were moving in water. Larry and Andy wanted their movement to be very direct, very precise, so we folded back the tentacles, sending them on their path as efficiently as possible, more menacing. What we did in the boards was to try and convey the feeling and emotion of a fast and menacing Sentinel, getting the way Larry and Andy wanted it to feel, but not necessarily the way it would look in the film.

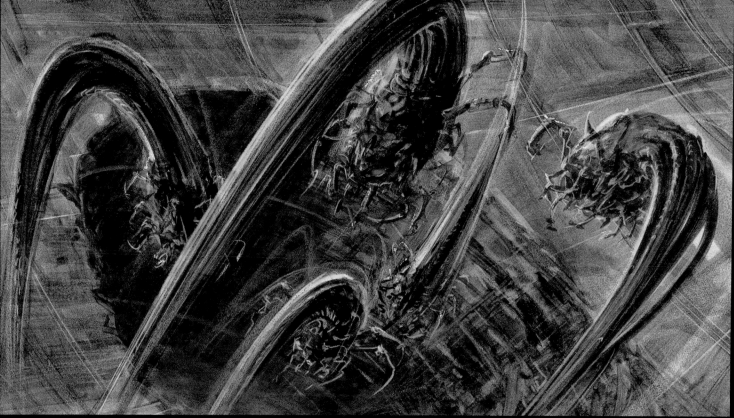

Kunitake: Here's where the Sentinels move from their efficiency mode with tentacles back, to attack mode, extending all their nasty appendages out for attack—which has pretty much translated to the screen as is. The Sentinels impact on the side of the ship, smashing against the hull and start cutting apart the ship.

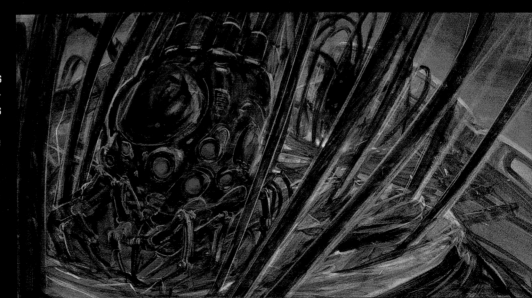

WARNING: HULL BREACH
WARNING: HULL BREACH
WARNING: HULL BREACH
WARNING: HULL BREACH

Steve Skroce: Drawing inside the Nebuchadnezzar was one of the more difficult things for me to do, just because it is such a small area and there's so much detail to everything, especially with all the chairs attached to the core.

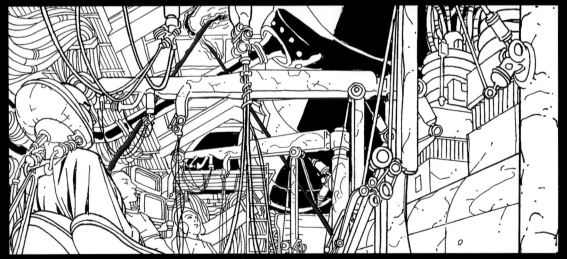

Trying to work out the perspectives and vanishing points, I sometimes found them going a million miles off the page, so it was a bit of a challenge.

Skroce: In this sequence, Tani did the exterior shots—what was happening outside the ship—and I did the interior.

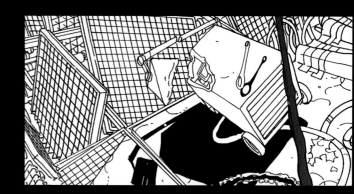

The kiss [below], the all-important kiss, happens in the film as it does in the boards.

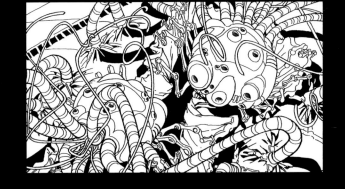

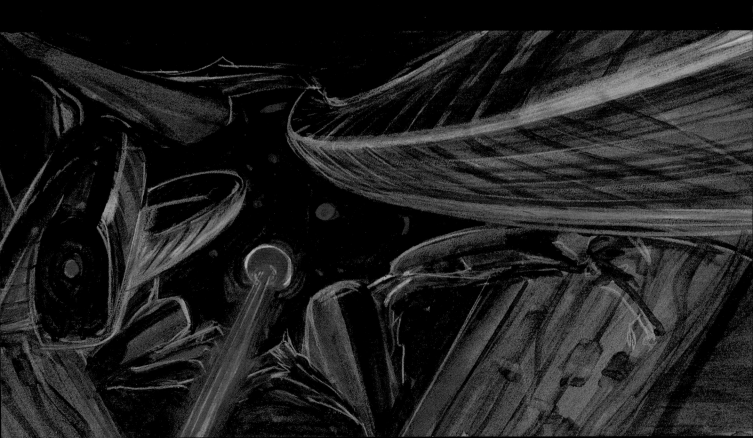

Skroce: These are the Sentinels breaking into the hull of the ship. Even with all the difficulties in drawing the interior of the Neb, at least there was great reference with the material that Geof had done; there's a lot of information in his illustrations.

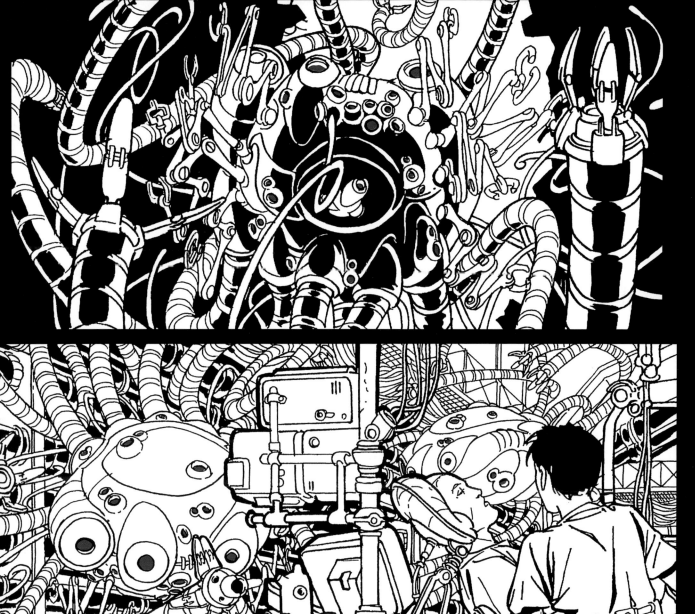

Skroce: Here's something that got cut from the movie [below], the belly of the Sentinel opening up. It was originally going to have mechanical arms with little components coming out and assembling something. You wouldn't be able to see what it was building, until it turned, allowing you to see it had just built a gun, a gun that was about to fire. It would've been cool, but an unnecessary beat.

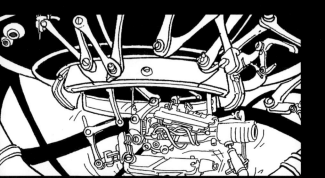

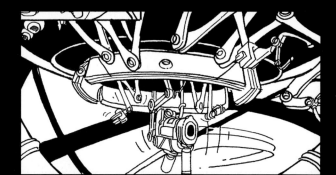

Kunitake: Here's the electromagnetic pulse destroying the Sentinels outside the Neb. Larry and Andy asked me to do this last shot to capture the essence of a great release of energy, stopping the attack.

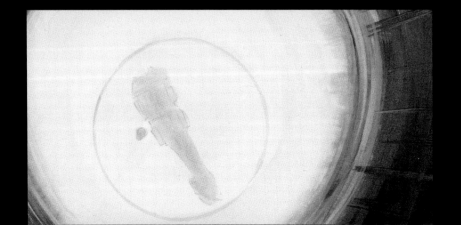

"I'VE DECIDED TO MAKE A FEW CHANGES."

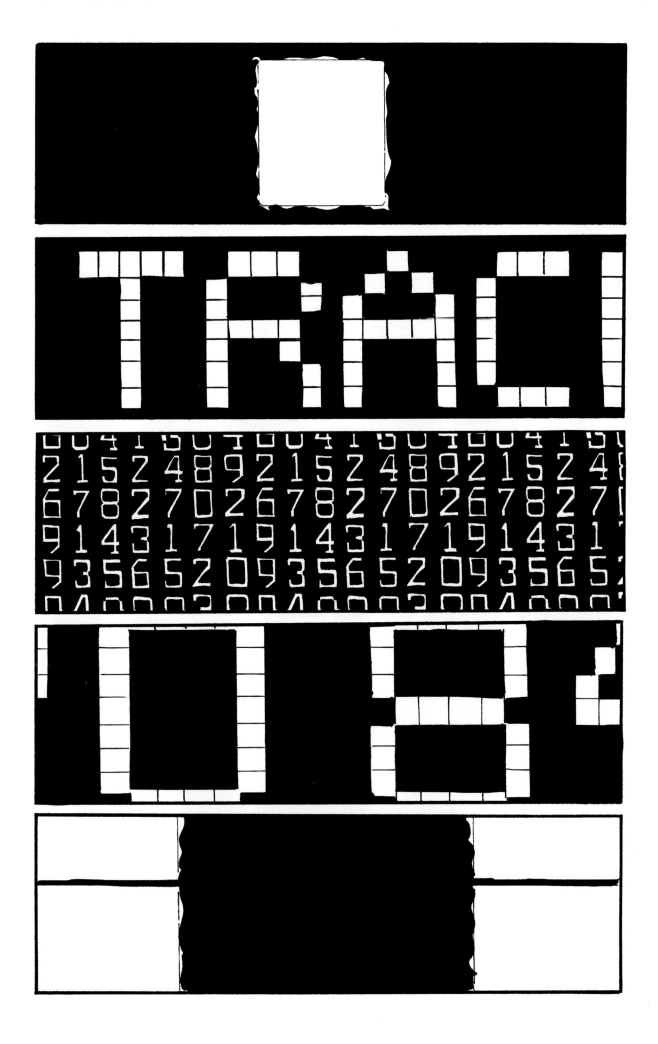

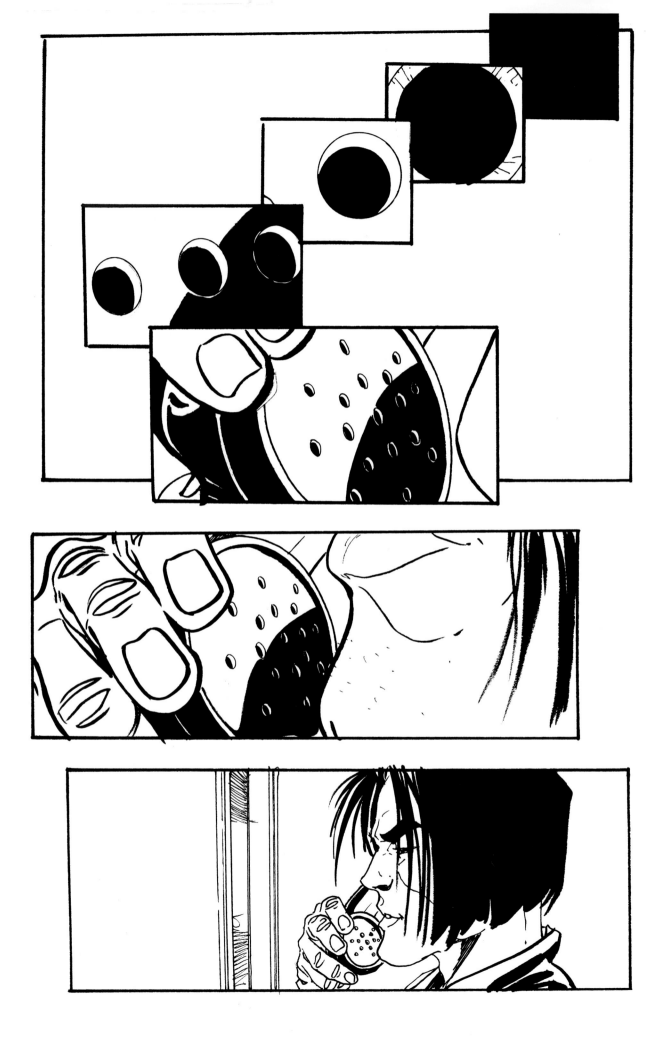

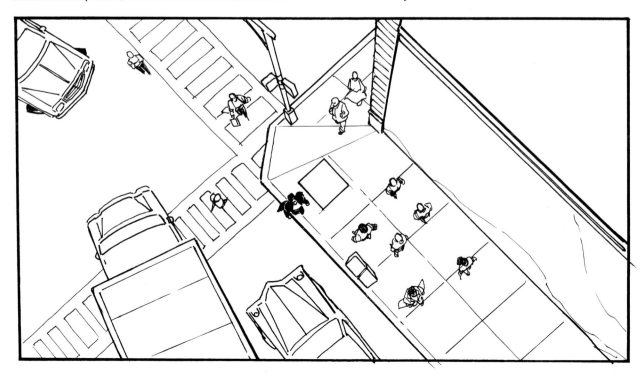

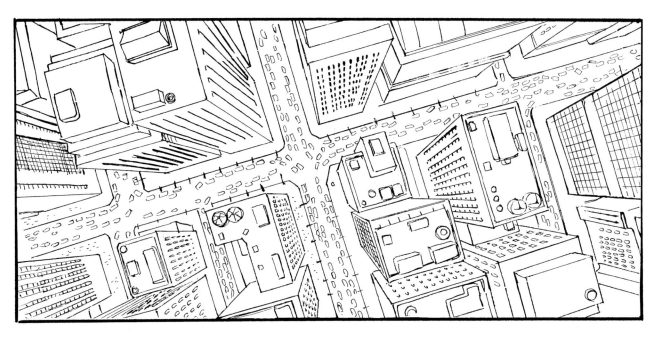

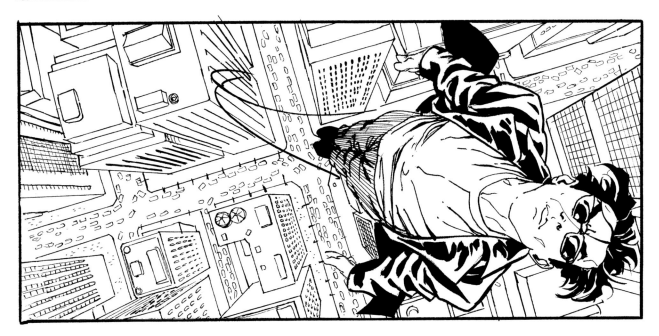

EXTERIOR NEB
CONCEPTUAL DESIGNS
+
COLOR RENDERINGS
OF GEOF DARROW DESIGNS

Tani Kunitake
Warren Manser

Tani Kunitake: I did the conceptual for the outside of the Neb, the ship, which was a big challenge. For one thing, I can't draw like Geof [Darrow]. I went into it more as a painting, rather than a drawing, working closely with Larry and Andy. Geof would have done it, but was tied up with other drawings at the time. I had his interior boards to work with and, of course, I was back and forth with Larry and Andy with sketches, two dozen ideas in all. They would zero in on a portion they liked and tell me to continue in this or that direction, talking about concepts for the equipment, like the mechanics of the hovering pods on the outside of the ship.

As they described it, these pods are electromagnetic displacement engines repelling the vehicle from surfaces all around. They'd ask, "How do we know it's a hover vehicle, other than it's hovering?" Just floating around is very boring, so we tried to figure out ways to put engines about the ship where they wouldn't normally be. The ship is not an assault vehicle, but they didn't want it to feel weak, so it had to look defensive. After going through a dozen sketches, they decided on a pattern, which is pretty much the way it's been rendered. The initial problem was seeing the outline, the perimeter of the Nebuchadnezzar in the dark, with it always shuttling around and hiding, or bolting down very dark tunnels. So we gave it all these spiny projections, giving it a kind of deep-sea angler-fish feel.

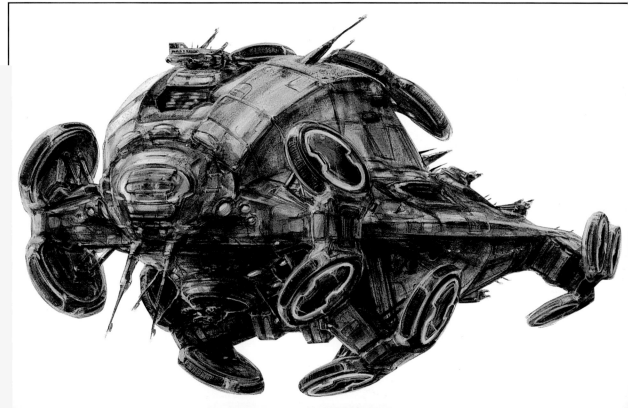

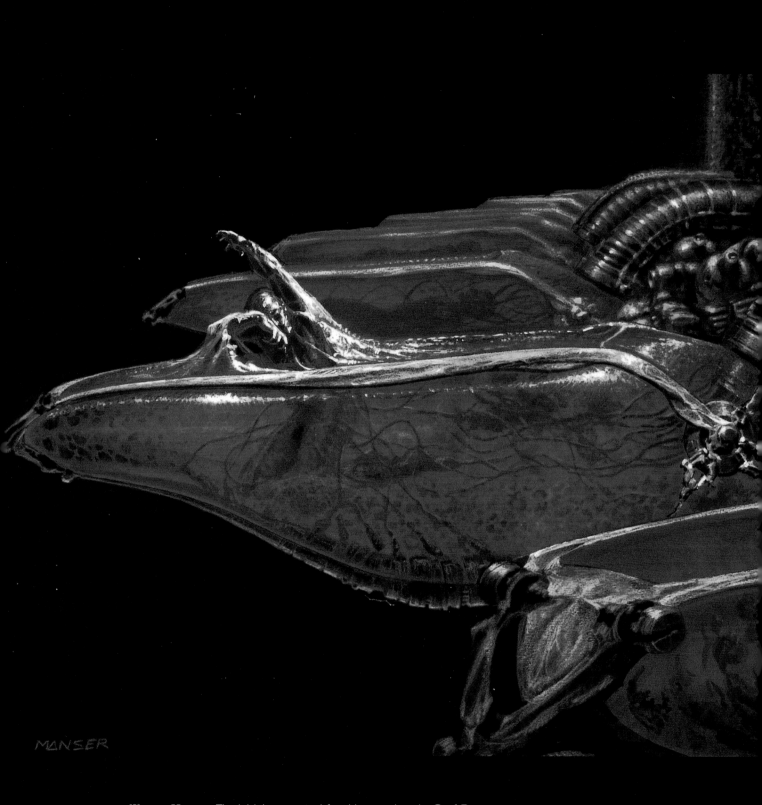

MANSER

Warren Manser: The initial conceptual for this was done by Geof Darrow with a really cool drawing of the pod. Conceptually, Geof had nailed it [see Conceptual Designs—page 257]. It's a fluid filled encasement with all sorts of organic and mechanical attachments keeping Neo alive, and absorbing all of his energy at the same time.

My take on this job was to try and keep as much of what we could from
the original concept and modify only as needed to conform to the reality
of building the set. My background is in industrial design, so I drew on
that to take something as complex as Geof's drawing to see how we
could make the pieces work as sets.

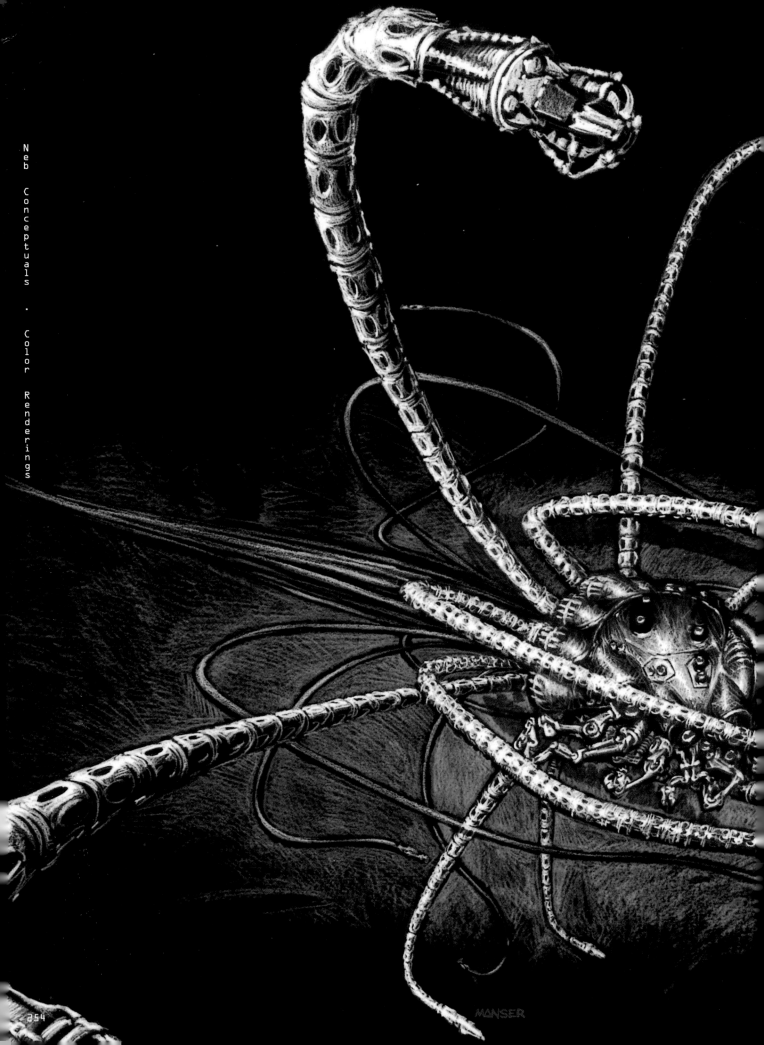

MANSER

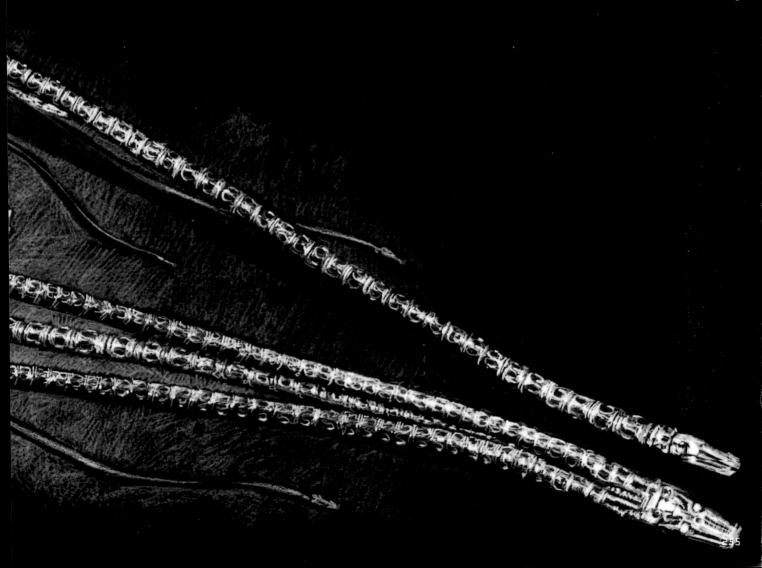

Manser: For the Sentinels Geof had done a really scary, kind of freakish-looking creature. He raised some wonderful questions—is it an octopus, a spider, or a completely mechanical device? By talking to Larry and Andy, I tried to mold these thoughts into a property that somebody could then sculpt and build and add to. Trying to juggle these things, we've got it looking like an octopus in one drawing [this page] with loose arms going everywhere, seemingly inescapable; then we've got the creature with its tentacles pinned back [page 256], transforming it into something that looks capable of moving at 200 miles per hour. The insect look and its glowing eyes were other major points to stress with my rendering of Geof's drawing. Some people are put off by somebody like Geof who has created such a foundation of strong material and say, "No, I want to make it my own." From the start, I realized I was hired to expand on what Geof had done, not change it.

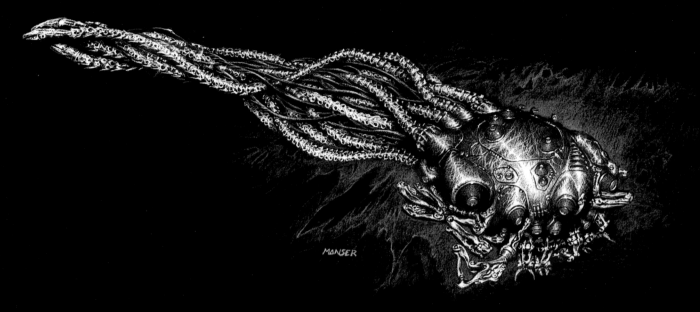

MANSER

Manser: Unfortunately, I was on the project for a very short time. I did the one pod image, a couple of takes on the Sentinel and a version of the claw, which picks Neo up and into the Neb [below]. Fortunately for the movie, but unfortunately for the directors, they had too many ideas—like the Bullet Time tricks—which came off spectacularly, but couldn't have been done on the film's budget in the States. So they shut down the art department to give some time to formulate a plan, to figure out how they were going to accomplish the movie. By the time THE MATRIX was back on track with a plan to film in Australia, I was on another project.

This was one movie I really wanted more time on, too. Larry and Andy are really talented guys. There is no pretense, they know their stuff and they know what they want to do. When I first met them, I was kind of shocked because, generally, in Hollywood you have giant egos, and everybody sort of caters to the director. I think the first time I met them, they were on their computers playing video games, and they were just, like, "Hey, how's it going?" Any time they came in to check out the drawings, it was never with an ego, and it was never their way or no way, it was, "This is what we're trying to do, and I see some of what we want in this and that, so let's go the first way." I really like that about them and can't stress enough how extremely different this is. These guys, Larry and Andy, are completely in tune with what they are trying to accomplish, making it really easy to be directed by them.

CONCEPTUAL DESIGNS

Geof Darrow

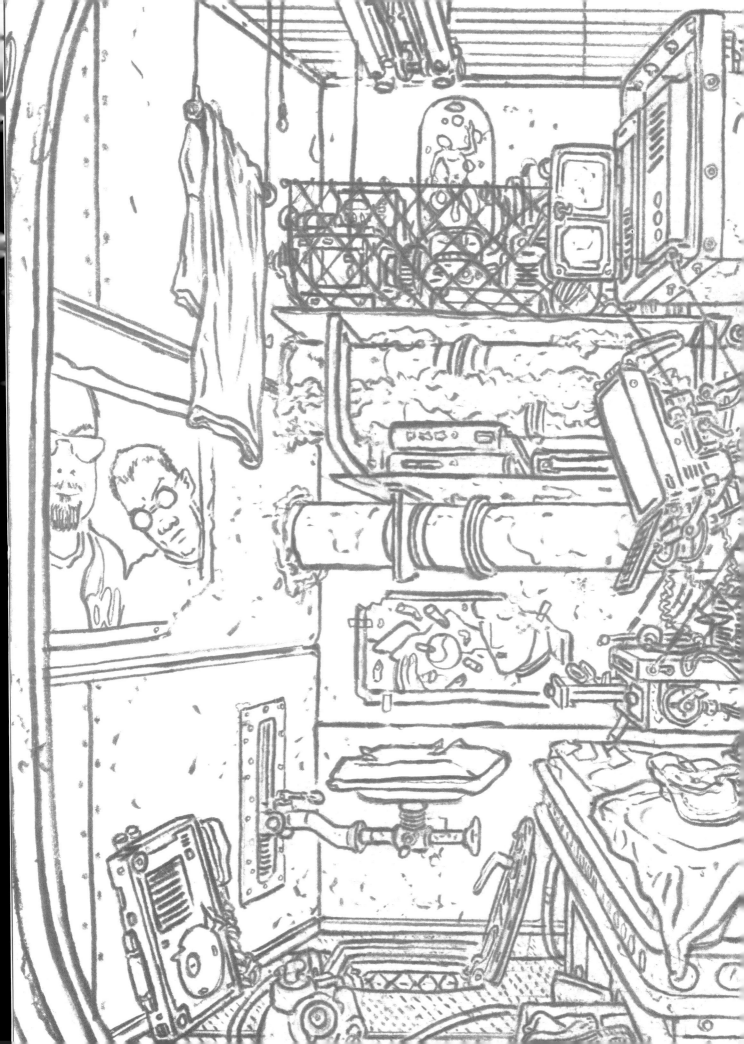

NEB CHAIR

Darrow: Originally, I did a version of the chair which was much bigger than this one. They didn't use it because it would have been too complicated to build, and on top of that, with the stuff going into his neck, an impossibility. I was glad because it meant I didn't have to draw it eight times for the Deck drawing [see inside], which would have made me crazy. It was bad enough drawing this one.

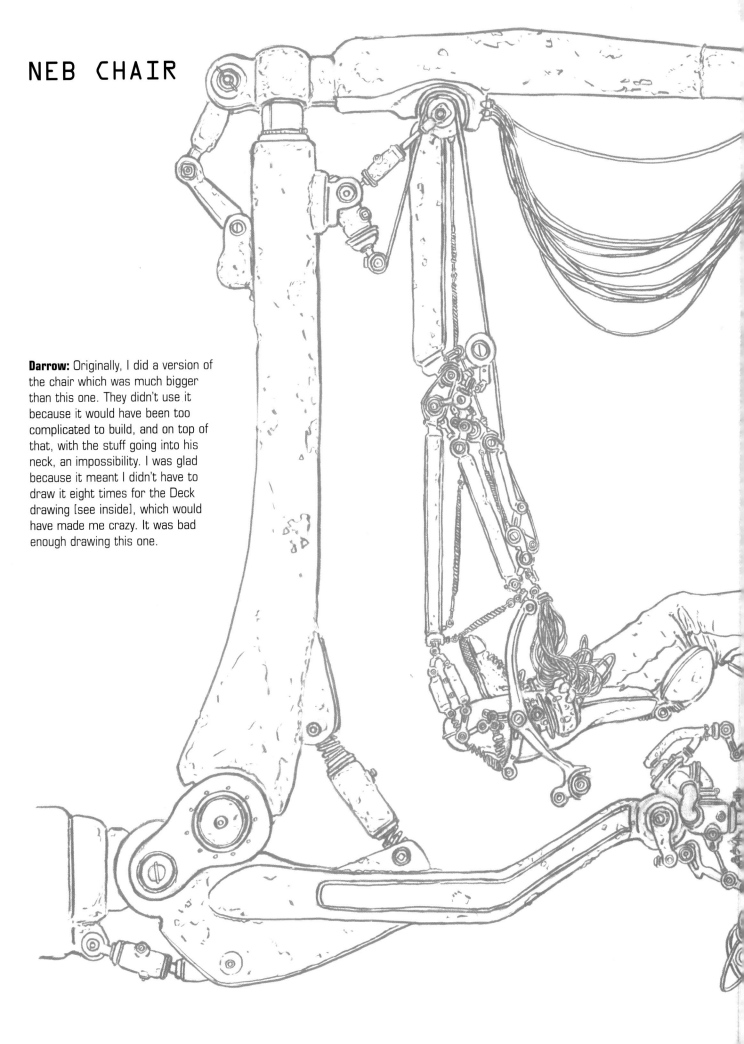

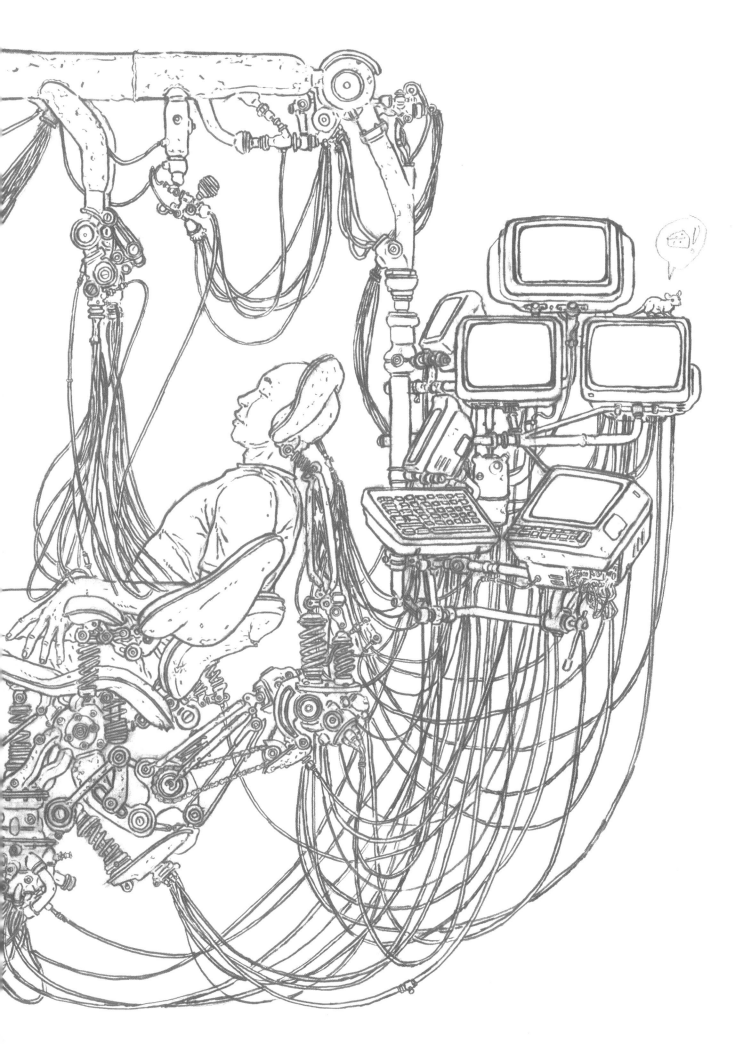

FETUS STALK

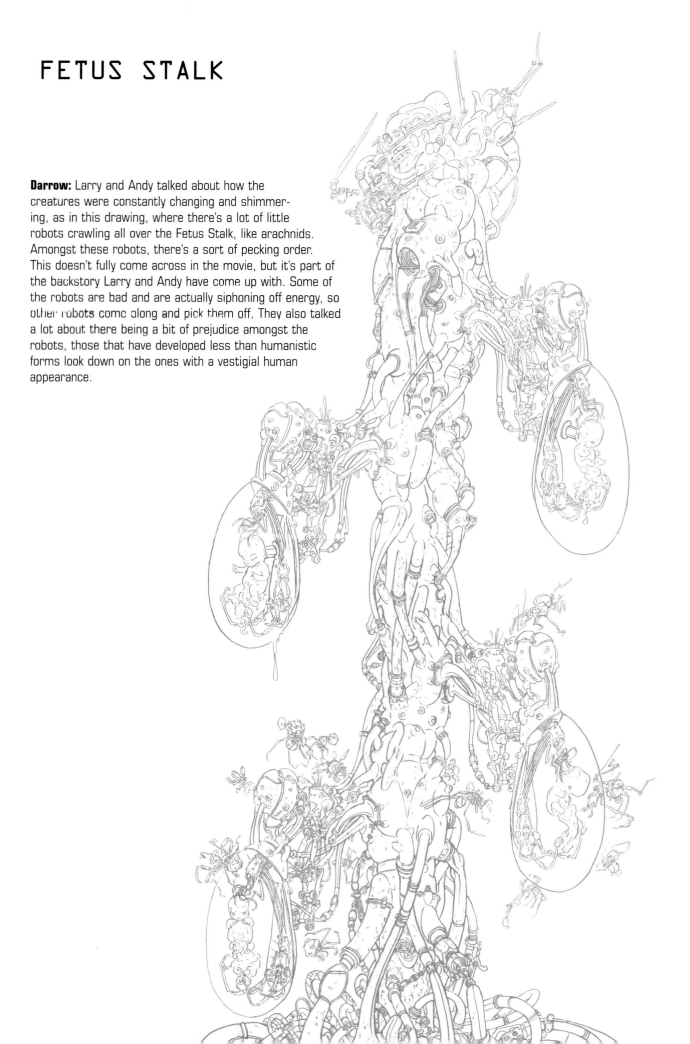

Darrow: Larry and Andy talked about how the creatures were constantly changing and shimmering, as in this drawing, where there's a lot of little robots crawling all over the Fetus Stalk, like arachnids. Amongst these robots, there's a sort of pecking order. This doesn't fully come across in the movie, but it's part of the backstory Larry and Andy have come up with. Some of the robots are bad and are actually siphoning off energy, so other robots come along and pick them off. They also talked a lot about there being a bit of prejudice amongst the robots, those that have developed less than humanistic forms look down on the ones with a vestigial human appearance.

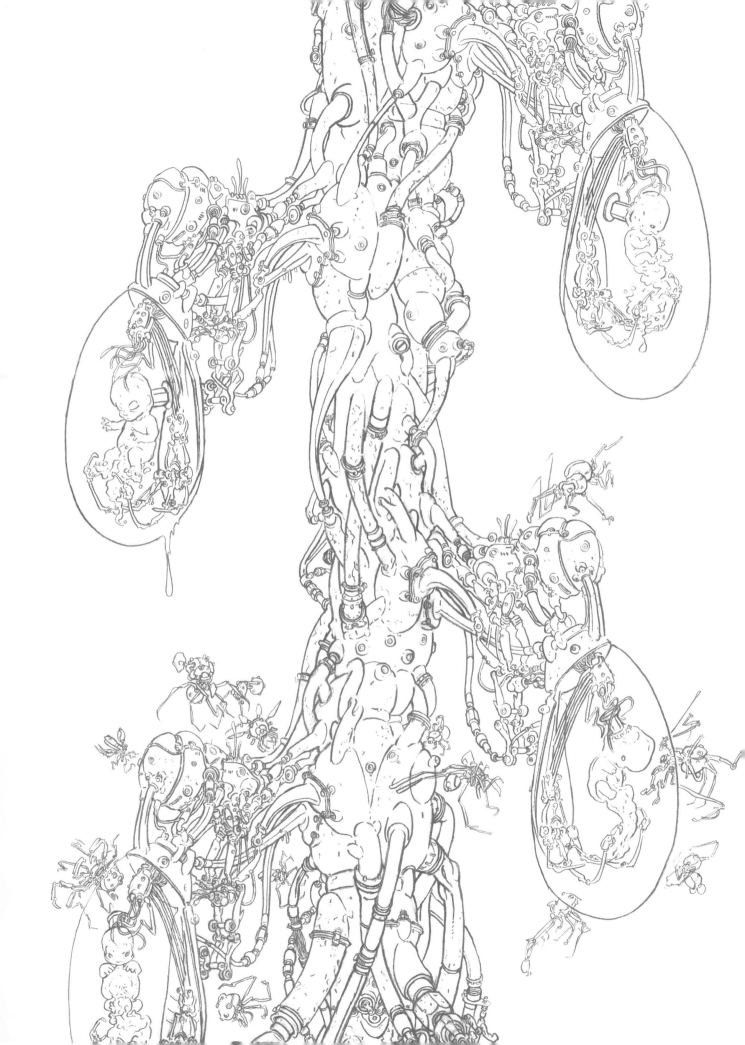

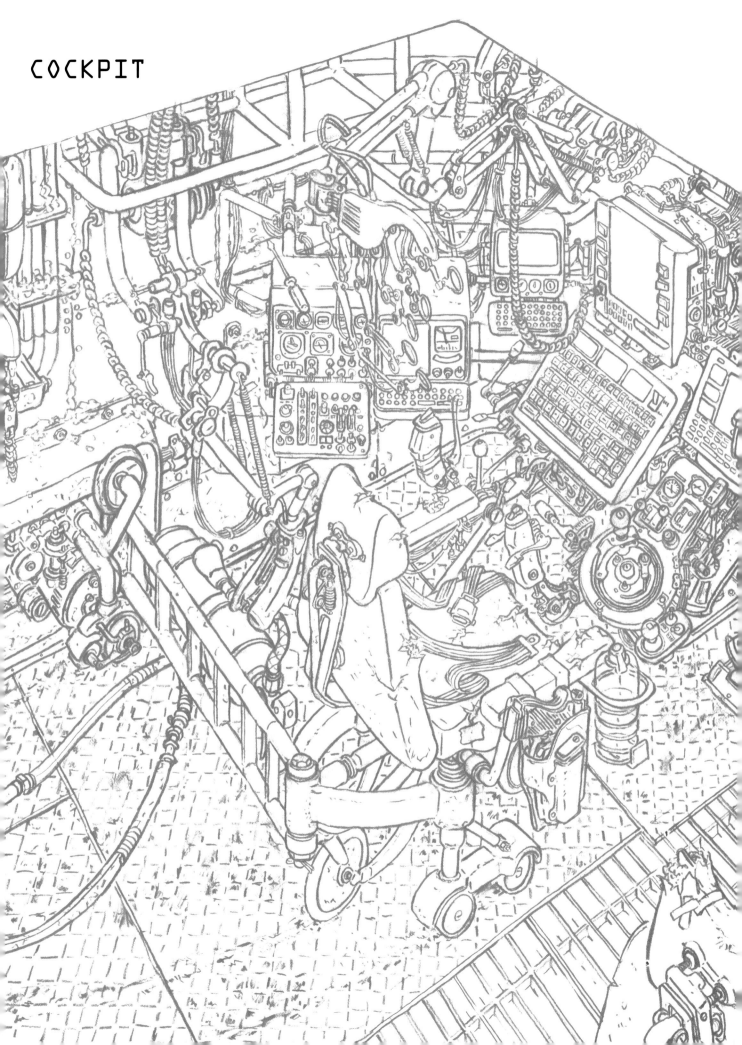

COCKPIT

Darrow: That's Larry there, his head floating [below]. Larry and Andy are in Neo's room, too [facing page]; there's a poster on the wall and that's them. If you look closely at this drawing, you'll see cup holders on the sides of the chairs and Larry and Andy asked, "What's with this one being broken?" I said it was broken because every now and then someone would run into it and it would be like… "Tank, you broke my cup holder." Larry and Andy laughed when I told them that, saying I've backstory on everything.

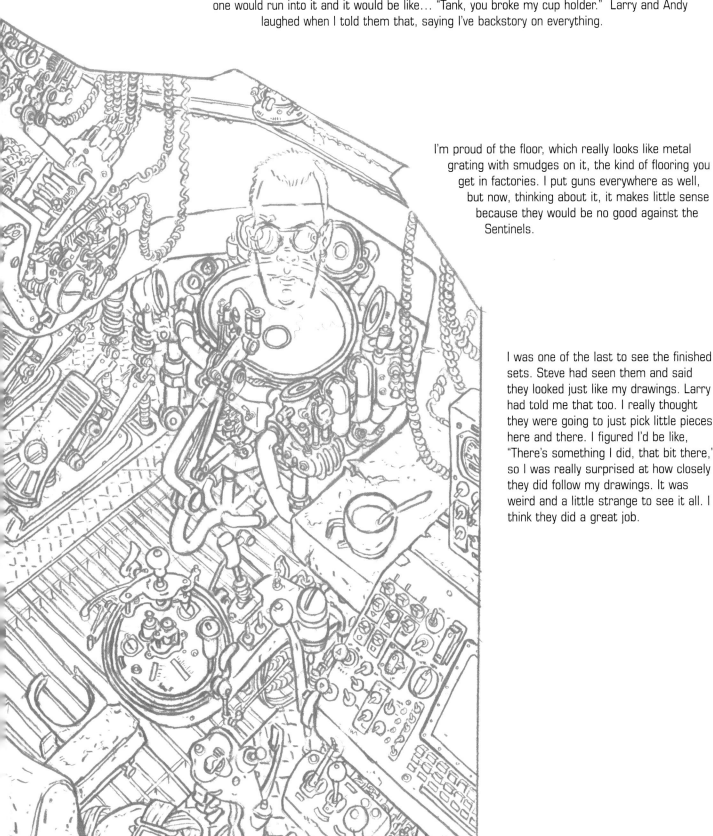

I'm proud of the floor, which really looks like metal grating with smudges on it, the kind of flooring you get in factories. I put guns everywhere as well, but now, thinking about it, it makes little sense because they would be no good against the Sentinels.

I was one of the last to see the finished sets. Steve had seen them and said they looked just like my drawings. Larry had told me that too. I really thought they were going to just pick little pieces here and there. I figured I'd be like, "There's something I did, that bit there," so I was really surprised at how closely they did follow my drawings. It was weird and a little strange to see it all. I think they did a great job.

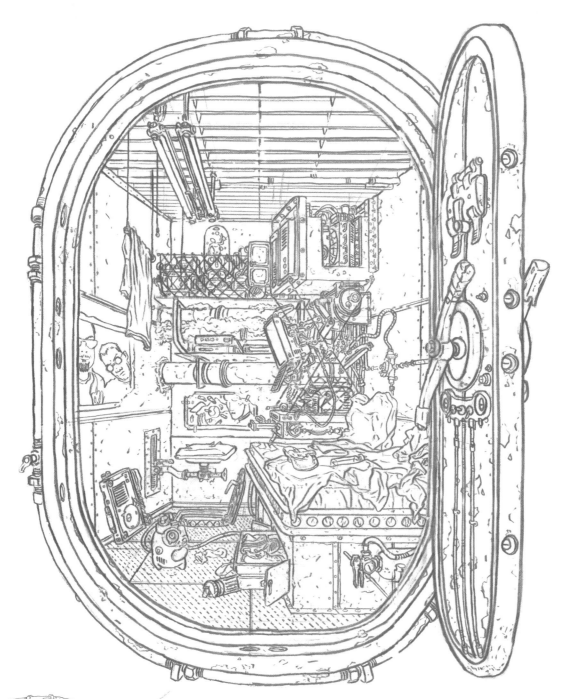

NEO'S ROOM

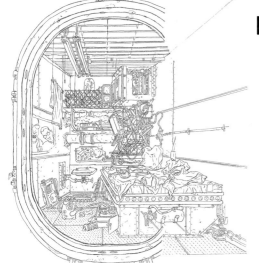

Darrow: In Neo's room, near the back wall by the floor, there's a porthole. I reasoned, if the Sentinels or something get on the ship, they could bolt the front door and get out the porthole, which would take them into the guts of the ship, and it would be harder to catch them there. Above the escape hatch is a chair that can be raised or lowered. For the shelves, I looked at ships which have this kind of netting, so that if the ship veers, it catches the contents of the shelf without breaking them. There is also a laptop computer and a place where they could actually plug in—the needle is coming off the back of the laptop apparatus. If they couldn't get up to the deck, they could punch into the Matrix or a training program from there. Many of these details didn't get into the film.

Darrow: This is one of the bugs [below], the one that gets put into Neo by the Agents. I wonder why I put the mouse in there. I must have been tired of drawing robots. Drawing mechanical stuff is fun, but it can get tiring.

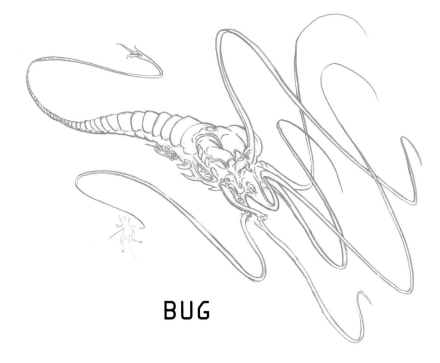

BUG

I was really pleased with this one [right]. I did a few different versions of the Sentinel, but Larry and Andy weren't seeing it, so they hired somebody else to give the Sentinel a try. He kept on turning in neat stuff, but it wasn't what they wanted, either. So one morning when we were going into Warner Bros., I asked Larry and Andy if I could take one more shot at it, and drew this in a couple of hours, and they said, "That's it!" They simplified it for the film, but basically, this is the Sentinel we see in the movie.

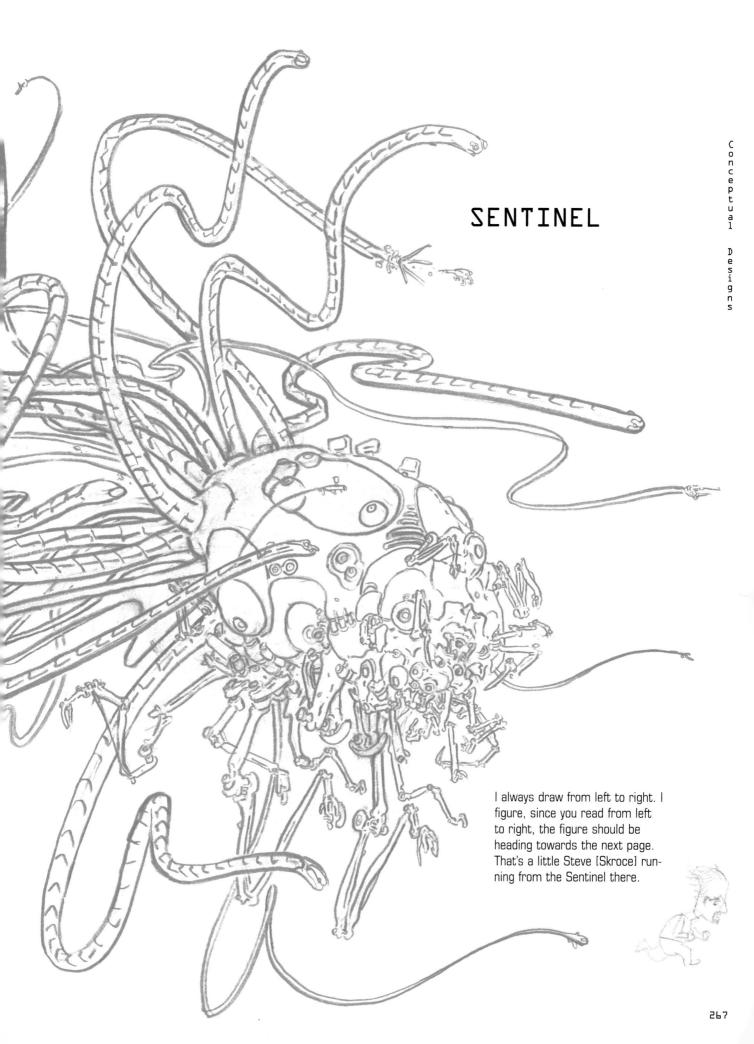

SENTINEL

I always draw from left to right. I figure, since you read from left to right, the figure should be heading towards the next page. That's a little Steve [Skroce] running from the Sentinel there.

Darrow: Here's the Fetus Harvester. The little spiders on its feet were the original body. When Larry and Andy looked at the initial drawing they said, "What if you put this arachnidlike creature on the end of tentacles?" In one of my previous drawings there was something similar to the canister on the back, which I combined into what Larry and Andy wanted with the little spiders. That's how it became this.

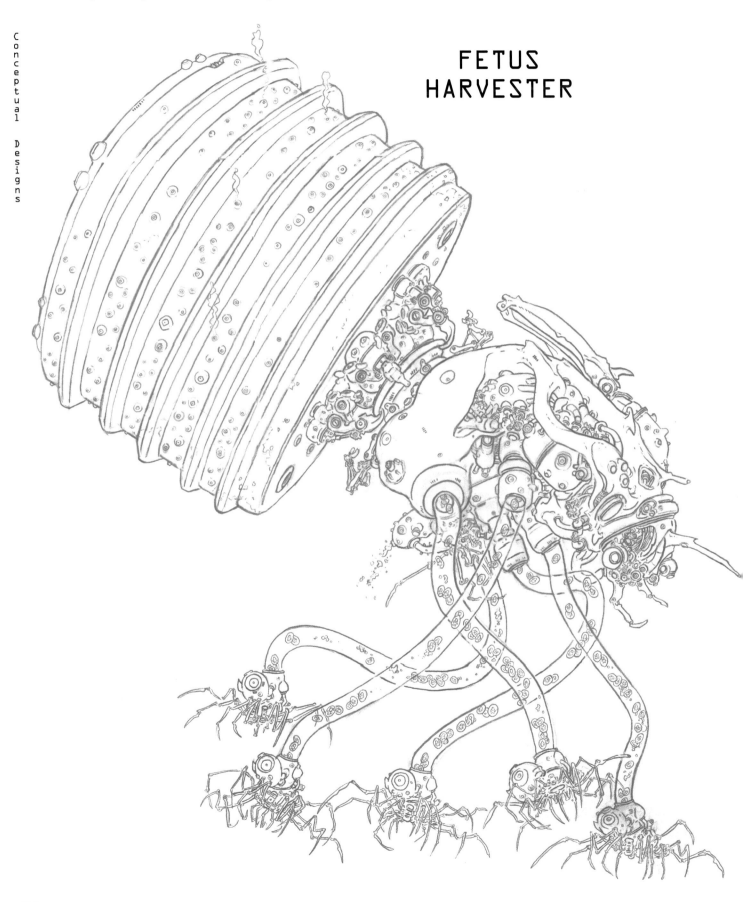

FETUS
HARVESTER

BATTLE SUIT

Darrow: There's a lot of material I drew that didn't get used for the film—from characters to equipment—conceptual material no one's going to see just yet. Here's a battle suit which wasn't used for the first film, but may or may not get used in the sequels.

I'm really looking forward to the next two films, but I'm scared to death, as well. I figure, they're going to find out what an imposter I am, so I'm nervous. I know Larry and Andy have a lot of this in their heads, they always saw THE MATRIX as more than one film, so they haven't written themselves into a corner, they know where it's going. It's inevitable, I'll be drawing Zion—a lot of fun, but a lot of work.

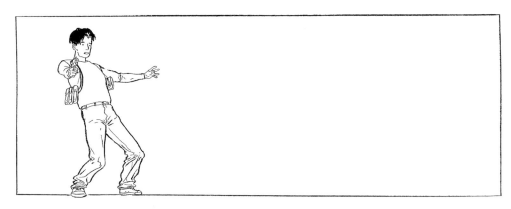

Editor: The rooftop Bullet Time sequence was done more than once. Here's one of the earlier passes, penciled by Geof Darrow and inked by Steve Skroce. The final version, the one closest to what John Gaeta and crew created via Bullet Time, was done by Steve [see page 168].

THE MATRIX

Larry & Andy Wachowski

What follows is the shooting script for THE MATRIX, although it's not exactly what people saw in theaters. While everything that follows was filmed, changes occurred during editing. An example of this is in the final speech by Neo (scene 219) which was altered when test audiences didn't know the word "chrysalis." Other differences exist, from small cuts to dialogue tweaks. This is, however, the last draft before filming.

Shooting Script

August 12, 1998

FADE IN:
On a computer
screen. So
close that it
has no bound-
aries.

A blinking
cursor pulses
in the elec-
tric darkness
like a heart
coursing with
phosphorous
light burn-
ing beneath
the derma of
black-neon
glass.

A phone

FADE IN:

INT. COMPUTER SCREEN

On a computer screen; so close it has no boundaries.

A blinking cursor pulses in the electric darkness like a
heart coursing with phosphorous light, burning beneath the
derma of black-neon glass.

A phone begins to ring; we hear it as though we were making
the call. The cursor continues to throb, relentlessly
patient, until--

                        MAN (V.O.)
                    Yeah?

Data now slashes across the screen, information flashing
faster than we can read:

                        SCREEN
                    Call trans opt: received. 2-19-98
                    13:24:18 REC:Log>.

                        WOMAN (V.O.)
                    Is everything in place?

                        SCREEN
                    Trace program: running.

We listen to the phone conversation as though we were on a
third line. The man's name is Cypher. The woman, Trinity.

                        TRINITY (WOMAN) (V.O.)
                    I said, is everything in place?

The entire screen fills with racing columns of numbers.
Shimmering like green-electric rivers, they rush at a 10-
digit phone number in the top corner.

                        CYPHER (MAN) (V.O.)
                    You weren't supposed to relieve
                    me.

                        TRINITY (V.O.)
                    I know, but I felt like taking a
                    shift.

The area code is identified. The first three numbers
suddenly fixed, leaving only seven flowing columns.

                        CYPHER (V.O.)
                    You like him, don't you? You like
                    watching him?

We begin moving toward the screen, closing in as each digit is matched, one by one, snapping into place like the wheels of a slot machine.

                    TRINITY (V.O.)
          Don't be ridiculous.

                    CYPHER (V.O.)
          We're going to kill him. Do you
          understand that? He's going to die
          just like the others.

                    TRINITY (V.O.)
          Morpheus believes he is the One.

Only two thin digits left.

                    CYPHER (V.O.)
          Do you?

                    TRINITY (V.O.)
          I... it doesn't matter what I
          believe.

                    CYPHER (V.O.)
          You don't, do you?

                    TRINITY (V.O.)
          If you have something to say, I
          suggest you say it to Morpheus.

                    CYPHER (V.O.)
          I intend to, believe me. Someone
          has to.

The final number pops into place--

                    TRINITY (V.O.)
          Did you hear that?

                    CYPHER (V.O.)
          Hear what?

                    SCREEN
          Trace complete. Call origin: #312-
          555-0690.

                    TRINITY (V.O.)
          Are you sure this line is clean?

                    CYPHER (V.O.)
          Yeah, 'course I'm sure.

We move, still closer, the electric hum of the green numbers growing into an ominous roar.

> TRINITY (V.O.)
> I better go.

She hangs up as we pass through the numbers, entering the netherworld of the computer screen. Suddenly, a flashlight cuts open the darkness and we find ourselves in--

2   **INT. HEART O' THE CITY HOTEL - NIGHT**   2

The hotel was abandoned after a fire licked its way across the polyester carpeting, destroying several rooms as it spooled soot up the walls and ceiling, leaving patterns of permanent shadow.

We follow four armed POLICE OFFICERS using flashlights as they creep down the blackened hall and ready themselves on either side of Room 303.

The biggest of them violently kicks in the door. The other cops pour in behind him, guns thrust before them.

> BIG COP
> Police! Freeze!

The room is almost devoid of furniture. There is a fold-up table and chair with a phone, a modem, and a Powerbook computer. The only light in the room is the glow of the computer.

Sitting there, her hands still on the keyboard, is TRINITY, a woman in black leather.

> BIG COP
> Hands behind your head! Now! Do
> it!

She slowly puts her hands behind her head.

3   **EXT. HEART O' THE CITY HOTEL - NIGHT**   3

A black sedan with tinted windows glides in through the police cruisers. AGENT SMITH, AGENT BROWN, and AGENT JONES get out of the car.

They wear dark suits and sunglasses even at night. They are also always hardwired; small Secret Service earphones in one ear, the cord coiling back into their shirt collars.

> AGENT SMITH
> Lieutenant?

LIEUTENANT
Oh shit.

AGENT SMITH
Lieutenant, you were given
specific orders--

LIEUTENANT
I'm just doing my job. You gimme
that Juris-my-dick-tion and you
can cram it up your ass.

AGENT SMITH
The orders were for your
protection.

The Lieutenant laughs.

LIEUTENANT
I think we can handle one little
girl.

Agent Smith nods to Agent Brown as they start toward the
hotel.

LIEUTENANT
I sent two units. They're bringing
her down now.

AGENT SMITH
No, Lieutenant, your men are
already dead.

4   **INT. HEART O' THE CITY HOTEL**   4

The Big Cop flicks out his cuffs, the other cops holding a
bead. They've done this a hundred times, they know they've
got her, until the Big Cop reaches with the cuffs and Trinity
moves--

It almost doesn't register, so smooth and fast, inhumanly
fast.

The eye blinks and Trinity's palm snaps up and the nose
explodes, blood erupting. Her leg kicks with the force of a
wrecking ball and he flies back, a two-hundred-fifty-pound
sack of limp meat and bone that slams into the cop farthest
from her.

Trinity moves again, bullets raking the walls, flashlights
sweeping with panic as the remaining cops try to stop a
leather-clad ghost.

A gun still in the cop's hand is snatched, twisted, and fired. There is a final violent exchange of gunfire and when it's over, Trinity is the only one standing.

A flashlight rocks slowly to a stop.

> TRINITY
> Shit.

5   **EXT. HEART O' THE CITY HOTEL**   5

Agent Brown enters the hotel while Agent Smith heads for the alley.

6   **INT. HEART O' THE CITY HOTEL**   6

Trinity is on the phone, pacing. The other end is answered.

> MAN (V.O.)
> Operator.

> TRINITY
> Morpheus! The line was traced! I
> don't know how.

> MORPHEUS (MAN) (V.O.)
> I know. They cut the hardline.
> This line is not a viable exit.

> TRINITY
> Are there any Agents?

> MORPHEUS (V.O.)
> Yes.

> TRINITY
> Goddamnit!

> MORPHEUS (V.O.)
> You have to focus. There is a
> phone. Wells and Lake. You can
> make it.

She takes a deep breath, centering herself.

> TRINITY
> All right--

> MORPHEUS (V.O.)
> Go.

She drops the phone.

7   INT. HALL   7

T
H
E
M
A
T
R
I
X
.
s
c
r
i
p
t
p
a
g
e
6

She bursts out of the room as Agent Brown enters the hall, leading another unit of police. Trinity races to the opposite end, exiting through a broken window onto the fire escape.

8   EXT. FIRE ESCAPE   8

In the alley below, Trinity sees Agent Smith staring at her. She can only go up.

9   EXT. ROOF   9

On the roof, Trinity is running as Agent Brown rises over the parapet, leading the cops in pursuit.

Trinity begins to jump from one roof to the next, her movements so clean, gliding in and out of each jump, contrasted to the wild jumps of the cops.

Agent Brown, however, has the same unnatural grace.

The roof falls away into a wide back alley. The next building is over 40 feet away but Trinity's face is perfectly calm, staring at some point beyond the other roof.

> COP
> That's it, we got her now.

The cops slow, realizing they are about to see something ugly as Trinity drives at the edge, launching herself into the air.

From above, the ground seems to flow beneath her as she hangs in flight, then hits, somersaulting up, still running hard.

> COP
> Jesus Christ--that's impossible!

They stare, slack-jawed, as Agent Brown duplicates the move exactly, landing, rolling over a shoulder up onto one knee.

It is a dizzying chase up and over the dark plateaued landscape of rooftops and sheer cliffs of brick. Ahead she sees her only chance, 50 feet beyond the point where her path drops away into a paved chasm, there is--

10   EXT. WINDOW   10

A window; a yellow glow in the midst of a dark brick building.

Trinity zeros in on it, running as hard as she can and--

Hurtles herself into the empty night space, her body leveling into a dive. She falls, arms covering her head as the whole world seems to spin on its axis--

A10   INT. BACK STAIRWELL   A10

And she crashes with an explosion of glass and wood, then falls onto a back stairwell, tumbling, bouncing down stairs bleeding, broken--

But still alive.

She wheels on the smashed opening above, her gun instantly in her hand, trained, waiting for Agent Brown but is met by only a slight wind that hisses against the fanged maw of broken glass.

Trinity tries to move. Everything hurts.

                    TRINITY
          Get up, Trinity. You're fine. Get
          up--just get up!

She stands and limps down the rest of the stairs.

11   EXT. STREET   11

Trinity emerges from the shadows of an alley and, at the end of the block, in a pool of white street light, she sees it--

The telephone booth.

Obviously hurt, she starts down the concrete walk, focusing in completely, her pace quickening, as the phone begins to ring.

Across the street, a garbage truck suddenly turns U-turns, its tires screaming as it accelerates. Trinity sees the headlights of the truck arcing at the telephone booth as if taking aim.

Gritting through the pain, she races the truck, slamming into the booth, the headlights blindingly bright, bearing down on the box of Plexiglas just as--

She answers the phone.

There is a frozen instant of silence before the hulking mass of dark metal lurches up onto the sidewalk--

Barrelling through the booth, bulldozing it into a brick wall, smashing it to Plexiglas pulp.

After a moment, a black loafer steps down from the cab of the garbage truck. Agent Smith inspects the wreckage. There is no body. Trinity is gone.

His jaw sets as he grinds his molars in frustration. Agents Jones and Brown walk up behind him.

                    AGENT BROWN
          She got out.

                    AGENT SMITH
          It doesn't matter.

                    AGENT BROWN
          The informant is real.

Agent Smith almost smiles.

                    AGENT SMITH
          Yes.

                    AGENT JONES
          We have the name of their next
          target.

                    AGENT BROWN
          The name is Neo.

The handset of the pay phone lays on the ground, separated in the crash like a severed limb.

                    AGENT SMITH
          We'll need a search running.

                    AGENT JONES
          It's already begun.

We are sucked towards the mouthpiece of the phone, closer and closer, until the smooth gray plastic spreads out like a horizon and the small holes widen until we fall through one--

Swallowed by darkness.

The darkness crackles with phosphorescent energy, the word "searching" blazing in around us as we emerge from a computer screen.

The screen flickers with windowing data as a search engine runs with a steady relentless rhythm.

We drift back from the screen and into--

12   **INT. NEO'S APARTMENT**   12

It is a studio apartment that seems overgrown with technology.

Weed-like cables coil everywhere, duct-taped into thickets
that wind up and around the legs of several desks. Tabletops
are filled with cannibalized equipment that lay open like an
autopsied corpse.

At the center of this technological rat-nest is NEO, a man
who knows more about living inside a computer than outside
one.

He is asleep in front of his PC. Behind him, the computer
screen suddenly goes blank. A prompt appears.

                    SCREEN
              Wake up, Neo.

Neo's eye pries open. He sits up, one eye still closed,
looking around, unsure of where he is. He notices the screen.

He types "CTRL X" but the letter "T" appears.

                    NEO
              What...?

He hits another and an "H" appears. He keeps typing, pushing
random functions and keys while the computer types out a
message as though it had a mind of its own.

He stops and stares at the four words on the screen.

                    SCREEN
              The Matrix has you.

                    NEO
              What the hell?

He hits the "ESC" button. Another message appears.

                    SCREEN
              Follow the white rabbit.

He hits it again and the message repeats. He rubs his eyes
but when he opens them, there is another message.

                    SCREEN
              Knock, knock, Neo.

Someone knocks on his door and he almost jumps out of his
chair. He looks back at the computer but the screen is now
blank.

Someone knocks again. Neo rises, still unnerved.

                         NEO
                    Who is it?

                         CHOI (O.S.)
                    It's Choi.

Neo flips a series of locks and opens the door, leaving the
chain on. A young Chinese MAN stands with several of his
friends.

                         NEO
                    You're two hours late.

                         CHOI
                    I know. It's her fault.

                         NEO
                    You got the money?

                         CHOI
                    Two grand.

He takes out an envelope and gives it to Neo through the
cracked door.

                         NEO
                    Hold on.

He closes the door. On the floor near his bed is a book,
Baudrillard's <u>Simulacra and Simulations</u>. The book has been
hollowed out and inside are several computer disks. He takes
one, sticks the money in the book and drops it on the floor.

Opening the door, he hands the disk to Choi.

                         CHOI
                    Hallelujah! You are my savior,
                    man! My own personal Jesus Christ!

                         NEO
                    If you get caught using that--

                         CHOI
                    I know, I know. This never
                    happened. You don't exist.

                         NEO
                    Right...

Neo nods as the strange feeling of unrealness suddenly
returns.

> CHOI
> Something wrong, man? You look a
> little whiter than usual.

> NEO
> I don't know... My computer...

He looks back at Choi, unable to explain what just happened.

> NEO
> You ever have the feeling that
> you're not sure if you're awake or
> still dreaming?

> CIIOI
> All the time. It's called
> mescaline and it is the only way
> to fly.

He smiles and slaps the hand of his nearest droog.

> CHOI
> It sounds to me like you need to
> unplug, man. A little R and R.
> What do you think, Dujour, should
> we take him with us?

> DUJOUR
> Definitely.

> NEO
> I can't. I have to work tomorrow.

> DUJOUR
> Come on. It'll be fun. I promise.

He looks up at her and suddenly notices on her black leather
motorcycle jacket dozens of pins: bands, symbols, slogans,
military medals and--

A small white rabbit. The room tilts.

> NEO
> Yeah, yeah. Sure, I'll go.

13   **INT. APARTMENT**   13

An older apartment; a series of halls connects a chain of
small high-ceilinged rooms lined with heavy casements.

Smoke hangs like a veil, blurring the few lights there are.

Dressed predominantly in black, people are everywhere, gathered in cliques around pieces of furniture like jungle cats around a tree.

Neo stands against a wall, alone, sipping from a bottle of beer; feeling completely out of place, he is about to leave when he notices a woman staring at him.

The woman is Trinity. She walks straight up to him.

In the nearest room, shadow-like figures grind against each other to the pneumatic beat of industrial music.

                    TRINITY
          Hello, Neo.

                    NEO
          How do you know that name?

                    TRINITY
          I know a lot about you. I've been
          wanting to meet you for some time.

                    NEO
          Who are you?

                    TRINITY
          My name is Trinity.

                    NEO
          Trinity? The Trinity? The Trinity
          that cracked the I.R.S. D-Base?

                    TRINITY
          That was a long time ago.

                    NEO
          Gee-zus.

                    TRINITY
          What?

                    NEO
          I just thought... you were a guy.

                    TRINITY
          Most guys do.

Neo is a little embarrassed.

                    NEO
          Do you want to go somewhere and
          talk?

TRINITY
No. It's safe here and I don't
have much time.

The music is so loud they must stand very close, talking
directly into each other's ear.

NEO
That was you on my computer?

She nods.

NEO
How did you do that?

TRINITY
Right now, all I can tell you, is
that you are in danger. I brought
you here to warn you.

NEO
Of what?

TRINITY
They're watching you, Neo.

NEO
Who is?

TRINITY
Please. Just listen. I know why
you're here, Neo. I know what
you've been doing. I know why you
hardly sleep, why you live alone
and why, night after night, you
sit at your computer; you're
looking for him.

Her body is against his; her lips very close to his ear.

TRINITY
I know because I was once looking
for the same thing, but when he
found me he told me I wasn't
really looking for him. I was
looking for an answer.

There is a hypnotic quality to her voice and Neo feels the
words, like a drug, seeping into him.

TRINITY
It's the question that drives us, the
question that brought you here. You
know the question just as I did.

> NEO
> What is the Matrix?

> TRINITY
> When I asked him, he said that no
> one could ever be told the answer
> to that question. They have to see
> it to believe it.

She leans close, her lips almost touching his ear.

> TRINITY
> The answer is out there, Neo. It's
> looking for you and it will find
> you, if you want it to.

She turns and he watches her melt into the shifting wall of
bodies.

A sound rises steadily, growing out of the music, pressing in
on Neo until it is all he can hear as we cut to--

14   **INT. NEO'S APARTMENT**   14

The sound is an alarm clock, slowly dragging Neo to
consciousness. He strains to read the clock-face: 9:15AM.

> NEO
> Shitshitshit.

15   **EXT. SKYSCRAPER**   15

The downtown office of Meta CorTechs, a software development
company.

16   **INT. META CORTECHS OFFICE**   16

The main offices are along each wall, the windows overlooking
downtown. RHINEHEART, the ultimate company man, lectures Neo
without looking at him, typing at his computer continuously.

Neo stares at two window cleaners on a scaffolding outside,
dragging their rubber squeegees down the surface of the
glass.

> RHINEHEART
> You have a problem with authority,
> Mr. Anderson.You believe that you
> are special, that somehow the rules
> do not apply to you. Obviously,
> you are mistaken.

His long, bony fingers resume clicking the keyboard.

>   RHINEHEART
>   This company is one of the top
>   software companies in the world
>   because every single employee
>   understands that they are part of
>   a whole. Thus, if an employee has
>   a problem, the company has a
>   problem.

He turns again.

>   RHINEHEART
>   The time has come to make a
>   choice, Mr. Anderson. Either you
>   choose to be at your desk on time
>   from this day forth, or you choose
>   to find yourself another job. Do I
>   make myself clear?

>   NEO
>   Yes, Mr. Rhineheart. Perfectly
>   clear.

17   **INT. NEO'S CUBICLE**   17

The entire floor looks like a human honeycomb, with a
labyrinth of cubicles structured around a core of elevators.

>   VOICE (O.S.)
>   Thomas Anderson?

Neo turns and finds a FEDERAL EXPRESS GUY at his cubicle
door.

>   NEO
>   Yeah. That's me.

Neo signs the electronic pad and the Fedex Guy hands him the
softpak.

>   FEDEX GUY
>   Have a nice day.

He opens the bag. Inside is a cellular phone. It seems the
instant it is in his hand, it rings. Unnerved, he flips it
open.

>   NEO
>   Hello?

>   MORPHEUS (V.O.)
>   Hello, Neo. Do you know who this
>   is?

Neo's knees give and he sinks into his chair.

                    NEO
          Morpheus...

                    MORPHEUS (V.O.)
          I've been looking for you, Neo. I
          don't know if you're ready to see
          what I want to show you, but
          unfortunately, we have run out of
          time. They're coming for you, Neo.
          And I'm not sure what they're
          going to do.

                    NEO
          Who's coming for me?

                    MORPHEUS (V.O.)
          Stand up and see for yourself.

                    NEO
          Right now?

                    MORPHEUS (V.O.)
          Yes. Now.

Neo starts to stand.

                    MORPHEUS (V.O.)
          Do it slowly. The elevator.

His head peeks up over the partition. At the elevator, he
sees Agent Smith, Agent Brown, and Agent Jones leading a
group of cops. A female employee turns and points out Neo's
cubicle.

Neo ducks.

                    NEO
          Holy shit!

                    MORPHEUS (V.O.)
          Yes.

One cop stays at the elevator, the others follow the Agents.

                    NEO
          What the hell do they want with
          me?!

                    MORPHEUS (V.O.)
          I'm not sure, but if you don't
          want to find out, you better get
          out of there.

                    NEO
          How?!

                    MORPHEUS (V.O.)
          I can guide you out, but you have
          to do exactly what I say.

The Agents are moving quickly towards the cubicle.

                    MORPHEUS (V.O.)
          The cubicle across from you is
          empty.

                    NEO
          But what if...?

                    MORPHEUS (V.O.)
          Go! Now!

Neo lunges across the hall, diving into the other cubicle
just as the Agents turn into his row.

Neo crams himself into a dark corner, clutching the phone
tightly to him.

                    MORPHEUS (V.O.)
          Stay here for a moment.

The Agents enter Neo's empty cubicle. A cop is sent to search
the bathroom.

Morpheus's voice is a whisper in Neo's ear.

                    MORPHEUS (V.O.)
          A little longer...

Brown is talking to another employee.

                    MORPHEUS (V.O.)
          When I tell you, go to the end of
          the row to the first office on the
          left, stay as low as you can.

Sweat trickles down his forehead.

                    MORPHEUS (V.O.)
          Now.

Neo rolls out of the cubicle, his eyes popping as he freezes
right behind a cop who has just turned around.

Staying crouched, he sneaks away down the row, shooting
across the opening to the first office on the left.

The room is empty.

> MORPHEUS (V.O.)
> Good. Outside there is a scaffold.

> NEO
> How do you know all this?

Morpheus laughs quietly.

> MORPHEUS (V.O.)
> The answer is coming, Neo. There
> is a window in front of you. Open
> it.

He opens the window. The wind howls into the room.

> MORPHEUS (V.O.)
> You can use the scaffold to get to
> the roof.

> NEO
> No! It's too far away.

> MORPHEUS (V.O.)
> There's a ledge. It's a short
> climb. You can make it.

Neo looks down; the building's glass wall vertigos into a
concrete chasm.

> NEO
> No way, no way, this is crazy.

> MORPHEUS (V.O.)
> There are only two ways out of
> this building. One is that
> scaffold. The other is in their
> custody. You take a chance either
> way. I leave it to you.

Click. He hangs up. Neo looks at the door, then back at the
scaffold.

> NEO
> This is insane! Why is this
> happening to me? What did I do?
> I'm nobody. I didn't do anything.

He climbs up onto the window ledge. Hanging onto the frame, he steps onto the small ledge. The scaffold seems even farther away.

                    NEO
            I'm going to die.

The wind suddenly blasts up the face of the building, knocking Neo off balance. Recoiling, he clings harder to the frame, and the phone falls out of his hand.

He watches as it is swallowed by the distance beneath him.

                    NEO
            This is insane! I can't do this!
            Forget it!

He climbs back into the office just as a cop opens the door.

                    NEO
            Shit!

19   **EXT. SKYSCRAPER**   19

        The Agents lead a handcuffed Neo out of the revolving doors, forcing his head down as they push him into the dark sedan.

        Trinity watches in the rear view mirror of her motorcycle.

                    TRINITY
            Shit.

20   **INT. INTERROGATION ROOM**   20

        Close on a camera monitor; wide angle view of a white room where Neo is sitting at a table alone. We move into the monitor, entering the room as if the monitor was a window.

        At the same moment, the door opens and the Agents enter. Agent Smith sits down across from Neo. A thick manila envelope slaps down on the table. The name on the file: "Anderson, Thomas A."

                    AGENT SMITH
            As you can see, we've had our eye
            on you for some time now, Mr.
            Anderson.

        He opens the file. Paper rattle marks the silence as he flips several pages. Neo cannot tell if he is looking at the file or at him.

                    AGENT SMITH
          It seems that you have been living
          two lives. In one life, you are
          Thomas A. Anderson, program writer
          for a respectable software
          company. You have a social
          security number, you pay your
          taxes, and you help your landlady
          carry out her garbage.

The pages continue to turn.

                    AGENT SMITH
          The other life is lived in
          computers where you go by the
          hacker alias Neo, and are guilty
          of virtually every computer crime
          we have a law for.

Neo feels himself sinking into a pit of shit.

                    AGENT SMITH
          One of these lives has a future.
          One of them does not.

He closes the file.

                    AGENT SMITH
          I'm going to be as forthcoming as
          I can be, Mr. Anderson. You are
          here because we need your help.

He removes his sunglasses; his eyes are an unnatural ice-
blue.

                    AGENT SMITH
          We know that you have been
          contacted by a certain individual.
          A man who calls himself Morpheus.
          Whatever you think you know about
          this man is irrelevant. The fact
          is that he is wanted for acts of
          terrorism in more countries than
          any other man in the world. He is
          considered by many authorities to
          be the most dangerous man alive.

He leans closer.

                    AGENT SMITH
          My colleagues believe that I am
          wasting my time with you but I
          believe you want to do the right
          thing.
                    (MORE)

                    AGENT SMITH   (cont'd)
                It is obvious that you are
                an intelligent man, Mr. Anderson,
                and that you are interested in the
                future. That is why I believe you
                are ready to put your past
                mistakes behind you and get on
                with your life.

Neo tries to match his stare.

                    AGENT SMITH
                We are willing to wipe the slate
                clean, to give you a fresh start
                and all we arc asking in return is
                your cooperation in bringing a
                known terrorist to justice.

Neo nods to himself.

                    NEO
                Yeah. Wow. That sounds like a real
                good deal. But I think I have a
                better one. How about I give you
                the finger--

He does.

                    NEO
                And you give me my phone call!

Agent Smith puts his glasses back on.

                    AGENT SMITH
                You disappoint me, Mr. Anderson.

                    NEO
                You can't scare me with this
                Gestapo crap. I know my rights. I
                want my phone call!

Agent Smith smiles.

                    AGENT SMITH
                And tell me, Mr. Anderson, what
                good is a phone call if you are
                unable to speak?

The question unnerves Neo and strangely he begins to feel the
muscles in his jaw tighten. The standing Agents snicker,
watching Neo's confusion grow into panic.

Neo feels his lips grow soft and sticky as they slowly seal
shut, melding into each other until all traces of his mouth
are gone.

Wild with fear, he lunges for the door but the Agents
restrain him, holding him in the chair.

> AGENT SMITH
> You are going to help us, Mr.
> Anderson, whether you want to or
> not.

Smith nods and the other two rip open his shirt. From a case
taken out of his suit coat, Smith removes a long, fiber-optic
wire tap.

Neo struggles helplessly as Smith dangles the wire over his
exposed abdomen. Horrified, he watches as the electronic
device animates, becoming an organic creature that resembles
a hybrid of an insect and a fluke worm.

Thin, whisker-like tendrils reach out and probe into Neo's
navel. He bucks wildly as Smith drops the creature which
looks for a moment like an uncut umbilical cord--

Before it begins to burrow, its tail thrashing as it worms
its way inside.

21   **INT. NEO'S APARTMENT - NIGHT**   21

Screaming, Neo bolts upright in bed.

He realizes that he is home. Was it a dream? His mouth is
normal. His stomach looks fine. He starts to take a deep,
everything-is-okay breath when--

The phone rings.

It almost stops his heart. It continues ringing, building
pressure in the room, forcing him up out of bed, sucking him
in with an almost gravitational force. He answers it, saying
nothing.

> MORPHEUS (V.O.)
> This line is tapped so I must be
> brief.

> NEO
> The Agents--

> MORPHEUS (V.O.)
> They got to you first, but they've
> underestimated how important you
> are. If they knew what I know, you
> would probably be dead.

> NEO
> What are you talking about? What
> the hell is happening to me?

> MORPHEUS
> You're the One, Neo. You see, you
> may have spent the last few years
> looking for me, but I've spent
> most of my life looking for you.

Neo feels sick.

> MORPHEUS (V.O.)
> Do you still want to meet?

> NEO
> ...yes.

> MORPHEUS (V.O.)
> Go to the Adams Street bridge.

Click. He closes his eyes, unsure of what he has done.

22   EXT. CITY STREET - NIGHT   22

It is just beyond the middle of the night, that time when it
seems there are no rules and everything feels unsafe. Neo's
boots scrape against the concrete. Every pair of eyes he
passes seems to follow him. Rain pours from a black sky.

As he reaches the bridge, headlights creep in behind him. He
turns just as the car slides quickly to a stop beside him.
The back door opens.

> TRINITY
> Get in.

23   INT. CAR   23

A large man named APOC is driving. Beside him is a beautiful
androgyne called SWITCH, aiming a large gun at Neo. Window
wipers beat heavily against the windshield.

> NEO
> What the hell is this?!

> TRINITY
> It's necessary, Neo. For our
> protection.

> NEO
> From what?

> TRINITY
> From you.

She lifts a strange steel and glass device that looks like a cross between a rib separator, speculum, and air compressor.

> SWITCH
> Take off your shirt.

He looks at the strange device and the gun still trained on him.

> NEO
> What? Why?

> SWITCH
> Stop the car.

Apoc does.

> SWITCH
> Listen to me, coppertop. We don't
> have time for 'twenty questions.'
> Right now there is only one rule.
> Our way or the highway.

> NEO
> Fine.

Neo opens the door.

> TRINITY
> Neo, please, you have to trust me.

> NEO
> Why?

> TRINITY
> Because you've been down there,
> Neo. You already know that road.
> You know exactly where it ends.

Neo stares out into sheets of rain railing against the dark street beyond the open door.

> TRINITY
> And I know that's not where you
> want to be.

He closes the door.

A23   **EXT. DARK STREET**   A23

A moment later the green street lights curve over the car's tinted windshield as it rushes through the wet underworld.

Neo grudgingly strips off his T-shirt.

> TRINITY
> Lie back.

Trinity aims the device at Neo, its glass snout forming a seal over his navel. Switch snaps a cable into the front seat cigarette lighter.

> NEO
> What is this thing?

> TRINITY
> We think you're bugged. Try to relax.

She turns a dial and the machine bears down on Neo's midsection, the cylinder sucking hard at his stomach.

Neo screams, squinting in pain as Trinity watches the needle on a pressure gauge climb steadily.

> TRINITY
> Come on, come on...

On a small monitor that projects an ultrasound-like image, we see Neo's insides begin to slither and churn. He gasps as something wiggles beneath his skin inside his stomach.

> SWITCH
> It's on the move.

> TRINITY
> Shit.

> SWITCH
> You're gonna lose it.

> TRINITY
> No I'm not. Clear.

The forboding word hangs in Neo's ear for a moment when Trinity squeezes a trigger. Electric current hammers into Neo and rigid convulsions take hold of him beneath the flickering car lamp until--

Something finally rockets wetly out of Neo's stomach through the extractor's coils.

> NEO
> Jesus Christ! It's real?! That thing is real?!

Trinity lifts a glass cage at the end of the tubing. Inside the small fluke-like bug flips and squirms, its tendrils flapping against the clear walls.

She unrolls the window and dumps it out.

25   **EXT. CAR**   25

It hits the pavement with a metallic tink, reverted back into a common wire tap, as the car disappears into the rainy night.

26   **EXT. HOTEL LAFAYETTE**   26

The car stops in a deserted alley behind a forgotten hotel.

27   **INT. HOTEL LAFAYETTE**   27

It is a place of putrefying elegance, a rotting host of urban maggotry.

Trinity leads Neo from the stairwell down the hall of the thirteenth floor. They stop outside room 1313.

                    TRINITY
              This is it.

Neo can hear his own heart pounding.

                    TRINITY
              Let me give one piece of advice.
              Be honest. He knows more than you
              can possibly imagine.

28   **INT. ROOM 1313**   28

Across the room, a DARK FIGURE stares out the tall windows veiled with decaying lace.

He turns and his smile lights up the room. A dull roar of thunder shakes the old building.

                    MORPHEUS
              At last.

He wears a long black coat and his eyes are invisible behind circular mirrored glasses. He strides to Neo and they shake hands.

                    MORPHEUS
              Welcome, Neo. As you no doubt have
              guessed, I am Morpheus.

                    NEO
              It's an honor.

                    MORPHEUS
          No, the honor is mine. Please.
          Come. Sit.

He nods to Trinity and she exits through a door to an
adjacent room. They sit across from one another in cracked,
burgundy-leather chairs.

                    MORPHEUS
          I imagine, right now, you must be
          feeling a bit like Alice, tumbling
          down the rabbit hole?

                    NEO
          You could say that.

                    MORPHEUS
          I can see it in your eyes. You
          have the look of a man who accepts
          what he sees because he is
          expecting to wake up.

A smile, razor-thin, curls the corner of his lips.

                    MORPHEUS
          Ironically, this is not far from
          the truth. But I'm getting ahead
          of myself. Can you tell me, Neo,
          why are you here?

                    NEO
          You're Morpheus, you're a legend.
          Most hackers would die to meet
          you.

                    MORPHEUS
          Yes. Thank you. But I think we
          both know there's more to it than
          that. Do you believe in fate, Neo?

                    NEO
          No.

                    MORPHEUS
          Why not?

                    NEO
          Because I don't like the idea that
          I'm not in control of my life.

                    MORPHEUS
          I know exactly what you mean.

Again, that smile that could cut glass.

                    MORPHEUS
          Let me tell you why you are here.
          You have come because you know
          something. What you know you can't
          explain but you feel it. You've
          felt it your whole life, felt that
          something is wrong with the world.
          You don't know what, but it's
          there like a splinter in your
          mind, driving you mad. It is this
          feeling that brought you to me. Do
          you know what I'm talking about?

                    NEO
          The Matrix?

                    MORPHEUS
          Do you want to know what it is?

Neo swallows hard and nods.

                    MORPHEUS
          The Matrix is everywhere, it's all
          around us, here even in this room.
          You can see it out your window or
          on your television. You feel it when
          you go to work, or go to church or
          pay your taxes. It is the world that
          has been pulled over your eyes to
          blind you from the truth.

                    NEO
          What truth?

                    MORPHEUS
          That you are a slave, Neo. Like
          everyone else, you were born into
          bondage, kept inside a prison that
          you cannot smell, taste, or touch.
          A prison for your mind.

The leather creaks as he leans back.

                    MORPHEUS
          Unfortunately, no one can be told
          what the Matrix is. You have to
          see it for yourself.

Morpheus opens his hands. In the right is a red pill. In the
left, a blue pill.

> MORPHEUS
> This is your last chance. After
> this, there is no going back. You
> take the blue pill and the story
> ends. You wake in your bed and you
> believe whatever you want to
> believe.

The pills in his open hands are reflected in the glasses.

> MORPHEUS
> You take the red pill and you stay
> in Wonderland and I show you how
> deep the rabbit hole goes.

Neo feels the smooth skin of the capsules, the moisture
growing in his palms.

> MORPHEUS
> Remember that all I am offering is
> the truth. Nothing more.

Neo opens his mouth and swallows the red pill. The Cheshire
smile returns.

> MORPHEUS
> Follow me.

29   INT. OTHER ROOM   29

He leads Neo into the other room, which is cramped with high-
tech equipment, glowing ash-blue and electric green from the
racks of monitors. Trinity, Apoc, Switch, and Cypher look up
as they enter.

> MORPHEUS
> Apoc, are we on-line?

> APOC
> Almost.

He and Trinity are working quickly, hard-wiring a complex
system of monitors, modules, and drives.

> MORPHEUS
> Neo, time is always against us.
> Will you take a seat there?

Neo sits in a chair in the center of the room and Trinity
begins gently fixing white electrode disks to him. Near the
chair is an old oval dressing mirror that is cracked. He
whispers to Trinity:

                              NEO
                       You did all this?

She nods, placing a set of headphones over his ears. They are
wired to an old hotel phone.

                         MORPHEUS
                    The pill you took is part of a
                    trace program. It's designed to
                    disrupt your input/output carrier
                    signal so we can pinpoint your
                    location.

                         NEO
                    What does that mean?

                         CYPHER
                    It means buckle up, Dorothy,
                    'cause Kansas is going bye-bye.

Distantly, through the ear phones, he hears Apoc pounding on
a keyboard. Sweat beads his face. His eyes blink and twitch
when he notices the mirror.

Wide-eyed, he stares as it begins to heal itself, a webwork
of cracks that slowly run together as though the mirror were
becoming liquid.

                         NEO
                    Did you...?

Cypher works with Apoc, checking reams of phosphorescent
data. Trinity monitors Neo's electric vital signs. Neo
reaches out to touch the mirror and his fingers disappear
beneath the rippling surface.

Quickly, he tries to pull his fingers out but the mirror
stretches in long rubbery strands like mirrored-taffy stuck
to his fingertips.

                         MORPHEUS
                    Have you ever had a dream, Neo,
                    that you were so sure was real?

A flash of lightning flickers white hot against Neo.

                         NEO
                    This can't be...

                         MORPHEUS
                    Be what? Be real?

The strands thin like rubber cement as he pulls away, until
the fragile wisps of mirror thread break.

                    MORPHEUS
          What if you were unable to wake
          from that dream, Neo? How would
          you know the difference between
          the dream world and the real
          world?

Neo looks at his hand; fingers distended into mirrored
icicles that begin to melt rapidly, dripping, running like
wax down his fingers, spreading across his palm where he sees
his face reflected.

                    NEO
          Uh-oh...

                    TRINITY
          It's going into replication.

                    MORPHEUS
          Apoc?

                    APOC
          Still nothing.

Morpheus takes out a cellular phone and dials a number.

                    MORPHEUS
          Tank, we're going to need the
          signal soon.

The mirror gel seems to come to life, racing, crawling up his
arms like hundreds of insects.

The mirror creeps up his neck as Neo begins to panic, tipping
his head as though he were sinking into the mirror, trying to
keep his mouth up.

                    NEO
          It's cold.

                    TRINITY
          I got a fibrillation!

                    MORPHEUS
          Shit! Apoc?

Streams of mercury run from Neo's nose.

                    APOC
          Targeting... almost there.

An alarm on Trinity's monitor erupts.

                         TRINITY
                    He's going into arrest!

                          APOC
                    Lock! I got him!

                        MORPHEUS
                    Now, Tank, now!

His eyes tear with mirror, rolling up and closing as a high-
pitched electric scream erupts in the headphones. It is a
piercing shriek like a computer calling to another computer--

Neo's body arches in agony and we are pulled like we were
pulled into the holes of the phone, sucked into his scream
and swallowed by darkness.

30   **INT. POWER PLANT**   30

Close on a man's body floating in a womb-red amnion. His body
spasms, fighting against the thick gelatin.

Metal tubes, surreal versions of hospital tubes, obscure his
face. Other lines like IVs are connected to limbs and cover
his genitals.

He is struggling desperately now. Air bubbles into the Jell-O
but does not break the surface. Pressing up, the surface
distends, stretching like a red rubber cocoon.

Unable to breathe, he fights wildly to stand, clawing at the
thinning elastic shroud, until it ruptures, a hole widening
around his mouth as he sucks for air. Tearing himself free,
he emerges from the cell.

It is Neo.

He is bald and naked, his body slick with gelatin. Dizzy,
nauseous, he waits for his vision to focus.

He is standing in an oval capsule of clear alloy filled with
red gelatin, the surface of which has solidified like curdled
milk. The IVs in his arms are plugged into outlets that
appear to be grafted to his flesh.

He feels the weight of another cable and reaches to the back
of his head where he finds an enormous coaxial plugged and
locked into the base of his skull. He tries to pull it out
but it would be easier to pull off a finger.

To either side he sees other tube-shaped pods filled with red
gelatin; beneath the wax-like surface, pale and motionless,
he sees other human beings.

Fanning out in a circle, there are more. All connected to a center core, each capsule like a red, dimly glowing petal attached to a black metal stem.

Above him, level after level, the stem rises seemingly forever. He moves to the foot of the capsule and looks out. The image assaults his mind.

Towers of glowing petals spiral up to incomprehensible heights, disappearing down into a dim murk like an underwater abyss.

His sight is blurred and warped, exaggerating the intensity of the vision. The sound of the plant is like the sound of the ocean heard from inside the belly of Leviathan.

From above, a machine drops directly in front of Neo. He swallows his scream as it seems to stare at him. It is almost insect-like in its design; beautiful housings of alloyed metal covering organic-like systems of hard and soft polymers.

The machine seizes hold of Neo, paralyzing him as the cable lock at the back of his neck spins and opens.

The cable disengages itself. A long clear plastic needle and cerebrum-chip slides from the anterior of Neo's skull with an ooze of blood and spinal fluid. The other connective hoses snap free and snake away as the machine lets Neo go.

Suddenly, the back of the unit opens and a tremendous vacuum, like an airplane door opening, sucks the gelatin and then Neo into a black hole.

31   INT. WASTE LINE   31

The pipe is a waste disposal system and Neo falls, sliding with the clot of gelatin.

Banking through pipe spirals and elbows, flushing up through grease traps clogged with oily clumps of cellulite.

32   INT. SEWER MAIN   32

Neo begins to drown when he is suddenly snatched from the flow of waste.

The metallic cable then lifts, pulling him up into the belly of the futuristic flying machine hovering inside the sewer main.

33   INT. HOVERCRAFT   33

The metal harness opens and drops the half-conscious Neo onto the floor. Human hands and arms help him up as he finds himself looking straight at Morpheus.

He smiles.

> MORPHEUS
> Welcome to the real world, Neo.

Neo passes out.

FADE TO BLACK.

34   **INT. HOVERCRAFT**   34

We have no sense of time. We hear voices whispering.

> MORPHEUS
> We've done it, Trinity. We found
> him.

> TRINITY
> I hope you're right.

> MORPHEUS
> I don't have to hope it. I know
> it.

Neo's eyes flutter open. We see Morpheus' face above us,
angelic in the fluorescent glow of a light stick.

> NEO (O.S.)
> ...am I dead?

> MORPHEUS
> Far from it.

FADE TO BLACK.

35   **INT. HOVERCRAFT - INFIRMARY**   35

He opens his eyes again, something tingling through him. He
focuses and sees his body pierced with dozens of acupuncture-
like needles wired to a strange device.

> DOZER
> He still needs a lot of work.

DOZER and Morpheus are operating on Neo.

> NEO
> What are you doing?

> MORPHEUS
> Your muscles have atrophied. We're
> rebuilding them.

Fluorescent light sticks burn unnaturally bright.

> NEO
> Why do my eyes hurt?

> MORPHEUS
> You've never used them before.

Morpheus closes Neo's eyes and Neo lays back.

> MORPHEUS
> Rest, Neo. The answers are coming.

36   INT. NEO'S ROOM   36

Neo wakes up from a deep sleep, feeling better. He begins to
examine himself. There is a futuristic IV plugged into the
jack in his forearm. He pulls it out, staring at the grafted
outlet.

He runs his hand over the short hair now covering his head.
His fingers find and explore the large outlet in the base of
his skull.

Just as he starts to come unglued, Morpheus opens the door.

> NEO
> Morpheus, what's happened to me?
> What is this place?

> MORPHEUS
> More important than what is when?

> NEO
> When?

> MORPHEUS
> You believe the year is 1997 when
> in fact it is much closer to 2197.
> I can't say for certain what year
> it is because we honestly do not
> know.

The wind is knocked from Neo's chest.

> MORPHEUS
> There is no reason for me to try
> to explain it when I can simply
> show it. Come with me.

37   INT. HOVERCRAFT   37

Like a sleepwalker, Neo follows Morpheus through the ship.

>   MORPHEUS
>   This is my ship, the
>   Nebuchadnezzar. It's a hovercraft.
>   Small like a submarine. It's
>   cramped and cold. But it's home.

They climb a ladder up to the main deck.

38   **INT. MAIN DECK**   **38**

Everyone is there.

>   MORPHEUS
>   This is the main deck. You know
>   most of my crew.

Trinity smiles and nods.

>   MORPHEUS
>   The ones you don't know. That's
>   Mouse, Cypher, and Switch. Those
>   two guys are Tank and Dozer.

The names and faces wash meaninglessly over Neo.

>   MORPHEUS
>   And this, this is the Core. This
>   is where we broadcast our pirate
>   signal and hack into the Matrix.

It is a swamp of bizarre electronic equipment. Vines of
coaxial hang and snake to and from huge monolithic battery
slabs, a black portable satellite dish and banks of life
systems and computer monitors.

At the center of the web, there are six ecto-skeleton chairs
made of a poly-alloy frame and suspension harness. Near the
circle of chairs is the control console and operator's
station where the network is monitored.

>   MORPHEUS
>   You want to know what the Matrix
>   is, Neo? The answer is right here.

He touches the back of Neo's head.

>   MORPHEUS
>   Help him, Trinity.

Neo allows himself to be helped into one of the chairs. He
feels Morpheus guiding a coaxial line into the jack at the
back of his neck. The cable has the same kind of cerebrum
chip we saw inside the plant.

                         MORPHEUS
                    This will feel a little weird.

There are several disturbing noises as he works the needle
in.

We move in as Neo's shoulders bunch and his face tightens
into a grimace until a loud click fires and his ears pop like
when you equalize them underwater.

He relaxes, opening his eyes as we pull back to a feeling of
weightlessness inside another place--

39   **INT. CONSTRUCT**   39

Neo is standing in an empty, blank-white space.

                         MORPHEUS
                    This is the Construct.

Startled, Neo whips around and finds Morpheus now in the room
with him.

                         MORPHEUS
                    It is our loading program. We can
                    load anything from clothes, to
                    weapons, to training simulations.
                    Anything we need.

Morpheus walks past Neo and when Neo turns he sees the two
leather chairs from the Hotel Lafayette set up in front of a
large-screen television.

                         MORPHEUS
                    Sit down.

Neo stands at the back of the chair as Morpheus sits.

                         NEO
                    Right now, we're inside a computer
                    program?

Morpheus smiles.

                         MORPHEUS
                    Is it so hard to believe? Your
                    clothes are different, the plugs
                    in your arms and head are gone.
                    Look at your hair, you were bald a
                    moment ago.

Neo touches his head.

                    MORPHEUS
          It's what we call residual self
          image. The mental projection of
          your electronic self. Wild, isn't
          it?

Neo's hands run over the cracked leather.

                    NEO
          This-- This isn't real?

                    MORPHEUS
          What is real? How do you define
          real? If you're talking about what
          you feel, taste, smell, or see,
          then real is simply electrical signals
          interpreted by your brain.

He picks up a remote control and clicks on the television. On
the television, we see images of the twentieth-century city
where Neo lived.

                    MORPHEUS
          This is the world you know. The
          world as it was at the end of the
          twentieth century. It exists now
          only as part of a neural-
          interactive simulation that we
          call the Matrix.

He changes the channel and we see a very different city as we
enter the television.

                    MORPHEUS
          You have been living inside a
          dreamworld, Neo. As in
          Baudrillard's vision, your whole
          life has been spent inside the
          map, not the territory. This is
          the world as it exists today.

In the distance, we see the ruins of a future city protruding
from the wasteland like the blackened ribs of a long-dead
corpse.

                    MORPHEUS
          'The desert of the real.'

Beneath us, the water is gone.

We turn and descend, spiraling down toward the lake bed which
is scorched and split like burnt flesh, where we find
Morpheus and Neo. Neo clings to the chair, trying to get his
bearings.

> MORPHEUS
> We have only bits and pieces of
> information. What we know for
> certain is that, at some point in
> the early twenty-first century,
> all of mankind was united in
> celebration. Through the blinding
> inebriation of hubris, we marveled
> at our magnificence as we gave
> birth to A.I.

> NEO
> A.I.? You mean artificial
> intelligence?

> MORPHEUS
> Yes. A singular consciousness that
> spawned an entire race of
> machines. I must say I find it
> almost funny to imagine the world
> slapping itself on the back,
> toasting the new age. I say almost
> funny.

He looks up and his sunglasses reflect the obsidian clouds
roiling overhead.

> MORPHEUS
> We don't know who struck first. Us
> or them. But we do know it was us
> that scorched the sky. At the
> time, they were dependent on solar
> power. It was believed they would
> be unable to survive without an
> energy source as abundant as the
> sun.

As we descend into the circular window of his glasses, there
is a flash of lightning.

> MORPHEUS
> Throughout human history, we have
> been dependent on machines to
> survive. Fate, it seems, is not
> without a sense of irony.

40   EXT. FETUS FIELDS   40

On the flash, we pull back from the darkness which reveals
itself to be the black eye of a fetus.

                    MORPHEUS
          The Machines discovered a new form
          of fusion. All they needed was a
          small electrical charge to
          initiate the reaction.

The fetus is suspended in a placenta-like husk, where its
malleable skull is already growing around the brain-jack.

                    MORPHEUS
          The human body generates more
          bioelectricity than a 120-volt
          battery and over 25,000 B.T.U.'s
          of body heat.

The husk hanging from a stalk is plucked by a thresher-like
farm machine.

                    MORPHEUS
          There are fields, endless fields
          where human beings are no longer
          born; we are grown.

We rise up, the field stretching in every direction to the
horizon, lightning tearing open the sky as a harvester sweeps
past us.

A40   INT. POWER PLANT   A40

From the yawning black of the waste port, we begin to pull
back as it snaps shut.

Red amniotic gel flows into the pod below us, pooling around
a tiny newborn that suckles its feed tube.

                    MORPHEUS
          For the longest time, I wouldn't
          believe it. But then I saw the
          fields with my own eyes, watched
          them liquify the dead so they
          could be fed intravenously to the
          living and standing there, facing
          the efficiency, the pure,
          horrifying precision, I came to
          realize the obviousness of the
          truth.

Still pulling back, we see the image of the power plant now
on the television as we return to the white space of the
construct.

41   INT. CONSTRUCT   41

Morpheus steps into view as he clicks off the television.

                         MORPHEUS
                  What is the Matrix? Control.

He opens the back of the television remote control.

                         MORPHEUS
                  The Matrix is a computer-generated
                  dreamworld built to keep us under
                  control in order to change a human
                  being into this.

He holds up a coppertop battery.

                         NEO
                  No! I don't believe it! It's not
                  possible!

                         MORPHEUS
                  I didn't say that it would be
                  easy, Neo. I just said that it
                  would be the truth.

                         NEO
                  Stop! Let me out! I want out!

42   INT. MAIN DECK   42

His eyes snap open and he thrashes against the chair, trying
to rip the cable from the back of his neck.

                         NEO
                  Get this thing out of me!

                         TRINITY
                  Easy, Neo. Easy.

Dozer holds him while Trinity unlocks it. Once it's out, he
tears away from them, falling as he trips free of the
harness.

                         NEO
                  Don't touch me! Get away from me!

On his hands and knees, he reels as the world spins. Sweat
pours off him as a pressure builds inside his skull as if his
brain had been put into a centrifuge.

                         NEO
                  I don't believe it! I don't
                  believe it!

                         CYPHER
                  He's going to pop!

Vomiting violently, Neo pitches forward and blacks out.

INT. NEO'S ROOM

He blinks, regaining consciousness. The room is dark. Neo is
stretched out on his bed.

                    NEO
          I can't go back, can I?

Morpheus is sitting like a shadow on a chair in the far
corner.

                    MORPHEUS
          No. But if you could, would you
          really want to?

Deep down, Neo knows that answer.

                    MORPHEUS
          I feel that I owe you an apology.
          There is a rule that we do not
          free a mind once it reaches a
          certain age. It is dangerous. They
          have trouble letting go. Their
          mind turns against them. I've seen
          it happen. I'm sorry. I broke the
          rule because I had to.

He stares into the darkness, confessing as much to himself as
to Neo.

                    MORPHEUS
          When the Matrix was first built
          there was a man born inside that
          had the ability to change what he
          wanted, to remake the Matrix as he
          saw fit. It was this man that
          freed the first of us and taught
          us the truth; as long as the
          Matrix exists, the human race will
          never be free.

He pauses.

                    MORPHEUS
          When he died, the Oracle
          prophesied his return and
          envisioned that his coming would
          hail the destruction of the
          Matrix, an end to the war and
          freedom for our people. That is
          why there are those of us that
          have spent our entire lives
          searching the Matrix, looking for
          him.

Neo can feel his eyes on him.

> MORPHEUS
> I did what I did because I believe
> the search is over.

He stands up.

> MORPHEUS
> Get some rest. You're going to
> need it.

> NEO
> For what?

> MORPHEUS
> Your training.

44   **INT. HOVERCRAFT**   44

There is no morning; there is only darkness and then the
fluorescent light sticks flicker on.

45   **INT. NEO'S ROOM**   45

Neo is awake in his bed, staring up at the lights. The door
opens and TANK steps inside.

> TANK
> Morning. Did you sleep?

> NEO
> No.

> TANK
> You will tonight. I guarantee it.
> I'm Tank. I'll be your operator.

He offers his hand and Neo shakes it. He notices that Tank
doesn't have any jacks.

> NEO
> You don't have...

> TANK
> Any holes? Nope. Me and my brother
> Dozer, we are 100 percent pure,
> old-fashioned, home-grown human.
> Born free. Right here in the real
> world. Genuine child of Zion.

> NEO
> Zion?

> TANK
>
> If this war ended tomorrow, Zion
> is where the party would be.

> NEO
>
> It's a city?

> TANK
>
> The last human city. The only
> place we got left.

> NEO
>
> Where is it?

> TANK
>
> Deep underground. Near the earth's
> core, where it's still warm. You
> live long enough, you might even
> see it.

Tank smiles.

> TANK
>
> Goddamn, I got to tell you, I'm
> fairly excited to see what you are
> capable of. I mean if Morpheus is
> right and all. We're not supposed
> to talk about any of that but if you
> are, well then this is an exciting
> time. We got a lot to do, so let's
> get to it.

46   **INT. MAIN DECK**   46

Neo is plugged in, hanging in one of the suspension chairs.

> TANK
>
> We're supposed to load all these
> operations programs first, but
> this is some major boring shit.
> Why don't we start with something
> a little fun?

Tank smiles as he plops into his operator's chair. He begins
flipping through a tall carousel loaded with micro discs.

> TANK
>
> How about some combat training?

Neo reads the label on the disk.

>   NEO
>   Jujitsu? I'm going to learn
>   jujitsu?

Tank slides the disk into Neo's supplement drive.

>   NEO
>   No way.

Smiling, Tank punches the "load" code. His body jumps against
the harness as his eyes clamp shut. The monitors kick wildly
as his heart pounds, adrenaline surges, and his brain
sizzles. An instant later his eyes snap open.

>   NEO
>   Holy shit!

>   TANK
>   Hey, Mikey, he likes it! Ready for
>   more?

>   NEO
>   Hell yes!

47   **INT. MAIN DECK**   47

Close on a computer monitor as grey pixels slowly fill a
small, half-empty box. It is a meter displaying how much
download time is left.

The title bar reads: "Combat Series 10 of 12," file
categories flashing beneath it: "Savate, Jujitsu, Ken Po,
Drunken Boxing..."

Morpheus walks in.

>   MORPHEUS
>   How is he?

>   TANK
>   Ten hours straight. He's a
>   machine.

Neo's body spasms and relaxes as his eyes open, breath
hissing from his lips. He looks like he just orgasmed.

>   NEO
>   This is incredible. I know kung
>   fu.

>   MORPHEUS
>   Show me.

They are standing in a very sparse Japanese-style dojo.

                    MORPHEUS
          This is a sparring program,
          similar to the programmed reality
          of the Matrix. It has the same
          basic rules. Rules like gravity.
          What you must learn is that these
          rules are no different than the
          rules of a computer system. Some
          of them can be bent. Others can be
          broken. Understand?

Neo nods as Morpheus assumes a fighting stance.

                    MORPHEUS
          Then hit me, if you can.

Neo assumes a similar stance, cautiously circling until he
gives a short cry and launches a furious attack.

It is like a Jackie Chan movie at high speed, fists and feet
striking from every angle as Neo presses his attack, but each
and every blow is blocked by effortless speed.

49   INT. MAIN DECK   49

While their minds battle in the programmed reality, the two
bodies appear quite serene, suspended in the drive chairs.

Tank monitors their Life Systems, noticing that Neo is wildly
and chaotically lit up as opposed to the slow and steady
rhythm of Morpheus.

50   INT. MESS HALL   50

MOUSE bursts into the room, interrupting dinner.

                    MOUSE
          Morpheus is fighting Neo!

All at once, everyone bolts for the door.

51   INT. DOJO   51

Neo's face is knotted, teeth clenched, as he hurls himself at
Morpheus.

                    MORPHEUS
          Good. Adaptation. Improvisation. But
          your weakness isn't your technique.

Morpheus attacks him and it is like nothing we have seen. His feet and fists are everywhere, taking Neo apart. For every blow Neo blocks, five more hit their marks until--

Neo falls.

Panting, on his hands and knees, blood spits from his mouth, speckling the white floor of the dojo.

                    MORPHEUS
          How did I beat you?

                    NEO
          You-- you're too fast.

                    MORPHEUS
          Do you think my being faster,
          stronger has anything to do with
          my muscles in this place?

Neo is frustrated, still unable to catch his breath.

                    MORPHEUS
          Do you believe that's air you are
          breathing now?

Neo stands, nodding slowly.

                    MORPHEUS
          Again.

Their fists fly with pneumatic speed.

52   INT. MAIN DECK   52

Everyone is gathered behind Tank watching the fight, like watching a game of Mortal Kombat.

                    MOUSE
          Jeeezus Keeerist! He's fast! Look
          at his neural-kinetics! They're
          way above normal!

53   INT. DOJO   53

Morpheus begins to press Neo, countering blows while slipping in several stinging slaps.

                    MORPHEUS
          Come on, Neo. What are you waiting
          for? You're faster than this.
          Don't think you are. Know you are.

Whack, Morpheus cracks Neo again. Neo's face twists with rage as the speed of the blows rises like a drum solo.

MORPHEUS
Come on! Stop trying to hit me and
just hit me.

Wham. A single blow catches Morpheus on the side of the head,
knocking off his glasses.

54   **INT. MAIN DECK**   54

There are several gasps.

MOUSE
I don't believe it!

55   **INT. DOJO**   55

Morpheus rubs his face, then smiles.

NEO
I know what you're trying to do--

MORPHEUS
I'm trying to free your mind, Neo,
but all I can do is show you the
door. You're the one that has to
step through. Tank, load the jump
program.

56   **INT. HOVERCRAFT**   56

Apoc and Switch exchange looks as Tank grabs for the disk.

57   **INT. CONSTRUCT - ROOFTOP - DAY**   57

Morpheus and Neo are again in the white space of the
Construct. Beneath their feet, we see the jump program rush
up at them until they are standing on a rooftop in a city
skyline.

MORPHEUS
Let it all go, Neo. Fear. Doubt.
Disbelief. Free your mind.

Morpheus spins, running hard at the edge of the rooftop. And
jumps. He sails through the air, his coat billowing out
behind him like a cape as he lands on the rooftop across the
street.

NEO
Shit.

Neo looks down at the street twenty floors below, then at
Morpheus an impossible fifty feet away.

                              NEO
                    Okie dokie. Free my mind. Right.
                    No problem.

He takes a deep breath. And starts to run.

58   INT. MAIN DECK   58

They are transfixed.

                              MOUSE
                    What if he makes it?

                              APOC
                    No way. Not possible.

                              TANK
                    No one's ever made their first
                    jump.

                              MOUSE
                    I know but what if he does?

                              APOC
                    He won't.

Trinity stares at the screen, her fists clenching as she
whispers.

                              TRINITY
                    Come on.

59   EXT. ROOFTOP   59

Summoning every ounce of strength in his legs, Neo launches
himself into the air in a single maniacal shriek--

But comes up drastically short.

His eyes widen as he plummets. Stories fly by, the ground
rushing up at him, but as he hits, the ground gives way,
stretching like a trapeze net. He bounces and flips, slowly
coming to a rest, flat on his back.

He laughs, a bit unsure, wiping the wind-blown tears from his
face. Morpheus exits the building and helps him to his feet.

                              MORPHEUS
                    Do you know why you didn't make
                    it?

                              NEO
                    Because... I didn't think I would?

Morpheus smiles and nods.

60   INT. MAIN DECK   60

They break up.

                        MOUSE
            What does it mean?

                        SWITCH
            It doesn't mean anything.

                        CYPHER
            Everyone falls the first time,
            right, Trinity?

But Trinity has already left.

Neo's eyes open as Tank eases the plug out. He tries to move
and groans, cradling his ribs. While Tank helps Morpheus, Neo
spits blood into his hand.

                        NEO
            I thought it wasn't real.

                        MORPHEUS
            Your mind makes it real.

Neo stares at the blood.

                        NEO
            If you are killed in the Matrix,
            you die here?

                        MORPHEUS
            The body cannot live without the
            mind.

61   INT. NEO'S ROOM   61

Trinity enters from the hall, carrying a tray of food.

                        TRINITY
            Neo, I saved you some dinner--

She sees him passed out on the bed. She sets the tray down
and pulls the blanket over him.

She pauses, her face close to his, then inhales lightly,
breathing in the scent of him before slowly pulling away.

62   INT. HALL   62

Trinity steps out of Neo's room to find Cypher watching her.

                    CYPHER
          I don't remember you ever bringing
          me dinner.

Trinity says nothing.

                    CYPHER
          There's something about him, isn't
          there?

                    TRINITY
          Don't tell me you're a believer
          now?

                    CYPHER
          I just keep wondering if Morpheus
          is so sure, why doesn't he take
          him to the Oracle? She would know.

                    TRINITY
          Morpheus will take him when he's
          ready.

She turns and he watches her walk away.

63   **EXT. CITY STREET - TRAINING PROGRAM - DAY**   63

Morpheus moves effortlessly through a crowded downtown street
while Neo struggles to keep up, constantly bumped and
shouldered off the path.

                    MORPHEUS
          The Matrix is a system, Neo, and
          that system is our enemy. But when
          you are inside and look around,
          what do you see; businessmen,
          lawyers, teachers, carpenters. The
          minds of the very people we are
          trying to save. But until we do,
          these people are still a part of
          the system and that makes them our
          enemy.

A cop writing a parking ticket stares at Neo from behind his
glasses.

                    MORPHEUS
          You have to understand that most
          of these people are not ready to
          be unplugged and many of them are
          so inured, so hopelessly dependent
          on the system that they will fight
          to protect it.

A beautiful woman in a red dress smiles at Neo as she passes
by.

                    MORPHEUS
          Were you listening to me, Neo? Or
          were you looking at the woman in
          the red dress?

                    NEO
          I was...

                    MORPHEUS
          Look again.

Neo turns just as Agent Smith levels a gun at his face. Neo
screams.

                    MORPHEUS
          Freeze it.

Everything except Morpheus and Neo freezes.

                    NEO
          This-- This isn't the Matrix?

                    MORPHEUS
          No, it's another training program
          designed to teach you one thing;
          if you are not one of us, you're
          one of them.

                    NEO
          What are they?

                    MORPHEUS
          Sentient programs. They can move
          in and out of any software still
          hardwired to their system. That
          means that anyone that we haven't
          unplugged is potentially an Agent.
          Inside the Matrix, they are
          everyone and they are no one.

Neo stares at the Agent.

                    MORPHEUS
          We've survived by hiding from
          them, running from them, but they
          are the gatekeepers, they're
          guarding all the doors, holding
          all the keys which means that
          sooner or later someone is going
          to have to fight them.

> NEO
> Someone?

> MORPHEUS
> I won't lie to you, Neo. Every
> single man or woman who has stood
> their ground, who has fought an
> Agent, has died. But where they
> failed, you will succeed.

> NEO
> Why?

> MORPHEUS
> I've seen an Agent punch through a
> concrete wall. Men have emptied
> entire clips at them and hit
> nothing but air. Yet their strength
> and their speed are still based in a
> world that is built by rules. Because
> of that, they will never be as strong
> or as fast as you can be.

Neo scratches his head.

> NEO
> What? Are you trying to tell me
> that I can dodge bullets?

> MORPHEUS
> No, Neo. I'm trying to tell you
> that when you're ready, you won't
> have to.

Morpheus's cell phone rings and he flips it open.

> TANK (V.O.)
> We got trouble.

64   **EXT. SEWER MAIN**   64

The Nebuchadnezzar blisters by, trailing a swirling,
supercharged, electromagnetic wake.

65   **INT. COCKPIT**   65

Morpheus slides into the co-pilot's chair next to Dozer.

                         MORPHEUS
              Did Zion send the warning?

                         DOZER
              No. Another ship. Big Brother I
              think, they're running a parallel
              pipeline.

Morpheus scans the decayed landscape of the sewer main that
rolls by as Neo and Trinity squeeze into the cockpit behind
him. An alarm begins to sound.

                         DOZER
              Shit, Squiddy's sweeping in quick.

                         MORPHEUS
              Set it down in there.

                         NEO
              Squiddy?

                         TRINITY
              A Sentinel. It's a killing machine
              designed for one thing.

                         DOZER
              Search and destroy.

Neo feels the ship rock to the side as it squeezes into a
tiny supply line.

66   **EXT. HOVERCRAFT**   66

The Nebuchadnezzar sets down, almost wedged into a pipe that
barely accommodates its size.

67   **INT. COCKPIT**   67

Morpheus clicks the intercom.

                         MORPHEUS
                   How we doing, Tank?

68   **INT. MAIN DECK**   68

Tank works furiously at the operator's station as the
ceaseless whir of the ship's turbines grind to a halt. The
main deck is plunged into dark silence. The rest of the crew
stands behind him as he whispers.

                         TANK
                   Power off-line. E.M.P. armed and
                   ready.

Tank's fingers curl around a small key that glows a dim red.

69   **INT. COCKPIT**   69

Neo leans into Trinity's ear.

>   NEO
> E.M.P?

>   TRINITY
> An electromagnetic pulse. It
> disables any electrical system in
> the blast radius. It's the only
> weapon we have against the
> machines.

Dozer looks up.

>   DOZER
> Now we wait.

Through the cockpit's windshield, the vast cavern of the
sewer main yawns before them. Strands of green haze curl
around mossy icicles that dangle into a pool of churning
frozen waste.

Neo begins to angle around Dozer but Morpheus grabs him.

>   MORPHEUS
> Don't move. It'll hear you.

Neo freezes and they wait. Without the Nebuchadnezzar's
heating systems, the temperature in the cockpit begins to
rapidly drop. The crew members huddle together, their breath
freezing into a uniform cloud as it gets colder and colder.

Dozer quietly reaches to brush away the frost on the
windshield and as his hand clears a swathe--

They see it.

In the darkness, a shifting shadow of mechanized death. It is
beautiful and terrifying. Black alloy skin flickers like
sequins beneath sinewy coils and skeletal appendages.

Neo can feel the hairs on the back of his neck rise as it
silently glides over them with shark-like malevolence until
it disappears into the darkness.

In the frozen little room, everyone breathes a little easier.

70   **INT. HALL**   70

The ship is quiet and dark. Everyone is asleep.

The core glows with monitor light. Cypher is in the
operator's chair as Neo comes up behind him.

T
H
E

M
A
T
R
I
X

.

s
c
r
i
p
t

p
a
g
e

5
6

                        CYPHER
              Whoa! Shit, Neo, you scared the
              Bejeezus out of me.

                        NEO
              Sorry.

                        CYPHER
              No, it's all right.

Neo's eyes light up as he steps closer to the screens that
seem alive with a constant flow of data.

                        NEO
              Is that...?

                        CYPHER
              The Matrix? Yeah.

Neo stares at the endlessly shifting river of information,
bizarre codes and equations flowing across the face of the
monitor.

                        NEO
              Do you always look at it encoded?

                        CYPHER
              Have to. The image translators
              sort of work for the construct
              programs but there's way too much
              information to decode the Matrix.
              You get used to it, though. Your
              brain does the translating. I
              don't even see the code. All I see
              is blonde, brunette, and redhead.
              You want a drink?

Neo nods and he pours a clear alcohol from a plastic jug.

                        CYPHER
              You know, I know what you're
              thinking 'cause right now I'm
              thinking the same thing. Actually,
              to tell you the truth, I've been
              thinking the same thing ever since
              I got here.

He raises the glass.

                    CYPHER
          Why, oh why, didn't I take that
          blue pill!?

He throws the shot down his throat. Neo does the same and it
almost kills him. Smiling, Cypher slaps him on the back.

                    CYPHER
          Good shit, eh? Dozer makes it.
          It's good for two things:
          degreasing engines and killing
          brain cells.

Red-faced, Neo finally stops coughing. Cypher pours him
another.

                    CYPHER
          Can I ask you something? Did he
          happen to tell you why he did it?

Neo looks up, unsure.

                    CYPHER
          Why you're here?

                    NEO
          ...yeah.

                    CYPHER
          Gee-zus! What a mindjob. You're
          here to save the world. You gotta
          be shitting me. What do you say to
          something like that?

Neo looks down at his drink.

                    CYPHER
          I'm going to let you in on a
          little secret here. Now don't tell
          him I told you this, but this
          ain't the first time Morpheus
          thought he found the One.

                    NEO
          Really?

                    CYPHER
          You bet your ass. It keeps him
          going. Maybe it keeps all of us
          going.

                    NEO
          How many were there?

                        CYPHER
            Five. Since I've been here.

                        NEO
            What happened to them?

                        CYPHER
            Dead. All dead.

                        NEO
            How?

                        CYPHER
            Honestly? Morpheus. He got them
            all amped up believing in bullshit.
            I watched each of them take on an
            Agent and I watched each of them die.
            Little piece of advice: you see an
            Agent, you do what we do; run. Run
            your ass off.

Neo gulps down another shot.

                        NEO
            Thanks... for the drink.

                        CYPHER
            Any time.

Cypher nods as Neo heads for the ladder.

                        CYPHER
            Sweet dreams.

A71   INT. RESTAURANT - NIGHT   A71

Chamber music and the ambiance of wealth soak the restaurant
around us as we watch a serrated knife saw through a thick,
gorgeous steak. The meat is so perfect, charred on the
outside, oozing red juice on the inside, that it could be a
dream.

We hear a voice that we recognize immediately.

                        AGENT SMITH
            Do we have a deal, Mr. Reagan?

A fork stabs the cube of meat and we follow it up to the face
of Cypher.

                    CYPHER
            You know, I know that this steak
            doesn't exist. I know that when I
            put it in my mouth, the Matrix is
            telling my brain that it is juicy
            and delicious. After nine years,
            do you know what I've realized?

He shoves it in, eyes rolling up, savoring the tender beef
melting in his mouth.

                    CYPHER
            Ignorance is bliss.

Agent Smith watches him chew the steak loudly, smacking it
between his teeth.

                    CYPHER
            Mmm so, so goddamn good.

                 AGENT SMITH
            Then we have a deal?

                    CYPHER
            I don't want to remember nothing.
            Nothing! You understand? And I
            want to be rich. Someone
            important. Like an actor. You can
            do that, right?

                 AGENT SMITH
            Whatever you want, Mr. Reagan.

Cypher takes a deep drink of wine.

                    CYPHER
            All right. You get my body back in
            a Power Plant, reinsert me into
            the Matrix, and I'll get you what
            you want.

                 AGENT SMITH
            Access codes to the Zion
            mainframe.

                    CYPHER
            I told you I don't know them. But
            I can give you the man who does.

                 AGENT SMITH
            Morpheus.

T
H
E

M
A
T
R
I
X

.

s
c
r
i
p
t

p
a
g
e

6
0

Close on breakfast, a substance with a consistency somewhere between yogurt and cellulite.

                    TANK
          Here you go, buddy. Breakfast of
          champions.

Tank slides it in front of Neo and takes a seat with the other crew members enjoying breakfast.

                    MOUSE
          If you close your eyes, it almost
          feels like you're eating runny
          eggs.

                    APOC
          Or a bowl of snot.

                    MOUSE
          But you know what it really
          reminds me of? Tastee Wheat. Did
          you ever eat Tastee Wheat?

                    SWITCH
          No, but technically neither did
          you.

                    MOUSE
          Exactly my point, because you have
          to wonder, how do the machines
          know what Tastee Wheat really
          tasted like? Maybe they got it
          wrong, maybe what I think Tastee
          Wheat tasted like actually tasted
          like oatmeal, or tuna fish. It
          makes you wonder about a lot of
          things. Take chicken for example.
          Maybe they couldn't figure out
          what to make chicken taste like
          which is why chicken tastes like
          everything. And maybe--

                    APOC
          Shut up, Mouse.

Neo scoops up a spoonful.

                    DOZER
          It's a single-celled protein
          combined with synthetic aminos,
          vitamins, and minerals. Everything
          your body needs. We grow it in a
          vat.

                    MOUSE
          Oh no, it doesn't have everything
          the body needs.

He sidles up to Neo.

                    MOUSE
          So I understand you've run through
          the Agent training program? You
          know, I wrote that program.

                    APOC
          Here it comes.

                    MOUSE
          So what did you think of her?

                    NEO
          Of who?

                    MOUSE
          The woman in the red dress. I
          designed her. She doesn't talk
          much but if you'd like to, you
          know, meet her, I could arrange a
          more personalized milieu.

                    SWITCH
          The digital pimp hard at work.

                    MOUSE
          Pay no attention to these
          hypocrites, Neo. To deny our
          impulses is to deny the very thing
          that makes us human.

Morpheus enters.

                    MORPHEUS
          I want everyone on twelve-hour
          standby. We're going in. I'm
          taking Neo to see her.

With that he turns and leaves.

                    NEO
          See who?

                    TANK
          The Oracle.

A72   INT. MAIN DECK   A72

Everyone is strapped into their chairs. Tank is at the
operator's station.

                              TANK
                    All right, everyone please observe
                    that the no smoking and fasten
                    seat belt signs have been turned
                    on. Sit back and enjoy your
                    flight.

          He strikes the enter key and we rush clockwise over the
          chairs, each body reacting as we cut--

B72   INT. HOTEL LAFAYETTE - ROOM 1313   B72

          Spinning counter clockwise around an old phone that rings
          inside the empty room until we spin full circle and find
          everyone now standing there.

          Morpheus answers the phone.

                              MORPHEUS
                    We're in.

73   EXT. HOTEL LAFAYETTE - DAY   73

          The door opens and for the first time since his release, Neo
          steps back into the Matrix. He squints at the sun which seems
          unnaturally bright. He is the only one without sunglasses.

          Apoc and Switch remain at the door as the others enter the
          alley.

                              MORPHEUS
                    We should be back in an hour.

          Cypher opens the driver's door of an old car. As Trinity,
          Morpheus, and Neo cross to the car, Cypher glances about
          quickly, then drops something inside a garbage can.

          It is a cellular phone and we see its blue display as the
          line connects.

74   INT. CAR   74

          Neo sits beside Trinity in the back. He cannot stop staring
          as the simple images of the urban street blur past his window
          like an endless stream of data rushing down a computer
          screen.

                              MORPHEUS
                    Almost unbelievable, isn't it?

          Neo nods as the car continues to wind through the crowded
          city.

                              NEO
                    God...

                    TRINITY
          What?

                    NEO
          I used to eat there... Really good
          noodles...

He is speaking in a whisper, almost as if talking to himself.

                    NEO
          I have these memories, from my
          entire life but... none of them
          really happened.

He turns to her.

                    NEO
          What does that mean?

                    TRINITY
          That the Matrix cannot tell you
          who you are.

                    NEO
          But an Oracle can.

                    TRINITY
          That's different.

                    NEO
          Obviously.

He turns to the window for a moment and then turns back.

                    NEO
          Did you go to her?

                    TRINITY
          Yes.

                    NEO
          What did she tell you?

                    TRINITY
          She told me...

She looks at him and suddenly she is unable to speak or even
breathe.

                    NEO
          What?

The car suddenly jerks to a stop.

MORPHEUS
We're here. Neo, come with me.

Neo and Morpheus get out of the car. Cypher looks into the
rearview mirror at Trinity.

CYPHER
Here we go again, eh, Trin?

He smiles as she turns to the window.

75   **EXT. BUILDING**   75

Tenement-like and vast, it is the kind of place where people
can disappear.

76   **INT. BUILDING**   76

Morpheus nods to a blind man who nods back. An elevator opens
and Neo follows Morpheus inside.

77   **INT. ELEVATOR**   77

The idea of learning one's fate begins to weigh upon Neo with
a steadily growing unease.

NEO
So is this the same oracle that
made the, uh, prophecy?

MORPHEUS
Yes. She's very old. She's been
with us since the beginning.

NEO
The beginning?

MORPHEUS
Of the Resistance.

NEO
And she knows what? Everything?

MORPHEUS
She would say she knows enough.

NEO
And she's never wrong.

MORPHEUS
Don't think of it in terms of
right and wrong. She is a guide,
Neo. She can help you find the
path.

NEO
She helped you?

                    MORPHEUS
Yes.

                    NEO
What did she tell you?

                    MORPHEUS
That I would find the One.

Ding. The elevator opens.

78   INT. HALL   78

The long dark hall beckons. Neo follows Morpheus out of the
elevator and the doors rattle shut behind him. With every
step, a disturbing sense of inevitability closes in around
him.

At the end of the hall, Morpheus steps to the side of a door.

                    MORPHEUS
          I told you that I can only show
          you the door. You have to step
          through it.

Neo blows out a breath. His hand reaches but stops, hovering
over the spherical handle. He backs away.

                    NEO
          Morpheus, I don't think this is a
          good idea.

                    MORPHEUS
Why?

                    NEO
          I told you I don't believe in this
          stuff. No matter what she says I'm
          not going to believe it, so what's
          the point?

                    MORPHEUS
What do you believe in?

                    NEO
          What do I believe in? Are you
          kidding me? What do you think? The
          world I grew up in, isn't real. My
          entire life was a lie. I don't
          believe in anything anymore.

                    MORPHEUS
          That's why we're here.

                    NEO
          Why? So I can hear some old lady
          tell me, what? That I'm this guy
          that everybody's been waiting for?
          That I'm supposed to save the
          world? It sounds insane.
          Unbelievable. And I don't care who
          says it, it's still going to sound
          insane and unbelievable.

                    MORPHEUS
          Faith is not a matter of
          reasonability. I do not believe
          things with my mind. I believe
          them with my heart. In my gut.

                    NEO
          And you believe I'm the One?

                    MORPHEUS
          Yes I do.

                    NEO
          Yeah? What about the other five
          guys? The five before me? What
          about them?

Morpheus tries to hide his heart being wrenched from his
chest.

                    NEO
          Did you believe in them too?

                    MORPHEUS
          I believed what the Oracle told
          me.... No, I misunderstood what she
          told me. I believed that it was
          all about me.

This is difficult for Morpheus to admit.

                    MORPHEUS
          I believed that all I had to do
          was point my finger and anoint
          whoever I chose. I was wrong, Neo.
          Terribly wrong. Not a day or night
          passes that I do not think of
          them. After the fifth, I lost my
          way. I doubted everything the
          Oracle had said. I doubted myself.

He looks up at Neo.

                    MORPHEUS
          And then I saw you, Neo, and my
          world changed. You can call it an
          epiphany, you can call it whatever
          the hell you want. It doesn't
          matter. It's not about a word.
          It's about this. So I can't
          explain it to you. All I can do is
          believe, Neo, believe that one day
          you will feel what I felt and know
          what I know; you are the sixth and
          the last. You are the One.

His eyes blaze.

                    MORPHEUS
          Until that time all I am asking
          from you is for you to hold on to
          whatever respect you may have for
          me and trust me.

Neo feels a rush from Morpheus's intensity, the unadulterated
confidence of a zealot.

                    NEO
          All right.

He reaches for the handle which turns without him even
touching it. A WOMAN wearing white opens the door.

                    PRIESTESS (WOMAN)
          Hello, Neo. You're right on time.

79   **INT. ORACLE'S APARTMENT**   79

It seems particularly normal.

                    PRIESTESS
          Make yourself at home, Morpheus.

                    MORPHEUS
          Thank you.

                    PRIESTESS
          Neo, come with me.

She leads Neo down another hall and into what appears to be a
family room.

There is another woman in white sitting on a couch watching a
soap opera. Scattered about the room are a half dozen
children. Some of them are playing, others are deep in
meditation. All of them exude a kind of Zen calm.

                              PRIESTESS
                    These are the other Potentials.
                    You can wait here.

Neo watches a little girl levitate wooden alphabet blocks.
Closer to him, a SKINNY BOY with a shaved head holds a spoon
which sways like a blade of grass.

In front of him is a pile of spoons bent and twisted into
knots. Neo crosses to him and sits. The boy smiles and hands
Neo the spoon which is now perfectly straight.

                              SPOON BOY
                    Do not try to bend the spoon. That
                    is impossible. Instead, only try
                    to realize the truth.

                              NEO
                    What truth?

                              SPOON BOY
                    That there is no spoon.

Neo nods, staring at the spoon.

                              NEO
                    There is no spoon.

                              SPOON BOY
                    Then you will see that it is not
                    the spoon that bends. It is only
                    yourself.

The entire room is reflected inside the spoon and as Neo
stares into it, it slowly begins to bend until--

A hand touches his shoulder.

                              PRIESTESS
                    The Oracle will see you now.

Spoon Boy smiles.

80   **INT. KITCHEN**   80

An OLD WOMAN is huddled beside the oven, peering inside
through a cracked door.

                              NEO
                    Hello?

                              ORACLE (OLD WOMAN)
                    I know. You're Neo. Be right with
                    you.

                    NEO
          You're the Oracle?

                    ORACLE
          Bingo. Not quite what you were
          expecting, right? I got to say I
          love seeing you non-believers.
          Always a pip. Almost done. Smell
          good, don't they?

                    NEO
          Yeah.

                    ORACLE
          I'd ask you to sit down, but
          you're not going to anyway. And
          don't worry about the vase.

                    NEO
          What vase?

He turns to look around and his elbow knocks a vase from the
table. It breaks against the linoleum floor.

                    ORACLE
          That vase.

                    NEO
          Shit, I'm sorry.

She pulls out a tray of chocolate chip cookies and turns. She
is an older woman, wearing big oven mitts, comfortable slacks,
and a print blouse. She looks like someone's grandma.

                    ORACLE
          I said don't worry about it. I'll
          get one of my kids to fix it.

                    NEO
          How did you know...?

She sets the cookie tray on a wooden hot pad.

                    ORACLE
          What's really going to bake your
          noodle later on is, would you
          still have broken it if I hadn't
          said anything.

Smiling, she lights a cigarette.

                    ORACLE
          You're cuter than I thought. I see
          why she likes you.

                                                            341

                    NEO
          Who?

                    ORACLE
          Not too bright though.

She winks.

                    ORACLE
          You know why Morpheus brought you
          to see me?

He nods.

                    ORACLE
          So? What do you think? You think
          you're the One?

                    NEO
          Honestly? I don't know.

She gestures to a wooden plaque, the kind every kitchen has,
except that the words are in Latin.

                    ORACLE
          You know what that means?
          It's Latin. Means, "Know Thyself."
          I'm gonna let you in on a little
          secret. Being the One is just
          like being in love. Nobody can
          tell you you're in love. You just
          know it. Through and through. Balls
          to bones.

She puts her cigarette down.

                    ORACLE
          Well, I better have a look at you.
          Open your mouth. Say "Ahh."

She widens his eyes, checks his ears, then feels the glands
in his neck. She nods then looks at his palms.

                    ORACLE
          Okay, now I'm supposed to say,
          "Hmmm, that's interesting but..."
          Then you say--

                    NEO
          But what?

                    ORACLE
          But you already know what I'm
          going to tell you.

                    NEO
          I'm not the One.

                    ORACLE
          Sorry, kid. You got the gift but
          looks like you're waiting for
          something.

                    NEO
          What?

                    ORACLE
          Your next life, maybe. Who knows.
          That's how these things go.

Neo almost has to laugh.

                    ORACLE
          What's funny?

                    NEO
          Morpheus. He almost had me
          convinced.

                    ORACLE
          I know. Poor Morpheus. Without him
          we are lost.

                    NEO
          What do you mean, without him?

The Oracle takes a long drag, regarding Neo with the eyes of
a Sphinx.

                    ORACLE
          Are you sure you want to hear
          this?

Neo nods.

                    ORACLE
          Morpheus believes in you, Neo and
          no one, not you or even me can
          convince him otherwise. He
          believes it so blindly that he's
          going to sacrifice his life to
          save yours.

                    NEO
          What?

> ORACLE
> You're going to have to make a
> choice. In one hand, you will have
> Morpheus's life. In the other
> hand, you will have your own. One
> of you is going to die. Which one,
> will be up to you.

Neo can't breathe.

> ORACLE
> I'm sorry, kiddo. I really am. You
> have a good soul and I hate giving
> good people bad news. But don't
> worry, as soon as you walk outside
> that door, you'll start feeling
> better. You'll remember that you
> don't believe any of this fate
> crap. You're in control of your
> own life, remember?

He tries to nod as she reaches for the tray of cookies.

> ORACLE
> Here, take a cookie. I promise by
> the time you're done eating it,
> you'll feel right as rain.

Neo takes a cookie, the tightness in his chest slowly
beginning to fade.

81   **INT. SITTING ROOM - DAY**   81

Morpheus rises from a couch as the Priestess escorts Neo out.
When they are alone, Morpheus puts his hand on Neo's
shoulder.

> MORPHEUS
> You don't have to tell anyone what
> she told you. What was said was
> said for you and you alone.

Neo nods and takes a bite of his cookie.

82   **INT. CAR**   82

Neo and Morpheus get in the car.

> MORPHEUS
> Let's go.

Cypher looks into the rearview mirror at Neo.

CYPHER
Well, good news or bad news?

MORPHEUS
Not now, Cypher.

Cypher slaps the car in gear and pulls into traffic. Trinity
looks at Neo who is staring at the final bit of cookie. He
puts it in his mouth and chews.

TRINITY
Are you all right?

NEO
...right as rain.

83   **SCENE OMITTED**   83

84   **INT. ROOM 1313 - DAY**   84

Mouse's cellular rings.

MOUSE
Welcome to Movie-Phone.

TANK (V.O.)
They're on their way.

85   **EXT. CITY STREET - DAY**   85

As they get out of the car, Cypher smiles at Neo.

CYPHER
Like the man says, welcome to the
real world.

Cypher, following the others into the hotel, nervously
glances around, wiping the sweat from his forehead.

86   **INT. MAIN DECK**   86

Sweat rolls down Cypher's face and neck. At the operator's
station, Tank is typing rapidly.

TANK
What is that...?

87   **INT. HOTEL LAFAYETTE - DAY**   87

Light filters down the throat of the building, through a
caged skylight at the top of the open elevator shaft. Six
figures glide up the dark stairs that wind around the antique
elevator.

Neo notices a black cat, a yellow-green-eyed shadow that slinks past them and pads quickly down the stairs.

A moment later, Neo sees another black cat that looks and moves identically to the first one.

> NEO
> Whoa. Deja vu.

Those words stop the others dead in their tracks.

88   **INT. MAIN DECK**   88

The monitors suddenly glitch as though the Matrix had an electronic seizure.

> TANK
> Oh shit! Oh shit!

89   **INT. HOTEL LAFAYETTE - DAY**   89

Trinity turns around, her face tight.

> TRINITY
> What did you just say?

> NEO
> Nothing. Just had a little deja
> vu.

> TRINITY
> What happened? What did you see?

> NEO
> A black cat went past us and then
> I saw another that looked just
> like it.

> TRINITY
> How much like it? Was it the same
> cat?

> NEO
> It might have been. I'm not sure.

Trinity looks at Morpheus who listens quietly to the rasping breath of the old building.

> NEO
> What is it?

> TRINITY
> A deja vu is usually a glitch in
> the Matrix. It happens when they
> change something.

She also listens as the staccato beat of helicopter blades grows ominously loud.

90   **INT. MAIN DECK**   90

Tank sees what was changed.

                         TANK
                    It's a trap!

91   **INT. STAIRCASE - DAY**   91

Morpheus looks up the stairs as he hears a helicopter.

                       MORPHEUS
                    Come on!

Apoc slaps a gun in Neo's hand.

                         APOC
                    I hope the Oracle gave you some
                    good news.

Neo nods, stuffing it into his belt.

92   **INT. BASEMENT - DAY**   92

Heavy bolt cutters snap through the main phone cable.

93   **INT. ROOM 1313 - DAY**   93

Hearing the helicopter, Mouse goes to the draped windows as his cellular rings. He answers it.

                       TANK (V.O.)
                    They cut the hardline! It's a
                    trap! Get out!

Mouse yanks open the curtain.

                        MOUSE
                    Oh no.

The windows are bricked up. Mouse spins as the rumble of combat boots builds, then explodes into the room.

94   **INT. MAIN DECK**   94

Tank watches helplessly.

                         TANK
                    No, no, no.

95   **INT. STAIRS - DAY**   95

Morpheus stops as Mouse's scream is drowned out by the report
of machine gun fire.

96   **INT. ROOM 1313 - DAY**   96

Mouse sails backwards as bullets pound him against the blood-
spattered brick window.

97   **INT. MAIN DECK**   97

Mouse's body thrashes against its harness, blood coughing
from his mouth in one final spasm, then lying perfectly
still. The flatline alarm softly cries out from the life
monitor.

98   **SCENE OMITTED**   98

99   **INT. STAIRWELL - DAY**   99

Flying downstairs, Morpheus stops, hearing police swarming
below.

A99   **INT. HALL - DAY**   A99

He turns and rushes down the hall of the eighth floor. At the
end of it, he finds the bricked-up windows.

                          CYPHER
                That's what they changed. We're
                trapped. There's no way out.

The sound of heavy bootsteps close around them with the
mechanical sureness of a vice.

                          MORPHEUS
                Give me your phone.

                          TRINITY
                They'll be able to track it.

                          MORPHEUS
                We have no choice.

Morpheus rips off his jacket.

100   **INT. MAIN DECK**   100

Tank answers the call.

                          MORPHEUS (V.O.)
                Tank, find a structural drawing of
                this building and find it fast.

101   **INT. HOTEL LAFAYETTE - DAY**   101

Flashlights probe the rotting darkness as the police search
every floor.

102   **INT. MAIN DECK**   102

The diagram windows onto the screen.

                         TANK
                    Got it.

                         MORPHEUS (V.O.)
                    I need the main wet-wall.

103   **INT. ROOM 1313 - DAY**   103

Agent Smith stands over Mouse's dead body, his hand going to
his earpiece.

104   **INT. ROOM 808 - DAY**   104

Morpheus is guided by Tank.

                         TANK (V.O.)
                    Now left and that's it in front of
                    you.

                         MORPHEUS
                    Good.

105   **INT. ROOM 1313 - DAY**   105

Agent Smith hears the line click dead.

                         AGENT SMITH
                    Eighth floor. They're on the
                    eighth floor.

A105   **INT. STAIRWELL - DAY**   A105

Agent Brown listens to his ear-piece.

106   **INT. STAIRWELL - DAY**   106

Boots clatter up the marble staircase.

A106   **INT. HALL - DAY**   A106

Cops flood the eighth floor, rushing everywhere.

107   **INT. ROOM 808 - DAY**   107

Several cops sweep through the room. It is empty. As they
pass the bathroom, we see a man-sized hole smashed through
the plaster and lath.

108   INT. WALL - DAY   108

They are inside the main plumbing wall, slowly worming their
way down the grease black stack pipes. Above them, light
fills the hole they made to get inside.

109   INT. HALL - DAY   109

Agent Brown and Agent Smith stand over Morpheus's jacket.

                          AGENT BROWN
                    Where are they?

110   INT. ROOM 608 - DAY   110

The cops search in silence, straining for a clue, when one
hears something strange near the bathroom.

111   INT. WALL - DAY   111

Cypher has slipped and is wedged between the wall and several
thick supply pipes.

112   INT. ROOM 608 - DAY   112

The cop leans in, his ear almost against the thin membrane of
plaster separating them. He can hear whispers, hisses, and a
grunt when--

The wall suddenly bulges, shatter-cracking as the Cop
realizes--

                          COP
                    They're in the walls!

113   INT. WALL - DAY   113

Trinity pulls Cypher free just as the Cop opens fire, bullets
punching shafts of light like swords into the box of soot-
black space.

Neo finds his gun first and begins blasting blindly through
the plaster and lath.

114   INT. ROOM 608 - DAY   114

The Cop spins out of the bathroom for cover, Neo's bullets
splintering the door jamb.

About to whirl back in, he freezes as something seems to
seize hold of him. The Cop's body starts to spasm and his
M-16 falls to the ground, long shadows springing up from the
mounted flashlight.

Neo listens for a moment, the gunfire quiet when he hears footsteps rising fast.

Two arms suddenly smash through the wall, punching Neo back against the iron stack pipe, fingers gouging into his neck.

> CYPHER
> It's an Agent!

Just as Neo's throat is about to collapse, Morpheus explodes through the tattered plaster and lath, diving on top of Agent Smith.

The two men crash to the wet terrazzo floor.

Before Agent Smith can find his weapon, Morpheus is on him, pinning him in an iron grip.

In the crawlspace, Trinity tries to scramble up past Cypher.

> TRINITY
> Morpheus!

Morpheus squeezes Agent Smith's throat.

> MORPHEUS
> Trinity, you must get Neo out. Do
> you understand? He is all that
> matters.

Neo suddenly glimpses what is happening but is powerless to stop it.

> NEO
> No. No! Morpheus! Don't!

> MORPHEUS
> Trinity! Go!

Trinity's fists ball in frustration. She yells down to Apoc.

> TRINITY
> Go!

> NEO
> We can't leave him!

> TRINITY
> We have to!

She grabs his ankle and they begin almost falling using the lath as a brake, skidding down the inside of the wall.

116   INT. BASEMENT - DAY   116

This part of the basement, a dark concrete cavern, was the main mechanical room. There are four enormous boilers, dinosaur-like technology that once pumped hot water like arteries.

Soldiers' blinding lights cut open the darkness as Trinity, Neo, and the others crash through the ceiling. Around them they hear a chorus of short, sharp coughs of grenade launchers from gas-masked figures.

Smoke blossoms from the green metal canisters. Trinity never stops moving. Searching the floor, she finds what she needs; the cover of the catch basin.

Cypher watches her pry open the grate, when a gas can bounces near him.

                         TRINITY
                    Come on!

Cypher seems to trip as the cloud envelops him.

Trinity watches Cypher disappear into the smoke, then follows the others down the wet-black hole.

117   INT. ROOM 608 - DAY   117

Morpheus and Agent Smith remain on the ground, locked in each other's death grip.

                         AGENT SMITH
                    The great Morpheus. We meet at
                    last.

                         MORPHEUS
                    And you are?

                         AGENT SMITH
                    Smith. I am Agent Smith.

                         MORPHEUS
                    You all look the same to me.

Agent Smith counters Morpheus and slowly begins to pry his hands from his throat. Striking like a viper, Morpheus drives a vicious head butt into Agent Smith's face. His nose and glasses shatter.

Agent Smith, unfazed, smiles, blood oozing from the shattered bridge of his nose and returns Morpheus's head butt with three of his own in pneumatic succession.

Morpheus staggers back, his body going slack when another kick buries him deep into crunching plaster and lath.

Morpheus turns in time to see a wall of men in the doorway.

> AGENT SMITH
> Take him.

The wall of Cops rush Morpheus, filling the tiny bathroom until he disappears under the tide.

118   **INT. MAIN DECK**   118

Tank reaches out to the screen as if reaching for Morpheus.

> TANK
> No!

119   **SCENE OMITTED**   119

120   **EXT. STREET - DAY**   120

A manhole cover cracks open. Two eyes peek out just as a truck rattles over it. The thunder dopplers away and the cover opens. Trinity climbs out.

121   **INT. MAIN DECK**   121

Tank is again at the monitors, searching the Matrix when the phone rings.

> TANK
> Operator.

> CYPHER (V.O.)
> I need an exit! Fast!

> TANK
> Cypher?

122   **EXT. STREET - DAY**   122

Cypher is standing at a public phone. Across the street is the burning paddy wagon that appears to have collided with an oncoming car.

> CYPHER
> There was an accident. A goddamn
> car accident. All of a sudden.
> (MORE)

                    CYPHER   (cont'd)
          Boom. Jesus, someone up there
          still likes me.

                    TANK (V.O.)
          I got you.

                    CYPHER
          Just get me outta here.

                    TANK (V.O.)
          Nearest exit is Franklin and Erie.
          An old T.V. repair shop.

Cypher hangs up and smiles as we hear fire trucks in the
distance.

                    CYPHER
          An actor. Definitely.

123   **INT. MAIN DECK**   123

The phone rings. Tank answers.

                    TRINITY (V.O.)
          Tank, it's me.

124   **EXT. STREET - DAY**   124

All four are moving quickly down a back street.

                    NEO
          Is Morpheus alive?

                    TRINITY
          Is Morpheus still alive, Tank?

                    TANK (V.O.)
          Yes. They're moving him. I don't
          know where yet.

                    TRINITY
          He's alive.

Again, inevitability seems to cinch around Neo.

                    TRINITY
          We need an exit!

                    TANK (V.O.)
          You're not far from Cypher.

                    TRINITY
          Cypher, I thought--

                              TANK (V.O.)
                    So did we. I sent him to Franklin
                    and Erie.

                              TRINITY
                    Got it.

A124   **EXT. T.V. REPAIR SHOP - DAY**   A124

        In a deserted alley, Cypher steps onto a dumpster in front of
        a small boarded-up window.

125   **INT. T.V. REPAIR SHOP - DAY**   125

        Dead machines, eviscerated and shrouded with dust, lay on
        metal shelves like bodies in a morgue. Plywood covering a
        window is ripped off and Cypher crawls inside.

        Deep in the back room, a phone that has not rung in years
        begins to ring.

126   **EXT. STREET - DAY**   126

        Trinity sees the T.V. repair shop.

127   **INT. MAIN DECK**   127

        Tank punches the exit command.

                              TANK
                    Got him.

        Cypher's body twitches in its harness, jerking itself awake.

128   **INT. T.V. REPAIR SHOP - DAY**   128

        Neo crawls through the window that Cypher opened.

129   **INT. MAIN DECK**   129

        Tank finishes loading the exit program as Cypher pulls back a
        heavy blanket, exposing a high-tech rifle.

130   **INT. T.V. REPAIR SHOP - DAY**   130

        The phone begins to ring as the others crawl in.

                              SWITCH
                    God, I love that sound.

131   **INT. MAIN DECK**   131

        Suddenly, a white bolt of lightning explodes against Tank's
        chair, blasting him into the air.

Cypher checks the gun, unable to believe he missed.

                         CYPHER
                    Shit.

Tank is on his feet, lunging when Cypher fires again, square
into his chest.

                         DOZER
                    No!

132   **INT. T.V. REPAIR SHOP - DAY**   132

The phone is still ringing.

                         TRINITY
                    You first, Neo.

Neo answers the phone when there is a click. There is no
signal. Nothing but silence.

                         TRINITY
                    What happened?

                         NEO
                    I don't know. It just went dead.

Trinity listens to the dead line and takes out the cellular.

133   **INT. MAIN DECK**   133

The operator phone begins to ring. Cypher steps over the
sizzling body of Dozer and looks at the monitor.

134   **INT. T.V. REPAIR SHOP - DAY**   134

Every unanswered ring wrings her gut a little tighter, until--

                         CYPHER (V.O.)
                    Hello, Trinity.

                         TRINITY
                    Cypher? Where's Tank?

                         CYPHER (V.O.)
                    He had an accident.

                         TRINITY
                    An accident?!

135   **INT. MAIN DECK/T.V. REPAIR SHOP [INTERCUT]**   135

He walks over to Trinity's body, staring down at it hanging
in its coma-like stillness.

                    CYPHER
          You know, for a long time, I
          thought I was in love with you,
          Trinity. I used to dream about
          you...

He nuzzles his face against hers, feeling the softness of it.

                    CYPHER
          You are a beautiful woman. Too bad
          things had to work out like this.

                    TRINITY
          You killed them.

                    APOC
          What?!

                    SWITCH
          Oh, God.

Wearing Tank's operator headgear, Cypher moves among the
silent bodies.

                    CYPHER
          I'm tired, Trinity. I'm tired of
          this war, I'm tired of fighting.
          I'm tired of this ship, of being
          cold, of eating the same goddamn
          goop every day. But most of all,
          I'm tired of this jagoff and all
          of his bullshit.

Cypher leans over, talking to Morpheus.

                    CYPHER
          Surprise, asshole. Bet you never
          saw this coming, did you? God, I
          wish I could be there when they
          break you. I wish I could walk in
          just as it happens, so right then,
          you'd know it was me.

                    TRINITY
          My God. Morpheus. You gave them
          Morpheus.

                    CYPHER
          He lied to us, Trinity! He tricked
          us! If he would've told us the
          truth, we would've told him to
          shove that red pill up his ass!

                    TRINITY
          That's not true, Cypher. He set us
          free.

                              CYPHER
                    Free? You call this free? All I do
                    is what he tells me to do. If I
                    have to choose between that and
                    the Matrix, I choose the Matrix.

                              TRINITY
                    The Matrix isn't real!

                              CYPHER
                    Oh, I disagree, Trinity. I
                    disagree. I think the Matrix can
                    be more real than this world. I
                    mean, all I do is pull a plug
                    here. But there, you have to watch
                    Apoc die.

She looks up at Apoc, her face going white.

                              APOC
                    Trinity?

He grabs hold of the cable in Apoc's neck, twists it, and
yanks it out.

                              CYPHER
                    Welcome to the real world, eh
                    baby?

Apoc seems to go blind for an instant, a scream caught in his
throat, his hands reaching for nothing, and then falls dead.

                              SWITCH
                    No!

                              TRINITY
                    But you're out, Cypher. You can't
                    go back.

                              CYPHER
                    That's what you think. They've
                    promised to take me back. They're
                    going to reinsert my body. I'll go
                    back to sleep and when I wake up,
                    I'll be fat and rich and I won't
                    remember a goddamned thing. It's
                    the American dream.

He laughs, his hand sliding around the neck of Switch as he
takes hold of her plug.

                              CYPHER
                    By the way, if you have anything
                    terribly important to say to
                    Switch, I suggest you say it now.

                    TRINITY
              Oh no, please don't.

Trinity's eyes find Switch and she knows she's next.

                    SWITCH
              Not like this. Not like this.

She suddenly feels her body severed from her mind as she is
murdered.

                    CYPHER
              Too late.

                    TRINITY
              Goddamn you, Cypher!

                    CYPHER
              Don't hate me, Trinity. I'm just
              the messenger. And right now I'm
              going to prove it to you.

He stands over Neo.

                    CYPHER
              If Morpheus was right, then
              there's no way I can pull this
              plug, is there?

She turns to Neo, eyes wide with fear and he knows he is
next.

                    CYPHER
              If Neo is the One, then in the
              next few seconds there has to be
              some kind of miracle to stop me.
              Right? How can he be the One if
              he's dead?

He takes hold of the cord.

                    CYPHER
              You never did answer me, Trinity,
              when I asked you before. Did you
              buy Morpheus's bullshit? Come on.
              You can tell me, did you? All I
              want is a little yes or no. Look
              into his eyes, Trinity, those big
              pretty eyes and tell me the truth.
              Yes or no.

Trinity stares at Neo as a single word falls soundlessly from
her lips.

                    TRINITY
              ...yes.

                            CYPHER
            No!

Charred and bloody, Tank levels the gun.

                            CYPHER
                    I don't believe it!

                            TANK
                    Believe it or not, you piece of
                    shit, you're still going to burn.

He fires a crackling bolt of lightning that knocks Cypher
flying backwards.

136   **SCENE OMITTED**   136

137   **INT. T.V. REPAIR SHOP - DAY**   137

        Trinity throws her arms around Neo and for a moment they are
        alone and alive until the phone rings.

                            NEO
                    Go. You first this time.

138   **INT. MAIN DECK**   138

        Trinity's eyes snap open, a sense of relief surging through
        her at the sight of the ship. As Tank unplugs her, she sees
        his charred wounds.

                            TRINITY
                    Tank, you're hurt.

                            TANK
                    I'll be all right.

                            TRINITY
                    Dozer?

        Tank's face tightens and she takes him into her arms.

139   **EXT. GOVERNMENT BUILDING - DAY**   139

        A government high-rise in the middle of downtown where a
        military helicopter sets down on the roof.

        Agent Jones gets out of the helicopter, flanked by columns of
        Marines. They open the roof access door and enter the top
        floor maintenance level of the building.

140   **INT. EXECUTIVE OFFICE - DAY**   140

        Agent Smith stands, staring out the windows at the city below
        shimmering with brilliant sunlight.

AGENT SMITH
Have you ever stood and stared at
it, Morpheus? Marveled at its
beauty. Its genius. Billions of
people just living out their
lives... oblivious.

Morpheus is handcuffed to a chair, stripped to the waist. He
is alternately shivering and sweating, wired to various
monitors with white disk electrodes. Beside him, Agent Brown
sucks a serum from a glass vial, filling a hypodermic needle.

AGENT SMITH
Did you know that the first Matrix
was designed to be a perfect human
world? Where none suffered, where
everyone would be happy. It was a
disaster. No one would accept the
program. Entire crops were lost.

Agent Brown jams the needle into Morpheus's shoulder and
plunges down.

AGENT SMITH
Some believed we lacked the
programming language to describe
your perfect world. But I believe
that, as a species, human beings
define their reality through
suffering and misery.

Agent Brown studies the screens as the life signs react
violently to the injection.

AGENT SMITH
The perfect world was a dream that
your primitive cerebrum kept
trying to wake up from. Which is
why the Matrix was redesigned to
this: the peak of your civilization.

He turns from the window.

AGENT SMITH
I say 'your civilization' because as
soon as we started thinking for you,
it really became our civilization,
which is, of course, what this is
all about.

He sits down directly in front of Morpheus.

                        AGENT SMITH
              Evolution, Morpheus. Evolution.

He lifts Morpheus's head.

                        AGENT SMITH
              Like the dinosaur. Look out that
              window. You had your time.

Morpheus stares hard at him, trying not to show the pain
racking his mind.

                        AGENT SMITH
              The future is our world, Morpheus.
              The future is our time.

Agent Smith looks at Agent Brown.

                        AGENT SMITH
              Double the dosage.

Agent Jones suddenly enters.

                        AGENT JONES
              There could be a problem.

141   **INT. MAIN DECK**   141

Tank drapes a sheet over his dead brother. The other bodies are
covered.

Neo looks at Morpheus whose body is covered with a cold sweat.

                        NEO
              What are they doing to him?

                        TANK
              They're breaking into his mind.
              It's like hacking a computer. All
              it takes is time.

                        NEO
              How much time?

                        TANK
              Depends on the mind. But eventually,
              it will crack and his alpha pattern
              will change from this to this.

Tank punches several commands on Morpheus's personal unit.
The monitor waves change from a chaotic pattern to an ordered
symmetrical one.

> TANK
> When it does, Morpheus will tell
> them anything they want to know.

> NEO
> What do they want?

> TANK
> The leader of every ship is given the
> codes to Zion's mainframe computer.
> If an Agent had those codes and got
> inside Zion's mainframe, they could
> destroy us.

He looks up at Trinity who is pacing relentlessly.

> TANK
> We can't let that happen, Trinity.
> Zion is more important than me. Or
> you or even Morpheus.

Trinity sees Cypher's dead body. Rage overtakes her and she
kicks him.

> TRINITY
> Goddamnit! Goddamnit!

> NEO
> There has to be something that we
> can do.

> TANK
> There is. We have to pull the
> plug.

> TRINITY
> You're going to kill him? Kill
> Morpheus?!

> TANK
> Trinity, we don't have any other
> choice.

142   **INT. GOVERNMENT BUILDING**   142

Morpheus is fighting to hold his mind together. The Agents
stand over him.

> AGENT SMITH
> Never send a human to do a
> machine's job.

                              AGENT BROWN
                    If, indeed, the insider has
                    failed, they will sever the
                    connection as soon as possible,
                    unless--

                              AGENT JONES
                    They are dead. In either case--

                              AGENT SMITH
                    We have no choice but to continue
                    as planned. Deploy the sentinels.
                    Immediately.

143   INT. MAIN DECK   143

Tank kneels beside Morpheus's body.

Neo suddenly sees it perfectly clear, fate rushing at him
like an oncoming train.

                              TANK
                    Morpheus, you were more than our
                    leader. You were... our father.
                    We will miss you, always.

Trinity can't bear to watch. As she closes her eyes, her
tears slip free.

Tank closes his eyes and takes hold of the plug.

Neo is paralyzed, his whole life is suddenly suspended by the
finality of this moment hurling at him with the speed of a
bullet.

                              NEO
                    Stop!

They both look at him.

                              NEO
                    Goddamnit! I don't believe this is
                    happening!

                              TANK
                    Neo, this has to be done!

                              NEO
                    Does it? I don't know. This can't
                    be just coincidence. It can't be!
                    Can it?

                              TANK
                    What are you talking about?

>   NEO
>   The Oracle. She told me this would
>   happen. She told me...

Neo stops, his stare fixed on Morpheus.

>   NEO
>   That I would have to make a
>   choice...

>   TRINITY
>   What choice?

He makes his choice. Turning, he walks to his chair.

>   TRINITY
>   What are you doing?

>   NEO
>   I'm going in.

>   TRINITY
>   You can't!

>   NEO
>   I have to.

>   TRINITY
>   Morpheus sacrificed himself so we
>   could get you out! There's no way
>   you're going back in!

>   NEO
>   Morpheus did what he did because
>   he believed that I'm something I'm
>   not.

>   TRINITY
>   What?

>   NEO
>   I'm not the One, Trinity. The
>   Oracle hit me with that too.

Trinity is stunned.

>   TRINITY
>   No, you... have to be.

>   NEO
>   I'm sorry, I'm not. I'm just
>   another guy. Morpheus is the one
>   that matters.

                    TRINITY
          No, Neo. That's not true. It can't
          be true.

                    NEO
          Why?

                    TRINITY
          Because...

Uncertainty swallows her words and she is unable to tell him
what she wants to.

                    TANK
          Neo, this is loco. They've got
          Morpheus in a military-controlled
          building. Even if you somehow got
          inside, those are Agents holding
          him. Three of them! I want
          Morpheus back, too, but what you
          are talking about is suicide.

                    NEO
          I know that's what it looks like,
          but it's not. I can't logically
          explain to you why it's not.
          Morpheus believed something and he
          was ready to give his life for
          what he believed. I understand
          that now. That's why I have to go.

                    TANK
          Why?

                    NEO
          Because I believe in something.

                    TRINITY
          What?

                    NEO
          I believe I can bring him back.

Trinity stares at him, hovering on the edge that he just
jumped off. Her jaw sets and she starts climbing into the
chair beside him.

                    NEO
          What are you doing?

                    TRINITY
          I'm coming with you.

                    NEO
          No, you're not.

> TRINITY
> No? Let me tell you what I
> believe. I believe Morpheus means
> more to me than he does to you.
> I believe that if you are serious
> about saving him then you are going
> to need my help and since I am the
> ranking officer on this ship, if
> you don't like it then I believe
> that you can go to hell, because
> you aren't going anywhere else.

There is nothing more to say except--

> TRINITY
> Tank, load us up.

144   **INT. EXECUTIVE OFFICE - DAY**   144

Agent Smith sits casually across from Morpheus who is hunched
over, his body leaking and twitching.

> AGENT SMITH
> I'd like to share a revelation
> that I've had during my time here.
> It came to me when I tried to
> classify your species. I've
> realized that you are not actually
> mammals.

The life signs continue their chaotic patterns.

> AGENT SMITH
> Every mammal on this planet
> instinctively develops a natural
> equilibrium with the surrounding
> environment. But you humans do
> not. You move to an area and you
> multiply and multiply until every
> natural resource is consumed and
> the only way you can survive is to
> spread to another area.

He leans forward.

> AGENT SMITH
> There is another organism on this
> planet that follows the same
> pattern. Do you know what it is? A
> virus.

He smiles.

                              AGENT SMITH
                    Human beings are a disease, a
                    cancer of this planet. You are a
                    plague. And we are... the cure.

A144   INT. CONSTRUCT   A144

Neo and Trinity stand in the white space of the construct as
he answers his ringing cell phone.

                              TANK (V.O.)
                    Okay. What do you need? Besides a
                    miracle...

                              NEO
                    Guns. Lots of guns.

145   INT. MAIN DECK   145

Neo and Trinity's bodies hang motionless in their drive
chairs as Tank hits load.

146   INT. CONSTRUCT   146

Racks of weapons appear and they begin to arm themselves.

                              TRINITY
                    No one has ever done anything like
                    this.

                              NEO
                    Yeah?

He snap cocks an Uzi.

                              NEO
                    That's why it's going to work.

147   INT. EXECUTIVE OFFICE - DAY   147

Agent Smith is again at the window.

                              AGENT SMITH
                    Why isn't the serum working?

                              AGENT BROWN
                    Perhaps we are asking the wrong
                    questions.

Agent Smith hides his knotting fist. He is becoming angry. It
is something that isn't supposed to happen to Agents.

                              AGENT SMITH
                    Leave me with him.

Agents Brown and Jones look at each other.

>   AGENT SMITH
>   Now!

They leave and Agent Smith sits beside Morpheus.

>   AGENT SMITH
>   Can you hear me, Morpheus? I'm
>   going to be honest with you.

He removes his earphone, letting it dangle over his shoulder.

>   AGENT SMITH
>   I hate this place. This zoo. This
>   prison. This reality, whatever you
>   want to call it, I can't stand it
>   any longer.

>   AGENT SMITH
>   It's the smell, if there is such a
>   thing. I feel saturated by it. I
>   can taste your stink and every
>   time I do, I fear that I've
>   somehow been infected by it.

He wipes sweat from Morpheus's forehead, coating the tips of
his fingers, holding them to Morpheus's nose.

>   AGENT SMITH
>   Repulsive, isn't it?

He lifts Morpheus's head, holding it tightly with both hands.

>   AGENT SMITH
>   I must get out of here, I must get
>   free. In this mind is the key. My
>   key.

Morpheus sneers through his pain.

>   AGENT SMITH
>   Once Zion is destroyed, there is
>   no need for me to be here. Do you
>   understand? I need the codes. I
>   have to get inside Zion. You have
>   to tell me how.

He begins squeezing, his fingers gouging into his flesh.

>   AGENT SMITH
>   You are going to tell me or you
>   are going to die.

Tank sits down beside Morpheus whose face is ashen like
someone near death. He takes hold of his hand.

> TANK
> Hold on, Morpheus. They're coming
> for you. They're coming.

149   EXT. GOVERNMENT BUILDING - DAY   149

A dark wind blows.

150   INT. GOVERNMENT BUILDING - DAY   150

In long black coats, Trinity and Neo push through the
revolving doors.

Neo is carrying a duffel bag. Trinity has a large metal
suitcase. They cut across the lobby to the security station,
drawing nervous glances.

Dark glasses, game faces.

Neo calmly passes through the metal detector which begins to
wail immediately. A security guard moves over toward Neo,
raising his metal detection wand.

> GUARD
> Would you please remove any
> metallic items you are carrying:
> keys, loose change--

Neo slowly sets down his duffel bag and throws open his coat,
revealing an arsenal of guns, knives, and grenades slung from
a climbing harness.

> GUARD
> Holy shit--

Neo is a blur of motion. In a split second, three guards are
dead before they hit the ground.

A fourth guard dives for cover, clutching his radio.

> GUARD 4
> Backup! Send in the backup!

He looks up as Trinity sets off the metal detector. It is the
last thing he sees.

The backup arrives. A wave of soldiers blocking the
elevators. The concrete cavern of the lobby becomes a white
noise roar of gunfire.

Slate walls and pillars pock, crack, and crater under a hail swarm of explosive tipped bullets.

They are met by the quivering spit of a subhandmachine gun and the razored whistle of throwing knives. Weapons like extensions of their bodies are used with the same deadly precision as their feet and their fists.

Bodies slump down to the marbled floor while Neo and Trinity hardly even break their stride.

151   INT. EXECUTIVE OFFICE   151

Agents Jones and Brown burst into the room. Agent Smith releases Morpheus.

                    AGENT BROWN
              What were you doing?

Agent Smith recovers, replacing his ear-piece.

                    AGENT JONES
              You don't know.

                    AGENT SMITH
              Know what?

Agent Smith listens to his earphone, not believing what he is hearing.

152   INT. ELEVATORS - DAY   152

They get in. Trinity immediately drops and opens the suitcase, wiring a plastique and napalm bomb.

Neo hits the emergency stop. He pulls down part of the false ceiling and finds the elevator shaft access panel.

153   INT. EXECUTIVE OFFICE - DAY   153

Agent Jones looks at Morpheus.

                    AGENT JONES
              I think they're trying to save
              him.

154   INT. ELEVATOR SHAFT - DAY   154

Neo ratchets down a clamp onto the elevator cable. Both of them lock on. He looks up the long, dark throat of the building and takes a deep breath.

                    NEO
              There is no spoon.

Neo whips out his gun and presses it to the cable, lower than they attached themselves.

BOOM! The cable snaps.

The counter-weights plummet, yanking Trinity and Neo up through the shaft as the elevator falls away beneath them, distending space, filling it with the sound of whistling metal as they soar to the top.

155   **INT. LOBBY - DAY**   155

The elevator hits the bottom.

BA-BOOM!

The massive explosion blows open the doors, fire clouds engulfing the elevator section of the lobby.

156   **INT. EXECUTIVE OFFICE - DAY**   156

The Agents hear the blast of fire alarms.

                         AGENT JONES
                    Lower level--

                         AGENT BROWN
                    They are actually attacking.

Another enormous explosion thunders above them, shaking the building. The alarm sounds, emergency sprinklers begin showering the room.

Agent Smith smashes a table.

                         AGENT SMITH
                    Find them and destroy them!

Agent Jones nods and touches his ear-piece.

157   **EXT. ROOF - DAY**   157

The roof-access tower is now engulfed in flames as Neo and Trinity stand amongst a pile of their fallen enemies.

Across the roof, the pilot inside the army helicopter watches the last of their ferocious onslaught.

                         PILOT
                    I repeat, we are under attack!

Suddenly his face, his whole body dissolves, consumed by spreading locust-like swarm of static as Agent Jones emerges.

Just as she drops the final Marine, Trinity sees what's coming. Neo sees her, the fear in her face, and he knows what is behind him.

Screaming, he whirls, guns filling his hands with thought-speed.

Fingers pumping, shells ejecting, dancing up and away, we look through the sights and gunsmoke at the Agent blurred with motion--

Until the hammers click against the empty metal.

                    NEO
               Trinity!

Agent Jones charges.

                    NEO
               ...help.

His gun booms as we enter the liquid space of--

Bullet-time.

The air sizzles with wads of lead like angry flies as Neo twists, bends, ducks just between them.

Agent Jones still running, narrows the gap, the bullets coming faster until Neo bent impossibly back, one hand on the ground as a spiraling gray ball shears open his shoulder.

He starts to scream as another digs a red groove across his thigh. He has only time to look up, to see Agent Jones standing over him, raising his gun a final time.

                    AGENT JONES
               Only human...

Suddenly Agent Jones stops. He hears a sharp metal click.

Immediately, he whirls around and turns straight into the muzzle of Trinity's .45--

Jammed tight to his head.

                    TRINITY
               Dodge this!

BOOM! BOOM! BOOM! The body flies back with a flash of mercurial light and when it hits the ground, it is the pilot.

Trinity helps Neo up.

                    TRINITY
               Neo, how did you do that?

                              NEO
                    Do what?

                              TRINITY
                    You moved like they moved. I've
                    never seen anyone move that fast.
                              NEO
                    It wasn't fast enough.

He checks his shoulder wound.

                              TRINITY
                    Are you all right?

                              NEO
                    I'm fine. Come on, we have to keep
                    moving.

Neo sees the helicopter.

                              NEO
                    Can you fly that thing?

                              TRINITY
                    Not yet.

She pulls out the cellular phone.

158   **INT. HOVERCRAFT**   158

Tank is back at the controls.

                              TANK
                    Operator.

                              TRINITY (V.O.)
                    Tank, I need a pilot program for a
                    military B-212 helicopter.

Tank is immediately searching the disk drawers.

                              TRINITY (V.O.)
                    Hurry!

His fingers flash over the gleaming laser disks finding one
that he feeds into Trinity's Supplement Drive punching the
"load" commands on her keyboard.

159   **EXT. ROOF - DAY**   159

Trinity's eyes flutter as information surges into her brain,
all the essentials of flying a helicopter absorbed at light-
speed.

                         TRINITY
                       Let's go.

160   **SCENE OMITTED**   160

161   **INT. EXECUTIVE OFFICE - DAY**   161

       Agent Jones throws open the door and enters, walking through
       the puddles pooling in the carpet. Over the rushing water and
       the alarms, Agent Smith hears a sound and understands the
       seriousness of the attack.

       He turns to the wall of windows as the helicopter drops into
       view--

       Neo is in the back bay, aiming the mounted .50 machine gun.

                       AGENT SMITH
                    No.

       The gun jumps and bullets explode through the window in a
       cacophony of crashing glass as the Agents go for their
       weapons.

       But Neo is too close, the .50 caliber too fast and bullets
       are everywhere, perforating the room.

       Agent Jones is hit first, his body jack-knifing back, blood
       arcing out with a sudden flash of light--

       Then Agent Brown, his gun still firing as his body falls. And
       finally Agent Smith.

       Neo stares at Morpheus, trying to will him into action.

                         NEO
                    Get up, Morpheus! Get up!

       Neo grabs the climbing rope and attaches one end to his
       harness.

162   **INT. HALL - DAY**   162

       Just outside the executive office, three Marines blister with
       snow-static.

163   **INT. EXECUTIVE OFFICE - DAY**   163

       Slowly, Morpheus lifts his face into the room's rain. When he
       finally opens his eyes, they are again dark and flashing with
       fire.

       He rises from the chair, snapping his handcuffs just as the
       Agents enter the adjoining room. Agent Smith stops and sees
       Morpheus run past the open door.

AGENT SMITH
Nooo!

He fires sweeping across the sheetrocked wall in a perfect
line.

For an instant, we see the bullets shred, puncturing the
wall, searing through the wet air with jet trails of chalk.

And as Morpheus starts his dive for the window, a bullet
buries itself in his leg, knocking him off balance.

NEO
He won't make it.

Morpheus lunges, out of control--

As Neo spins, every move a whip crack, snapping the other
rope-end on to a bolted bar as--

Morpheus begins to fall, when Neo hurls himself into the wide
blue empty space, flying for a moment.

The rope snaking out behind him; an umbilical cord attached
to a machine.

As their two bodies, set in motion, rushing at each other on
a seemingly magnetic course until they collide.

Almost bouncing free of each other, arms, legs scrambling,
hands searching in furious desperation, finding hold and
clinging.

Until the line ends, snapping taut, cracking their fragile
embrace. Morpheus tumbles, legs flipping over, falling down--

The ground deliriously distant as Neo snatches hold of his
mentor's still handcuffed wrist.

NEO
Gotcha!

164   **EXT. GOVERNMENT BUILDING - DAY**   164

Trinity pulls the copter up and away as Agent Smith stands in
the shattered window, aiming his gun out through the curtain
of rain.

Ponk. Ponk. Ponk. The rear hull is punched full of holes and
smoke and oil pour out like black blood.

TRINITY
Shit-shit-no!

Neo hears the helicopter begin to die.

                              NEO
                        Uh oh--

Trinity throws the helicopter towards the roof of the nearest
building.

Morpheus and Neo cling to one another as they and the machine
above them begin to fall.

The engine grinds, the chopping blades start to slow while--

Trinity guides the parabolic fall over the nearest roof where--

Neo and Morpheus drop safely, rolling free as the rope goes
slack. Neo gets to his feet, trying to detach himself but--

The helicopter is falling too fast, arcing over the roof like
a setting sun--

The coils of slack snap taut, yanking Neo off his feet,
dragging him with ferocious speed towards the edge even as--

Trinity lunges for the back door, her gun in one hand,
grabbing for the rope with the other--

Neo flies like a skipping stone, hurtling at the parapet,
when his feet hit the rain gutter and he levers up just as--

Trinity fires, severing the cord from the helicopter, falling
free of it as it smashes, blades first into a glass
skyscraper.

Holding onto the rope as she swings, connected to Neo, who
stands on the building's edge watching her arc beneath him as
the helicopter explodes--

She bounces against a shatterproof window that spider-cracks
out while flames erupt behind her.

165   **INT. MAIN DECK**   165

Tank stares at the screen, his mouth agape.

                              TANK
                  I knew it! He's the One.

166   **SCENE OMITTED**   166

167   **EXT. ROOFTOP - DAY**   167

Neo pulls Trinity up into his arms. Both shaking, they hold
each other again.

                    MORPHEUS
          Do you believe it now, Trinity?

Trinity looks at Neo.

                    NEO
          Morpheus, the Oracle... she told
          me--

                    MORPHEUS
          She told you exactly what you
          needed to hear. That's all. Sooner
          or later, Neo, you're going to
          realize just like I did the
          difference between knowing a path
          and walking a path.

168   INT. MAIN DECK   168

     The phone rings.

                    MORPHEUS (V.O.)
          Tank.

                    TANK
          Goddamn! It's good to hear your
          voice, sir!

                    MORPHEUS (V.O.)
          We need an exit.

                    TANK
          Got one ready, sir. Subway. State
          and Balbo.

                    MORPHEUS (V.O.)
          We're on our way--

169   EXT. ROOFTOP - DAY   169

     We rush at the roof access door as it suddenly slams open and
     the three Agents charge out. But Neo, Trinity, and Morpheus
     are already gone.

                    AGENT SMITH
          Damnit!

                    AGENT BROWN
          The trace was completed.

                    AGENT JONES
          We have their position.

AGENT BROWN
Sentinels are standing by.

AGENT JONES
Order the strike.

Agent Smith can't stand listening to them. He moves to the
edge of the building, looking out at the surrounding city.

AGENT SMITH
They're not out yet.

170   INT. SUBWAY STATION - DAY   170

An old man sits hunched in the far corner of the station,
shadows gathered around him like blankets. Mumbling, he
nurses from a bottle of Thunderbird when--

A phone begins to ring.

Neo leads Trinity and Morpheus bounding over a set of
turnstiles towards the ringing phone inside a graffiti-
covered booth.

NEO
Let's go! You first, Morpheus.

Morpheus gets in and answers the phone.

Lost in the shadow, the Old Man watches as Morpheus
disappears, the phone dropping, dangling by its cord. His
eyes grow wide, glowing white in the dark.

171   EXT. ROOFTOP - DAY   171

Agent Smith stares, his face twisted with hate. He will never
be free of the Matrix.

He starts to turn from the edge of the building when he
suddenly hears it, his head whipping back around, staring--

172   INT. SUBWAY - DAY   172

Through the Old Man's eyes as the world begins to rumble.

Trinity hangs up the phone, then turns to Neo.

The rumble grows, the ground beginning to shake.

TRINITY
Neo, I want to tell you
something... but I'm afraid of
what it could mean if I do.

Behind her, the phone begins to ring.

                              TRINITY
                    Everything the Oracle told me, has
                    come true, everything but this...

                              NEO
                    But what?

The rumble rises, drowning her voice. Neo is drawn towards
her, their lips close enough to kiss when a train blasts into
the station.

For a moment, they are frozen by the strobing lights of the
train until Trinity turns, unable to say what she wants to
say.

The phone rings once more before she lifts the receiver when,
in the darkness of the far corner, Neo sees the old man in
the flashing train-light as he becomes--

Agent Smith, raising a fistful of black gun-metal.

                              NEO
                    No!

The gun fires, the bullet flying at her, bursting through the
plastic window just as Trinity disappears.

The handset hanging in the air as the bullet hits, shattering
the ear-piece.

173   INT. HOVERCRAFT   **173**

Trinity blinks, shivering as her conscious exits the
Construct.

                              TRINITY
                    Neo!

                              TANK
                    What the hell just happened?

                              TRINITY
                    An Agent! You have to send me
                    back!

                              TANK
                    I can't!

174   INT. SUBWAY STATION - DAY   **174**

The destroyed phone dangles in the empty booth. Neo turns to
Agent Smith whose gun stares at him like a third eye.

                         AGENT SMITH
                        Mr. Anderson.

175   **INT. MAIN DECK**   175

        Morpheus and Trinity stand behind Tank riveted to the
        scrolling code.

                          TRINITY
                       Run, Neo. Run.

176   **INT. SUBWAY STATION - DAY**   176

        Neo looks at the dead escalator that rises up behind him.
        Slowly he turns back and in his eyes we see something
        different, something fixed and hard like a gunfighter's
        resolve.

        There is no past or future in these eyes. There is only what
        is.

177   **INT. MAIN DECK**   177

        Trinity is unable to understand.

                          TRINITY
                      What is he doing?

                         MORPHEUS
                   He's beginning to believe.

178   **INT. SUBWAY STATION - DAY**   178

        Neo whip-draws his gun flashpoint speed of lightning as--

        Smith opens fire.

        Gun report thunders through the underground, both men
        blasting, moving at impossible speed.

        For a blinking moment we enter Bullet-time.

        Gun flash tongues curl from Neo's gun, bullets float forward
        like a plane moving across the sky, cartridges cartwheel into
        space.

        An instant later they are nearly on top of each other,
        rolling up out of a move that is almost a mirrored reflection
        of the other--

        Each jamming their gun tight to the other's head.

        They freeze in a kind of embrace; Neo sweating, panting,
        Agent Smith machine-calm. Agent Smith smiles.

                        AGENT SMITH
                   You're empty.

Neo pulls the trigger. Click.

                        NEO
                   So are you.

The smile falls. Agent Smith yanks his trigger.

CLICK.

Agent Smith's face warps with rage and he attacks, fists
flying at furious speed, blows and counters, Neo retreating
as--

A knife-hand opens his forearm, and a kick sends him slamming
back against a steel column. Stunned, he ducks just under a
punch that crunches into the beam, steel chunks exploding
like shrapnel.

Behind him, Neo leaps into the air, delivering a neck-
snapping reverse round-house. Agent Smith's glasses fly off
and he glares at Neo; his eyes ice blue.

                        AGENT SMITH
                   I'm going to enjoy watching you
                   die, Mr. Anderson.

Agent Smith attacks with unrelenting fury, fists pounding Neo
like jackhammers.

179   **INT. HOVERCRAFT**   179

Trinity watches Neo as his body jerks, mouth coughing blood,
his life signs going wild.

                        TRINITY
                   Jesus, he's killing him!

180   **INT. SUBWAY STATION - DAY**   180

Agent Smith grabs hold of him, lifting him into the air,
hurling him against the curved wall of the train tunnel,
where he falls inches from the electrified third-rail.

The Agent is about to jump down and press his attack when he
hears something. From deep in the tunnel, like an animal cry,
a burst of high-speed metal grinding against metal.

The sound of an oncoming train.

Neo tries to get up. Agent Smith jumps down onto the tracks and drop-kicks him in the face. The world again begins to shake, rumbling as the train nears.

                    AGENT SMITH
          Do you hear that, Mr. Anderson?

Agent Smith grabs Neo in a choke-hold forcing him to look down the tracks, the train's headlight burning a hole in the darkness.

                    AGENT SMITH
          That is the sound of
          inevitability.

Neo sees it coming and he starts to fight.

                    AGENT SMITH
          It is the sound of your death.

There is another metal screech, much louder, closer, as Agent Smith tightens his hold. Neo is unable to breathe.

                    AGENT SMITH
          Good-bye, Mr. Anderson.

The train roars at them, swallowing Agent Smith's words. The veins bulge in Neo's head, as he grits through the pain.

He is not ready to die.

                    NEO
          My name is Neo.

Impossibly, he hurls himself straight up, smashing Smith against the concrete ceiling of the tunnel.

They fall as the sound and fury of the train explodes into the station. Neo backflips up off the tracks just as--

The train barrels over Agent Smith.

Neo stands, knees shaking, when the train slams on its emergency brake. With an ear-splitting shriek of tortured rails, the train slows, part of it still in the station.

Neo turns, limping, starting to run, racing for the escalator--

As the train comes to a stop and the doors of the last car open; Agent Smith bursts out in furious pursuit, his glasses again intact.

T
H
E

M
A
T
R
I
X

.

s
c
r
i
p
t

p
a
g
e

1
1
2

Tank searches the Matrix.

                    TRINITY
          What just happened?

                    TANK
          I don't know. I lost him.

                    MORPHEUS
          He's on the run--

Suddenly, a siren sounds.

                    TANK
          Oh shit!

Morpheus bolts to the ladder.

182   INT. COCKPIT   182

Morpheus climbs into the cockpit. On the hologram radar, he
sees the Sentinels.

                    TRINITY
          Oh no.

Trinity is behind him.

                    TRINITY
          How long?

                    MORPHEUS
          Five minutes. Maybe six.

Morpheus lifts the headset.

                    MORPHEUS
          Tank, charge the E.M.P.

                    TANK (V.O.)
          Yes, sir.

                    TRINITY
          You can't use that until Neo is
          out!

                    MORPHEUS
          I know, Trinity. Don't worry. He's
          going to make it.

A BUSINESSMAN walks along the sidewalk, wheeling and dealing
into his cell phone when it disappears, snatched by Neo as he
flashes by.

                         MAN
                What the shit-- My phone!

The man turns to call for help and when he turns back, it is
Agent Smith.

Neo is in a full-out sprint, spinning and weaving away from
every pedestrian, every potential Agent. He flips open the
cell phone and dials long distance.

184   INT. HOVERCRAFT   184

Tank answers.

                         TANK
                Operator.

                         NEO (V.O.)
                Mr. Wizard, get me the hell out of
                here!

185   EXT. CITY STREET - DAY   185

Neo dives down an alley, Agent Smith starting to gain.

                         NEO
                Hurry, Tank! I got some serious
                pursuit!

186   INT. HOVERCRAFT   186

The keyboard clicking, Tank searches for an exit. Trinity
screams into the headset.

                         TRINITY
                Neo, you better get your ass back
                here!

187   EXT. ALLEY   187

Agent Smith stops and takes aim.

                         NEO
                I'm trying, Trinity. I'm trying.

A bullet shatters the image of Neo in a truck's rearview
mirror.

188   **INT. MAIN DECK**   188

Tank speed-reads the reams of Matrix code.

> TANK
> I got a patch on an old exit.
> Wabash and Lake. A hotel. Room
> 303.

189   **SCENE OMITTED**   189

190   **EXT. OPEN MARKET**   190

Neo spins away, turning and finds himself in an open market
that teems with people.

He kamikazes his way down the little avenues lined with
vendors and shops, careening through the labyrinth, out of
control. And at every turn there is an Agent, appearing from
crowds, behind fish counters, tent flaps, and crates.

191   **SCENE OMITTED**   191

192   **EXT. ALLEY**   192

He dives from the maze down a service alley but it is a dead
end.

Neo turns back as the Agents emerge from the market.

> NEO
> Uh, help! Need a little help!

193   **INT. MAIN DECK**   193

Tank frantically scans the monitor like a road map.

> TANK
> The door.

194   **EXT. ALLEY**   194

Neo dives for it but--

> NEO
> It's locked.

> TANK (V.O.)
> Kick it in!

Peeling back, Neo almost kicks the door from its hinges,
lunging from the Agents' bullets.

195   **INT. APARTMENT BUILDING - STAIRCASE**   195

Neo springs up the old crooked apartment building stairs.

A195   INT. APARTMENT BUILDING - HALL   A195

He is halfway down the hall, running in sharp long strides
when a door explodes open at the end.

                    TANK (V.O.)
              Shit! The door on your left.

Neo lurches, kicking in an apartment door.

                    TANK (V.O.)
              No! Other left!

He whirls back to his other left, battering through the door
which splinters, perforated by bullets.

An old woman watches TV as Neo blurs past her and into her
kitchen, where another woman is chopping vegetables.

                    TANK (V.O.)
              That window!

Neo throws it open, leaping for the fire escape just as a
knife buries itself in the window casing.

                    TANK (V.O.)
              Down! Down!

B195   EXT. APARTMENT BUILDING - FIRE ESCAPE   B195

Tumbling down the rattling fire escape, Neo leaps the last
ten feet into the alley below with Agent Brown right behind
him.

Neo scrapes himself to his feet, broken and bleeding,
charging for the end of the alley.

196   INT. MAIN DECK   196

Finger on the monitor, Tank traces Neo's path.

                    TANK
              That's it! You're almost there!
              That fire escape at the end of the
              alley!

197   EXT. HEART O' THE CITY HOTEL - DAY   197

Agent Smith suddenly pauses as if recognizing something; the
faded neon buzzes: Heart O' The City Hotel.

198   INT. HOVERCRAFT   198

Tank loads the exit.

                            TANK
                I'm going to make the call.

                          MORPHEUS
                Do it!

Suddenly, the lights go red.

                           TRINITY
                No.

Morpheus looks up.

                          MORPHEUS
                Here they come.

199   **EXT. SEWER MAIN**   199

        The Sentinels open and shift like killer kaleidoscopes as
        they attack, slamming down onto the Nebuchadnezzar.

200   **INT. HOVERCRAFT**   200

        The hovercraft booms down as they hit. Morpheus opens the
        lock on the E.M.P. detonator.

        Trinity watches him.

                          MORPHEUS
                He's going to make it.

201   **EXT. ALLEY - DAY**   201

        Neo scrambles up the fire escape, bullets sparking and
        ricocheting around him as Agents Brown and Jones close the
        gap.

A201   **INT. HALL - DAY**   A201

        On the third floor, he kicks in the window, jumping into the
        hall. The doors count backwards: 310... 309...

202   **INT. MAIN DECK**   202

        Another systems alarm sounds.

                            TANK
                They've burned through the outer
                hull.

                           TRINITY
                Hurry, Neo.

203   INT. HALL - DAY   203

Neo can hear the phone ringing. 305... 304...

Agent Brown reaches the broken window behind him just as Neo
grabs the handle of 303, throwing open the door to find--

Agent Smith, waiting, .45 cocked.

Neo can't move-- can't think--

BOOM.

204   INT. MAIN DECK   204

Neo's body jerks, and everyone hears it as the life monitors
snap flatline.

Trinity screams. Morpheus stumbles back in disbelief.

                    MORPHEUS
          No, it can't be. It can't be.

Lasers suddenly sear through the main deck as the Sentinels
slice open the hull.

205   INT. HALL - DAY   205

Three holes in his chest, Neo falls to the blue shag
carpeting, blood smearing down the wallpaper. Agent Smith
stands over him, still aiming, taking no chances.

                    AGENT SMITH
          Check him.

206   INT. MAIN DECK   206

Amid the destruction raining around her, Trinity takes hold
of Neo's body.

                    TRINITY
          Neo...

207   INT. HALL - DAY   207

Kneeling beside him, Agent Brown checks his vital signs.

                    AGENT BROWN
          He's gone.

Agent Smith smiles, standing over him.

                    AGENT SMITH
          Good-bye, Mr. Anderson.

In tears, Morpheus takes hold of the E.M.P. switch.

Trinity whispers in Neo's ear.

                         TRINITY
          Neo, please, listen to me. I
          promised to tell you the rest. The
          Oracle, she told me that I'd fall
          in love and that man, the man I
          loved would be the One. You see?
          You can't be dead, Neo, you can't
          be because I love you. You hear
          me? I love you!

Her eyes close and she kisses him, believing in all her heart
that he will feel her lips and know that they speak the
truth.

209   INT. HOTEL HALL - DAY   209

He does. And they do.

His eyes snap open.

210   INT. MAIN DECK   210

Trinity screams as the monitors jump back to life. Tank and
Morpheus look at each other.

It is a miracle.

                         TRINITY
                    Now get up!

211   INT. HALL - DAY   211

Holding his chest, Neo struggles to get up. At the end of the
hall, the Agents wait for the elevator when Agent Smith
glances back. He rips.off his sunglasses looking at Neo as if
he were looking at a ghost.

Neo gets to his feet all three Agents grabbing for their
guns. As one, they fire.

                          NEO
                     No!

Neo raises his hands and the bullets, like a cloud of
obedient bees, slow and come to a stop. They hang frozen in
space, fixed like stainless steel stars.

The Agents are unable to absorb what they are seeing.

Neo plucks one of the bullets from the air. We see him and the hall reflected in the bright casing. We move closer until the bullet fills our vision and the distorted reflection morphs, becoming the 'real' image.

He drops the bullet and the others fall to the floor.

Neo looks out, now able to see through the curtain of the Matrix. For a moment, the walls, the floor, even the Agents become a rushing stream of code.

212   INT. MAIN DECK   212

All three stare transfixed with awe as the scrolling code accelerates, faster and faster, as if the machine language was unable to keep up or perhaps describe what is happening.

They begin to blur into streaks, shimmering ribbons of light that open like windows, as--

Each screen fills with brilliant saturated color images of Neo standing in the hall.

                    TANK
              How...?!

                    MORPHEUS
              He is the One. He is the One!

An explosion shakes the entire ship.

213   INT. HALL   213

Agent Smith screams, his calm machine-like expression shredding with pure rage.

He rushes Neo. His attack is ferocious but Neo blocks each blow easily. Then with one quick strike to the chest he sends Agent Smith flying backwards.

For the first time since their inception, the Agents know fear.

Agent Smith gets up, bracing himself as Neo charges him and springs into a dive. But the impact doesn't come. Neo sinks into Agent Smith, disappearing, his tie and coat rippling as if he were a deep pool of water.

Spinning around he looks to the others and feels something, like a tremor before a quake, something deep, something that is going to change everything.

Suddenly a searing sound stabs through his ear-piece as his chest begins to swell, then balloon as--

Neo bursts up out of him. And with a final death scream, Agent Smith explodes like an empty husk in a brilliant cacophony of light, his shards spinning away, absorbed by the Matrix until--

Only Neo is left.

Neo faces the remaining Agents. They look at each other, the same idea striking simultaneously--

They run.

214   **INT. MAIN DECK**   214

Sentinels are everywhere destroying the ship.

                        TRINITY
                    Neo!

215   **INT. HALL**   215

Again he hears her. He reacts to the ringing phone, rushing towards it even as--

216   **INT. MAIN DECK**   216

A Sentinel descends towards Morpheus. On the screen we see Neo dive for the phone.

                        TRINITY
                    Now!

Morpheus turns the key.

217   **INT. OVERFLOW PIT**   217

A blinding shock of white light floods the chamber; Sentinels blink and fall instantly dead, filling the pit with their cold metal carcasses.

218   **INT. HOVERCRAFT**   218

In the still darkness, only the humans are alive.

                        TRINITY
                    Neo?

His eyes open. Tears pour from her smiling eyes as he reaches up to touch her.

And she kisses him; it seems like it might last forever.

                                          FADE TO BLACK.

Close on a computer screen as in the opening. The cursor
beating steadily, waiting. A phone begins to ring.

It is answered and the screen fills instantly with the trace
program. After a long beat, we recognize Neo's voice.

> NEO (V.O.)
> Hi. It's me. I know you're out
> there. I can feel you now.

We close in on the racing columns of numbers shimmering
across the screen.

> NEO (V.O.)
> I imagine you can also feel me.

The numbers begin to lock into place.

> NEO (V.O.)
> You won't have to search for me
> anymore. I'm done running. Done
> hiding. Whether I'm done fighting,
> I suppose, is up to you.

We glide in towards the screen.

> NEO (V.O.)
> I believe deep down, we both want
> this world to change. I believe
> that the Matrix can remain our
> cage or it can become our
> chrysalis, that's what you helped
> me to understand. That to be free,
> truly free, you cannot change your
> cage. You have to change yourself.

We dive through the numbers, surging up through the darkness,
sucked towards a tight constellation of stars.

> NEO (V.O.)
> When I used to look out at this
> world, all I could see was its
> edges, its boundaries, its rules
> and controls, its leaders and
> laws. But now, I see another
> world. A different world where all
> things are possible. A world of
> hope. Of peace.

We realize that the constellation is actually the holes in
the mouthpiece of a phone. Seen from inside.

> NEO (V.O.)
> I can't tell you how to get there,
> but I know if you can free your
> mind, you'll find the way.

220   **EXT. PHONE BOOTH/STREET**   220

We shoot through the holes as Neo hangs up the phone. He
steps out of the phone and slides on a pair of sunglasses. He
looks up and we rise.

Higher and higher, until the city is miles below.

After a moment, Neo blasts by us, his long black coat
billowing like a black leather cape as he flies faster than a
speeding bullet.

                                                    FADE OUT.

SCENE NOTES
Phil Oosterhouse

DELETED SCRIPT EXCERPTS
Larry and Andy Wachowski

Scene 4 TRACE PROGRAM - Originally, Trinity wasn't even in this scene. It was a conversation between a character named Eddie who has just secretly reentered the Matrix to see his girlfriend, Christie, one more time. Eddie had been recently recruited by Morpheus and, as a result, had left Christie behind in the Matrix. When this scene was changed, the script no longer addressed what hap-

This is the part of the book usually written by the directors. They give their comments on how they shot certain scenes, what scenes broke their hearts when they had to be cut and why they wrote the script in the first place. On top of that, they might give funny anecdotes about what happened to them while they were making the film: heart-warming stories like how they got through the trying times when they thought it was never going to happen and the pure elation they felt when the film was finally released to widespread critical acclaim and box office success. After reading a section like this, you feel somehow closer to the directors, like you've taken the journey with them.

That's how it usually works.

Larry and Andy, however, were too busy so they asked me to do it. I was their assistant on THE MATRIX so, basically, I spent every moment with them while they were making the film. I saw the whole process, from the first draft of the script, to the completion of the storyboards (which eventually convinced Warner Bros. to make the film), to the casting process, then preproduction, principal photography, editing, all the way through the final sound mix. When you consider that, it is almost like they wrote this section... or maybe not. Anyway, I gave it my best shot. I hope you enjoy it.

Scene 1 TRACE PROGRAM - Originally, Trinity wasn't even in this scene. It was a conversation between a character named Eddy who had secretly reentered the Matrix to see his girlfriend, Christie, one more time. Eddy had been recently recruited by Morpheus and, as a result, had left Christie behind in the Matrix. When this scene was changed, the script no longer addressed what happens when people are separated by Morpheus's crusade. That's the problem with working with an idea as rich as THE MATRIX, there's no way you can explore all of its implications in two hours. It's a good thing they're doing sequels.

As the scene turned out, it is a great, kick-ass introduction to Trinity.

```
FADE IN:
On a computer screen; so close that it has no boundaries.

A blinking cursor pulses in the electric darkness like a heart coursing with
phosphorous light, burning beneath the derma of black-neon glass.

A phone begins to ring, we hear it as though we were making the call. The cursor
continues to throb, relentlessly patient, until--

                    WOMAN'S VOICE
          Hello?

Data now slashes across the screen, information flashing faster than we can read.

                    SCREEN
          Call received: AT&T 3125558315

                    MAN'S VOICE
          Christie?

                    SCREEN
          2-19-94 13:24:18 REC:Log>

We listen to the phone conversation as though we were on a third line.

                    CHRISTIE
          Eddy!? Is it really you?

                         EDDY
          It's me. God, it's good to hear your
          voice.
                    SCREEN
          Trace program: Running.
```

                    CHRISTIE
          Eddy, where are you? Where have you
          been?

The entire screen fills with racing columns of numbers. They rush, shimmering like
green-electric rivers at a 10-digit phone number in the top corner.

                    EDDY
          I can't tell you. I'm not supposed
          to be here. I'm not supposed to be
          talking to you.

                    CHRISTIE
          Why? Eddy, what kind of trouble are
          you in?

The area code is identified. The first three numbers suddenly fixed, leaving only
seven flowing columns.

                    EDDY
          I had to call you. Christie, I miss
          you. I want to come back to you but I
          can't. I've seen things--

We begin moving toward the screen, closing in as each digit is matched, one by
one, snapping into place like the wheels of a slot machine.

                    CHRISTIE
          Eddy--

                    EDDY
          Jesus Christie, I dream about you and
          every time I wake up without you I want
          to go back to sleep.

                    CHRISTIE
          Eddy, the police were here--

Only two thin digit lines left.

                    EDDY
          What? Oh fuck.

                    CHRISTIE
          And these Agents, Special Agents--

                    EDDY
          Shit, they could have a trace on the
          line! Christie, I have to see you.

The final number pops into place--

                    SCREEN
          Trace complete. Call origin #3125550690

                    EDDY
          Please, Christie, tonight at midnight.
          You know where. Please come.

                    SCREEN
          750 N. Wabash.

                    EDDY
          Christie... I love you.

He hangs up and the line goes dead.
We continue closing in on the glowing green numbers of the address as we hear the crackle of a police radio.

                              RADIO
              Attention all units, Attention all units.

Scene 2 TRINITY CHASE - Look for the map of Australia torn into the wallpaper.

Scene 4 TRINITY CHASE - This scene was the first of Carrie-Anne's wall running scenes. One of the most impressive things about the film was the actors' insane dedication to the kung fu training. Keanu, Laurence, Carrie-Anne, and Hugo all could have done two or three films in the time it took to train for and shoot THE MATRIX. Doing in six months what normally takes years, Yuen Wo Ping transformed four Hollywood actors into kung fu masters. This was the first scene with kung fu wire work that was shot. Carrie-Anne nailed it, putting the pressure on the other actors to do the same.

Scene 9 TRINITY CHASE - As you can see from the boards, Trinity and Agent Brown used to jump onto a moving elevated train in this scene. However, the train was scrapped when the decision was made to shoot in Sydney instead of Chicago. They considered building an elevated train in Sydney but it probably would have doubled our budget.

Scene 11 TRINITY CHASE - In the earlier version of this scene, Eddy doesn't make it to the phone booth. The Agents use a sports car instead of a garbage truck to run him over, then place a trace on him, trying to find Morpheus. As a result, Morpheus is forced to unplug Eddy before he gives them away. Love costs Eddy his life.

EXT. STREET

Eddy emerges from the shadows of an alley, and at the end of the block, in a pool of white street light, he sees it.

The telephone booth.

He lurches down the concrete walk so focused on his goal he does not see a speeding sports car suddenly veer off the road aiming straight for him.

It plows into Eddy, rolling him over the hood, bouncing him into the air, swerving as it slams on its brakes while Eddy hits the ground.

The car door opens and Agent Smith gets out.

Eddy is trying to stand when Smith shoots, blowing a hole in his knee. Eddy screams.

Agent Smith slips his gun into the shoulder holster and touches his ear piece. A moment later, the tinted four door rolls up and Agent Brown gets out with a black briefcase.

                         AGENT SMITH
                       Start the trace.

Both men work very quickly and efficiently. Agent Brown attaching white-disk electrodes to Eddy's head and chest while Agent Smith prepares a large hypodermic needle, pumping a clear liquid into Eddy's neck.

The electrodes are connected to several monitors and a computer in the briefcase. Agent Brown begins typing with unnatural speed.

Eddy's eyes glaze as he begins convulsing.

                          AGENT SMITH
                 I want information. Information.
                 Full access. Understood.

Words scramble as they spit from Eddy's mouth. His eyes begin to go white,
rolling up into his head when--

The phone rings.

Agents Smith and Brown exchange looks. Agent Smith stands, enters the booth and
answers the phone.

                          AGENT SMITH
                 Hello, Morpheus.

Silence.

                          AGENT SMITH
                 You've lost another one. How many
                 is that? I've lost count but I'm
                 sure you haven't. This one? He was
                 weak, even weaker than the last.

The phone crackles with static.

                          AGENT SMITH
                 Will it be the next that finally
                 gives you away? What did you expect
                 fighting inevitability? No matter,
                 it won't be long now. Every loss
                 brings me closer to you, Morpheus.
                 Closer to Zion.

The line goes dead.

Suddenly, Eddy's body seizes up. He reaches into the air, grabbing at nothing,
screaming.

                          EDDY
                 Nooo!

And then his body collapses. Perfectly still. Perfectly dead.

Agent Smith looks at the phone then drops the handset, letting it hang from its
spiral-metal cord as he gets out of the booth.

We hear him talking to Agent Brown, their voices, as always, muted and monotone.

                          AGENT SMITH (V.O.)
                 Anything?

Dangling before the phone, we move toward the ear piece.

                          AGENT BROWN (V.O.)
                 A name.

                          AGENT SMITH (V.O.)
                 Neo.

The gray plastic of the phone widens before us, spreading out like a smooth perfect landscape marked by small black holes.

                          AGENT SMITH (V.O.)
                 We'll need a search running.

AGENT BROWN (V.O.)
It has already begun.

Still closer, until we fall into one of those holes and are swallowed by –

Darkness.

Scene 14 NEO'S APARTMENT - A lot of people have asked about the significance of the numbers that show up in the film. In this scene, the clock reads 9:18 because this is the birthday of Andy's wife

Scene 15 CORTECHS CAPTURE - The addition of Meta to CorTechs saved us billions in lawsuits, or so we were told by the lawyers.

Scene 16 CORTECHS CAPTURE - For safety reasons, the window cleaners in this scene ended up being played by our stunt coordinator, Glenn Boswell, and stuntman, Lou Horvath. Be sure to notice their expert window cleaning technique.

Scene 17 CORTECHS CAPTURE - Day one of shooting. Everyone was nervous, all the Warner Bros. guys were out, making sure Larry and Andy knew what they were doing. No one really knew how it was going to go. As it turned out, the day was flawless. The actors were fantastic, Larry and Andy got every setup they wanted and we finished on time.

Scene 18 CORTECHS CAPTURE - Complete contrast to scene 17. The shot of the phone dropping took nearly half a day and wasn't used. It was reshot on a bluescreen stage. We ran out of sun at the end of the day and had to rebuild the office onstage to get the remaining interior setups. More kudos for Keanu's dedication, however: he was actually out on the ledge, thirty-four stories up because he wanted to be.

Scene 20 INTERROGATION ROOM - The bug went through many conceptions before the finished product. Like many of the CG creatures in this film, it took a long time to create a creature that looked like it belonged in the scene. There were countless conversations about details like tentacle motion (flailing or not) and the texture and opacity of the sac. In the film, you also might notice a difference in the prosthetic Neo stomach that the bug bur-rows into, and Keanu's stomach when the Agents rip open his shirt. The stomach model was made before Keanu was deep into training. Keanu warned us that his stomach would look nothing like that when we got to shooting, and he was right.

Scene 28 LAFAYETTE PILLS - The Red Pill and Morpheus intro scene. What character could ask for a better intro-duction, complete with thunder and lightning accents? When these storyboards were drawn, not a lot of consider-ation was given to how the images would be duplicated on film. Larry and Andy drew what they wanted, figuring that the logistics could be sorted out later. Most of the time this wasn't a problem but certain shots proved to be much more complicated than anticipated. For example, the shot of Morpheus with pills reflected in his glasses was simple in theory, but proved very difficult to match to the storyboard. Eventually, it was shot with Laurence wearing green glasses. Reflection plates of Neo grabbing the pill were later composited onto his glasses. The scene was always a great read and, as a result, was a pretty enjoyable shooting day.

Scene 29 LAFAYETTE MIRROR - A much less enjoyable shooting day. This was another good example of a sequence that was boarded without knowing if it would be possible to film. In the end, there were something like fifty visual effects setups. Every shot with Keanu and the mirror gel had to be shot once with all the elements in the shot, once with a greenscreen, and then John Gaeta, the visual effects supervisor, would step in and film the shot again, without Keanu but with a cube, pyramid or ball in his place. Even though it was a grueling day that stretched into a couple of days, the finished product looks fantastic and makes it all worthwhile.

Scene 30 POWER PLANT - A great scene and another in which Keanu should be commended for his dedication. It was the last scene on the schedule because Keanu had to be shaved completely bald, including his eyebrows. He also lost considerable weight for this scene so that he looked like he'd been lying inactive in gel for years. If that wasn't enough, he had to spend four hours at the beginning of each day in prosthetic makeup as the jacks were put on his body. There were internet rumors circulating throughout production that we had built a fully animatronic Keanu for this scene and the tougher action. That was untrue but there was a prosthetic Keanu head made for the close up of the Docbot removing the plug from his neck.

Scene 31 POWER PLANT - Three underwater camera housings were broken shooting this scene. There was one point in the waterslide in which the stuntman and cameraman built up so much speed that they slammed into the top of the tube, shattering the camera housing.

Scene 35 NEO WAKES UP - Eight hours of prosthetic makeup for this scene. Those are real acupuncture needles in Keanu's face and forehead. The needles were provided and placed by Longie, the cast masseur whose official title is Master of Pressure Points. Throughout the shoot, the cast would get worn down and Longie would be called in to heal their wounds. He was so effective that by the end of the shoot, they all would have joined a cult if Longie had told them to.

Scene 39 HISTORY PROGRAM - This scene was shot in a stage that was completely painted white. The camera-men wore white suits to cut down on reflection in Morpheus's glasses. The sunglasses presented constant reflection problems for Bill Pope, the director of photography. As a result, nearly every scene was a challenge and Bill conquered all of them. We'll see how he does on the sequels when everybody has a fully reflective chrome head.

Scene 40 HISTORY PROGRAM - In order to translate the boards for this scene to film, John Gaeta decided the best option was to create them all digitally. The result is visually stunning and also the most complex completely computer-generated shot in history. Running time: 34 seconds. The Fetus Harvesters were designed by Geof Darrow.

Scene A40 HISTORY PROGRAM - A lot of people questioned how we got a baby to be so well behaved while shooting this scene, especially with a jack in the back of its neck. Fortunately, it isn't a real baby, just a very convincing prosthetic constructed by MEG in Australia.

Scene 48 CONSTRUCT KUNG FU - Again, the actors deserve credit for their preparation. This scene took a whole week to shoot. Laurence and Keanu had to do these moves take after take and they kicked ass despite the intense heat. Because Larry and Andy were shooting at speeds as high as 300fps, Bill Pope needed to use huge lights to get enough illumination. The lights gave off enormous amounts of heat and once even began to singe the rice paper on the dojo walls. Wo Ping did a great job choreographing this scene and his wire team did some amazing work as well. The most difficult wire work appears in this scene.

You'll notice that these boards bear little resemblance to the film. That's mostly due to the fact that Wo Ping hadn't been hired when they were drawn. He made the sequence what it became in the final scene. The only boards that were actually used were the last four pages in which Neo runs up the pole and flips over Morpheus' head. The stunt doubles for Laurence and Keanu, Chyna McCoy and Chad Stahelski, also did a great job. Keanu had had neck surgery before shooting began and this forced Chad to double for him on any impacts. Chad's excellent at being thrown into walls.

Scene 57 CONSTRUCT ROOFTOP - Larry and Andy couldn't find a section of Sydney big enough to recreate the first three boards in this sequence, the effect of the city rushing up at their feet. Sydney just doesn't have the urban sprawl we have become accustomed to in America. In the early visual effects meetings when discussing how the shot should look, they described the city looking like a circuit board as it rushes up at Neo and Morpheus. So, John Gaeta took the existing helicopter shot of Sydney and merged it with a photo of an actual circuit board to fill in the gaps. If you step frame by frame through the final shot, you can actually see the circuit board mixed in with the city.

Scene 63 TRAINING PROGRAM - All the storyboards you see in this book were drawn largely because they were needed to create a visual effects budget. This scene wasn't storyboarded for a couple of reasons. One, we ran out of time. Two, it seemed pretty straightforward. Nonetheless, long after the VFX budget was done, we realized that because it wasn't storyboarded, it wasn't included in the budget. After some long, tense meetings, the issue finally got resolved. However, the scene still had to be shot and it was one of the worst shooting days on record. There were incredibly loud jackhammers at a construction site across the street that made it impossible to talk, let alone shoot. We got about two-thirds of the setups we wanted and had to finish on a greenscreen stage.

For the extras, Larry and Andy requested twins. We had multiple sets of real twins and triplets. To fill in the gaps, Manex created more to give the impression that Mouse got lazy and duplicated people instead of creating unique ones.

There was a funny moment involving the woman in the red dress, Fiona Johnson. She came by for a costume fitting and was waiting just outside the set for Larry and Andy to finish. Across the street, some guy pulling out of his garage was so distracted by her beauty that he actually drove his car through the garage door. The bottom of the door scraped over the entire length of his car, ruining his new paint job. The guy drove away humiliated, his windshield wipers twisted lamely out of position.

Scene 64 SENTINEL SIGHTING - Another scene that was created digitally to match the boards.

Scene 71 NEO TAKES A DRINK - The section where Cypher tells Neo there were five potential Ones before him was shot and then cut in postproduction for reasons only Larry and Andy know.

Scene A71 STEAK - This scene alternated between being cut, indispensable, moved around and then, finally, put back in its original position. It's a good scene, giving you more insight into why Cypher would sell everyone out. Plus, every time we did a take, they had to replace Cypher's steak and we got to eat the other ones. The steaks were provided by a restaurant called Level 41 and were probably the best in Sydney.

Scene 72 TASTEE WHEAT - The food in this scene was originally cockroach. No one tells Neo what it is.

                    MORPHEUS
          Sit down Neo. Let's get you something to eat.

    Piled onto plates are pieces of a large black shelled creature. Everyone begins
    grabbing and cracking open shells, pulling out the meat and dipping it into bowls
    of butter-flavored topping.

                    BUZZ
          So, Neo, how'd you like the orientation
          program?

    He sucks at a long piece that looks a lot like a crab leg.

                      NEO
          It was... effective.

    Neo struggles, trying to break open the shell.

                    BUZZ
          I created Eve, you know.

    Buzz laughs.

                    BUZZ
          And I can create anyone else if your
          heart desires.

                              JAZZ
                   Buzz is our local porno shop.

                              BUZZ
                   Don't listen to these prudes, Neo.
                   We're men, we have urges.

        He leans close, licking the artificial butter from his lips.

                              BUZZ
                   If you've ever fantasized about screwing
                   any woman or hell, any man. On disk I
                   already got Marilyn Monroe, Betty Page,
                   Cokie Roberts--

                              APOC
                   Cokie Roberts?

                              BUZZ
                   Oh... that brain.

        Jazz hands him a piece of white meat. Neo dips and eats it.

                              NEO
                   What is this?

                              JAZZ
                   You're going to learn Neo, there are some questions
                   you don't want to know the answers to.

        Suddenly the lights dim and Tank, who left for a moment, returns carrying a small
        fruit cake with a single candle on it.

                              MORPHEUS
                   Here's a little something we do, Neo, to
                   celebrate your first day out.

        He raises his polyplastic glass, everyone does the same.

                              MORPHEUS
                   Happy Birthday, Neo.

        Neo stares at the burning candle.

                              MORPHEUS
                   Be careful what you wish for.

Scene 79 SPOON BOY - Rowan Witt, who played Spoon Boy, appears in Dark City with a shaved head as well. By the time we got around to casting THE MATRIX, his hair had grown back and he had long curly locks that his mother loved. He was cast as Spoon Boy and as it got closer and closer to shooting, his mother kept try- ing to convince Larry and Andy that maybe Spoon Boy didn't need to be bald. Eventually, she was convinced and on the day his head was shaved, his mother saved his hair in a plastic bag which Rowan carried around the set. In the end, he looked great and did a great job. Finally, in a testament to how long it took to complete this film, we saw the Witts again during postproduction while Rowan was shooting a commercial. His long curly locks had returned.

Bending spoons came courtesy of Dfilm.

Scene 87 DEJA VU - Great cat acting here. How did they get it to do exactly the same thing twice, complete with identical meows? Wow, that cat was good.

    A lot of people have asked if the animals in the Matrix are also hooked up in pods. Unfortunately, they are not, they're all computer generated images.

Scene 108 LAFAYETTE TRAP - Owen Paterson constructed a great set for this scene. It must have been 100 feet high and about two feet wide. The actors were on wires, sliding down the walls. Two smaller walls were also built for the dialogue parts of the scene. The set was built mainly because it allowed the storyboard [see page 124] to be shot by blacking out the scaffolding surrounding the set.

Scenes 134/135 TV REPAIR SHOP - A great acting scene. I've been surprised by how many people identify with Cypher in this film, people that would rather live on in ignorant bliss if the Matrix was a reality. As for me, I imagine I couldn't get enough cold goop. The building this was shot in was allegedly haunted by a man that had shot himself in the basement. I didn't go down there but there was one take in which a shadowy figure could be seen lurking behind Trinity as she talked on the phone. It was a frightening night at dailies when that came up on screen. Larry and Andy wanted to use it in the film but the lawyers couldn't reach the spirit in time to get legal clearance.

Speaking of improbable postmortem appearances, if you believe Joey Pants, Cypher didn't really die in this scene and will be back for the sequels.

Scene 140 GOVERNMENT BUILDING - Another great acting scene. Hugo took this great speech by Agent Smith and made it even better. Like the pod sequence, this scene didn't change much from the first draft of the script to the last. It has to be one of the all time great film speeches. The city out the window is actually a huge photograph of Sydney, called a translite, with additional buildings strategically placed to block Sydney landmarks like the Harbor bridge. When we shot it, it was the largest translite ever made.

Scene 150 GOVERNMENT LOBBY - This scene took a very long time to shoot. Steve Courtley and Brian Cox, the special effects supervisors, had built about a hundred extra pillars and walls for this scene and we used over half of them. If anything went wrong on a take, however, it took at least two hours to reset everything that was blown up. After each take, the air filled with toxic dust and we had to wear face masks while huge fans were brought in to clear the air. As a result, each take became like an Olympic event. The actors would be outside the set, pumping themselves up, knowing that they might only get one chance to get the action right. After a few days, everyone was convinced that there was nothing else to life except sitting around in this dingy warehouse waiting for pillars to be reset. This scene also contained two of the film's most difficult wire stunts, Trinity's flip off the wall and Neo's triple kick.

It's funny how the boards began to take on a life of their own. The soldier in this scene [see page page 150] became known as Prince Charles because Steve's drawing resembled the Prince of Wales. The lucky stuntman, Alex Kuzelicki, selected to perform the Prince got to be repeatedly kicked in the head before flipping head over heels and crashing to the ground. He must have done it twenty times on two separate days.

Scene 152 ELEVATOR SHAFT - This is another scene shot almost exactly as storyboarded.

Scene 157 GOVERNMENT ROOF - Bullet Time. Three years of development went into the boards for this scene [see pages 168 through 170]. John Gaeta had to invent technology to make what Steve Skroce had storyboarded possible on film. Larry and Andy wanted the action to occur in slow motion while the camera appeared to move at normal speed. Up to this point such an effect had been nearly impossible to achieve. The scene was shot once on the actual rooftop, once on a greenscreen stage with the Bullet Time rig, and then plates were shot on the rooftop without any actors. The Bullet Time rig consisted of a lot of still cameras lined up in a virtual camera move. The cameras were timed to go off milliseconds after each other. The VFX crew took the resulting photographs which basically were steps along the camera move and fed them into a computer. The computer then interpolated the intermediate frames until the virtual camera move was complete.

Trinity's "Dodge This" moment can be matched almost exactly to frames of film [see pages 173 through 174].

Scene 158 PILOT PROGRAM - A note for helicopter fanatics. Yes, we do realize that the actual helicopter is a B-212 but the graphic on Tank's screen is a B-206. Sorry about that.

Scene 161 HELICOPTER RESCUE - This was one of the first scenes to be boarded and it was never certain how it was going to be shot. As it turned out, it was shot mostly inside on stage. We had the body of a helicopter mounted to a crane that was raised and lowered in the shot to simulate hovering. The office set was three stories high with a huge water tank underneath. The water from the sprinklers drained into this tank in between shots. The Agents had to wear wetsuits under their suits so they didn't freeze in between takes. The whole crew had to wear knee high boots to wade through the soaked set. Air guns were placed under the floor to simulate bullets hitting the water. This has to be one of the best action scenes on record.

Scene 164 HELICOPTER RESCUE - Any shot in this scene with the actors in it was shot on stage in front of a greenscreen while stuntmen performed the shots hanging from the helicopter as it weaves between buildings throughout Sydney. Shooting this scene was front page news on every station in Sydney the night it was shot.

The helicopter crash [see pages 203 through 206], was another scene boarded without really knowing how it would be shot. In the end it was shot with models but it was still a massive undertaking. The model building was at least forty feet high. It was constructed entirely of mirrored glass and surrounded by greenscreens. A quarter scale helicopter was then placed on a green rig. The rig was lowered into the building and blown up. It was such a huge, dangerous shoot that it had to be shot out in the desert. Only the special effects crew were allowed near it and they were operating in underground bunkers. The lowering of the helicopter and the explosion were set off remotely from the bunkers. Larry and Andy used to joke that this one shot probably cost more than BOUND, their first film.

Before it was shot, there were probably two months of meetings about what kind of glass would be used on the mini-building and how to get it to ripple. The whole scene was previsualized in CGI before it was shot. Eventually, John Gaeta and Steve Courtley sorted it all out.

Scenes 170, 172, 174, 176, 178 EL FIGHT - A set which seemed like we would never leave. I think this scene was originally scheduled for five days and ended up taking twelve or fifteen. The subway station was constructed over an outside railroad track. It was freezing cold and everyone got sick, making it particularly brutal for the actors. Every shot seemed like a struggle. It was hard while we were shooting but, in the end, the difficulty of the shoot made the final scene even more intense.

Scenes 204, 206, 208 SENTINEL ATTACK - These Sentinel scenes were strange shooting days because we had to plot the destruction for Sentinels that were to be added later. The Sentinel action had to be matched by John Gaeta during postproduction. So on the set, things ground to a standstill as Larry and Andy tried to plot out how a Sentinel would destroy the ship. At that point, it wasn't even entirely determined how exactly the Sentinels would move. It's a good thing they figured it out because, somehow, John Gaeta running up to Neo and Trinity's chair with a cube on a green stick is no substitute for the real thing. It looked good in the end but on the day, I think everyone's head was throbbing.

PRELIMINARY THUMBNAILS

Before the boards were completed, numerous notebooks
were filled with initial sketches by Larry and Andy
Wachowski. Used as a starting point, these preliminary
sketches would go back and forth between the artists
and the brothers, allowing them to zero in, visually,
on what Larry and Andy were after. Here's a selection
from this part of preproduction.

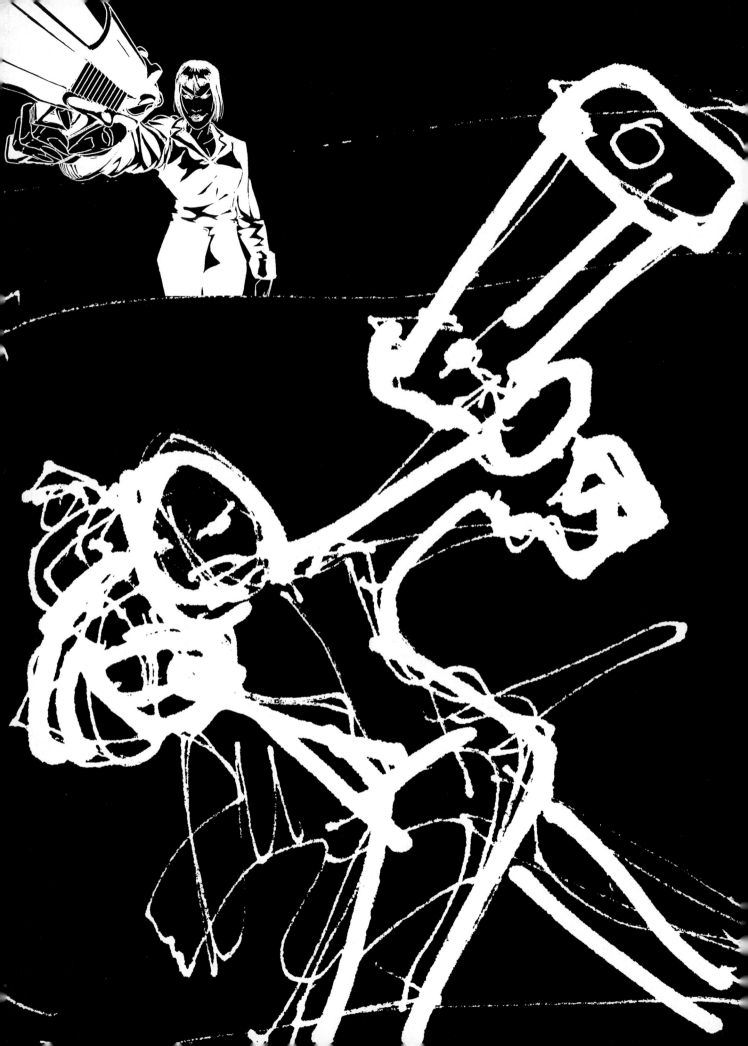

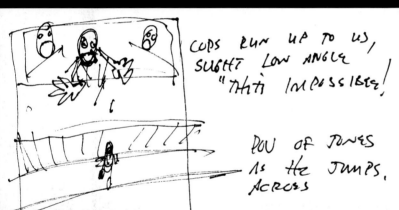

COPS RUN UP TO US,
SLIGHT LOW ANGLE
"THAT'S IMPOSSIBLE!"

POV OF JONES
AS HE JUMPS.
ACROSS

LOWER?

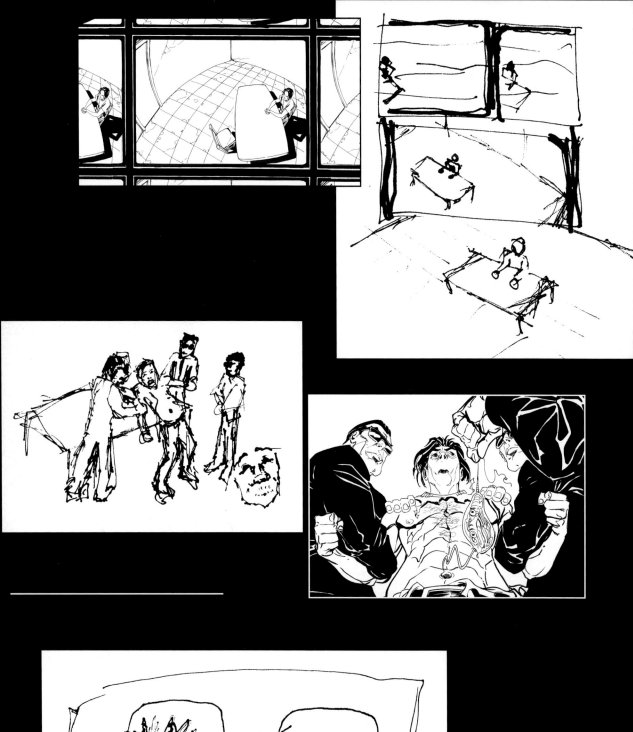

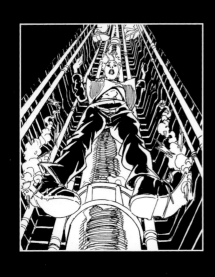
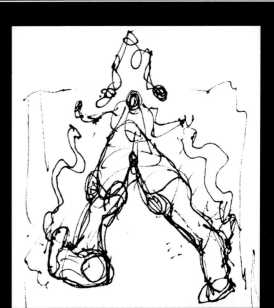

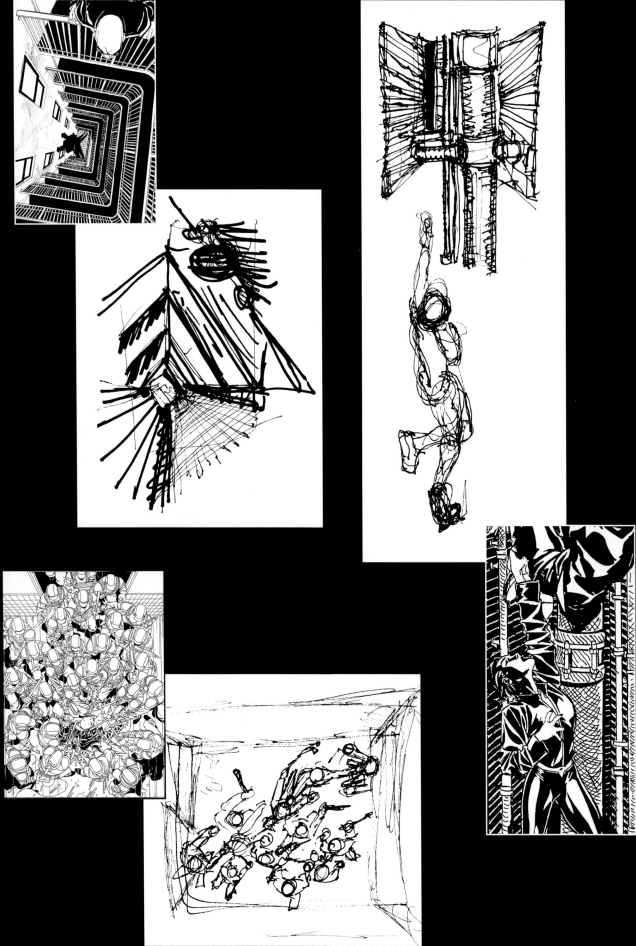

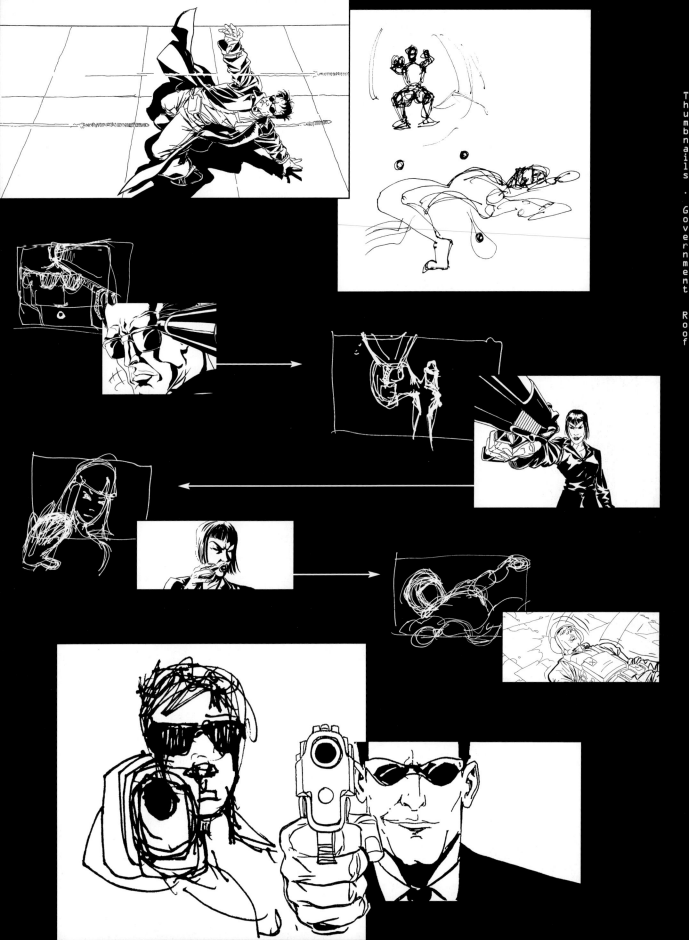

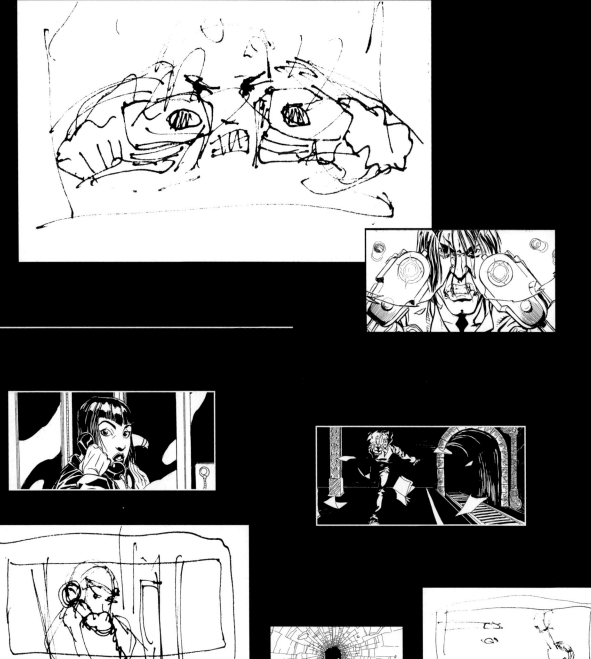
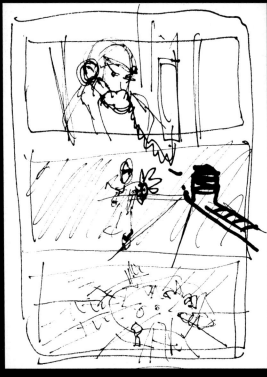
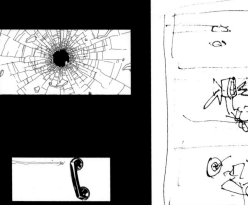

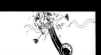

"I NEED THE MAIN WET WALL."

The following three sections of storyboards are not
in the film. They are based on early drafts of the
script and included here, with commentary, to add
insight into the preproduction process.

Lafayette Trap

Original Sequence

Steve Skroce: A lot got changed for this scene, characters juggled around. Here's how it was originally illustrated, with Trinity in the place Neo has in the final boards [see page 125].

Skroce: Again, here's how this shot was initially drawn. After I first drew it, Larry and Andy changed their minds about the order the characters should be in while hanging in the wet wall. That's why, in this version, Trinity is where she is. In the film, and the redrawn board [see page 124], she's at the bottom.

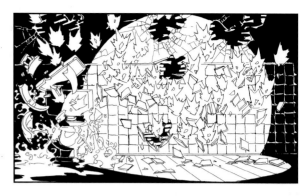

Skroce: In case you're wondering what's happening here [above], the agent is taking over the soldier.

Skroce: You can see more of Larry and Andy's comic-book influence here. They wanted a classic comic-book look to this page, which is seen with the gas can, sort of an abbreviation of the scene. Instead of having to draw it all, they had me show the gas can, which becomes the panel for Morpheus pulling the manhole cover off in the basement of the hotel.

And that's Cypher there in the middle, slinking away.

Skroce: The basic gist here is retained in the later version, with Morpheus sacrificing himself. Only in the film, the sacrifice occurs earlier, straight from the wet wall into the bathroom where he fights Agent Smith.

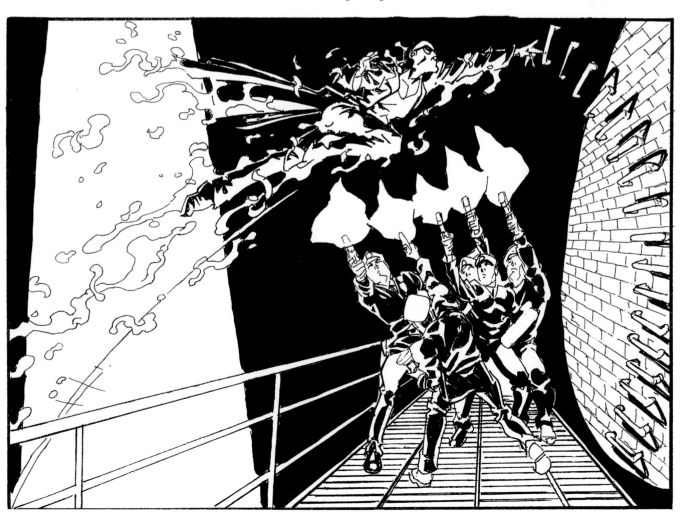

Skroce: This is a close-up of Neo's face as the cops scurry up behind Morpheus. Morpheus has no escape and is heading up towards a manhole to go to street level.

Skroce: This next bit was to be a much larger-scale fight between Morpheus, the cops, and the Agents. Morpheus is exploding out of the manhole cover into the street where he is surrounded by a zillion cops with guns turned on him.

Here's a really cool idea that was dropped, where one of the Agents comes up to Morpheus with a special gun. It's an idea Larry and Andy had about a gun that fires tranquilizer needles, which was to work with compressed air. In this shot [below], we see a close-up of the gun and see all the little puffs escaping through the vents as the gun is fired.

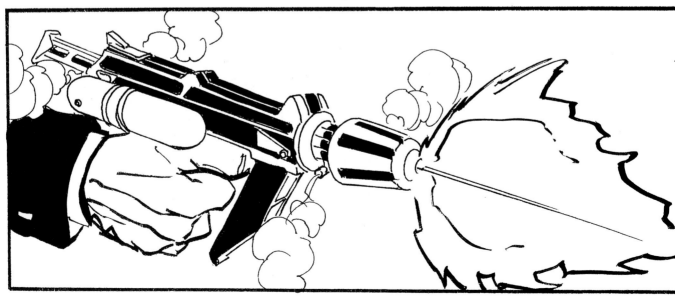

Skroce: This scene only got better with Morpheus deflecting the little needles with the manhole cover and then whipping the cover like a superhuge discus. He nails the Agent in the stomach, sending him flying back into a police truck.

The truck was going to get knocked up on two wheels from the incredible impact, windows exploding, the frame buckling like it's just been smashed by a speeding car. Larry and Andy had this all worked out, how they were going to do it, with wires and thin sheet metal. You can almost hear the shattering glass.

Skroce: Here's Morpheus kicking back, getting busy with the cops. This shot where all the cops jump on top of Morpheus evolved into the overhead shot with Agent Smith kicking his butt in the bathroom, where all the cops come in [see page 134]. This one [bottom] is my own idea, the "69 throw," as we called it. For some reason it didn't make it into the film.

CUT

"IN LONG BLACK COATS, TRINITY AND NEO PUSH
THROUGH THE REVOLVING DOORS."

Government Lobby

Original Sequence

Steve Skroce: Originally, the Government Lobby scene was set in a hotel lobby, like a Marriott with big open spaces and couches. There were a couple of cops down there hanging around in the lobby to make sure there was no trouble. In this panel (left), trouble walks in with Neo and Trinity, and we have a shoot 'em up, which is quite a bit different from what we wound up with in the movie.

Skroce: Some elements from these initial boards were kept, such as the paper getting torn in half as the guy gets shot [see page 138].

In these two panels [above and right] the idea was to have Neo lift his right arm with his gun in his pocket, firing at something off panel. Then the camera would swing around, over his left shoulder, and we'd see one of the cops drop to his knees with a smoldering bullethole in his head.

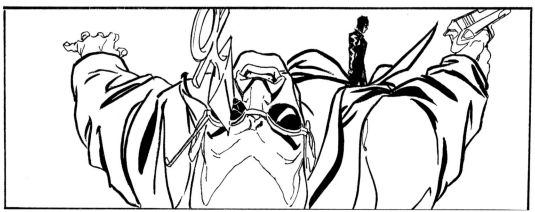

Skroce: Here's Neo spraying the ceiling to scare everyone out of the hotel, to safely get as many people out as possible. The two are still about to set the bomb in the elevator, blowing up the lobby, so they're trying to lessen innocent casualties.

"I REPEAT, WE'RE UNDER ATTACK."

Government Roof

Original Sequence

Steve Skroce: The Government Roof scene was going be different, because it was here where the main fighting was to happen. From an aerial shot, we were going to speedily push through the black smoke from the elevator explosion, not knowing where we were until we got through it. Then we would see an overhead shot of Neo and Trinity going to town on a bunch of soldiers on the rooftop.

Skroce: The roof is on fire from the explosion of the elevator shaft. Some of these shots are in the movie but have been moved to the Government Lobby scene.

Skroce: This is a different take on Neo diving for the gun before doing the one-handed flip seen in the Government Lobby scene [page 144].

Skroce: After doing the big flip, Neo lands, and the camera starts to pull back.

Skroce: Here's Trinity beating up a soldier. That's supposed to be the bridge of his teeth coming out there [center].

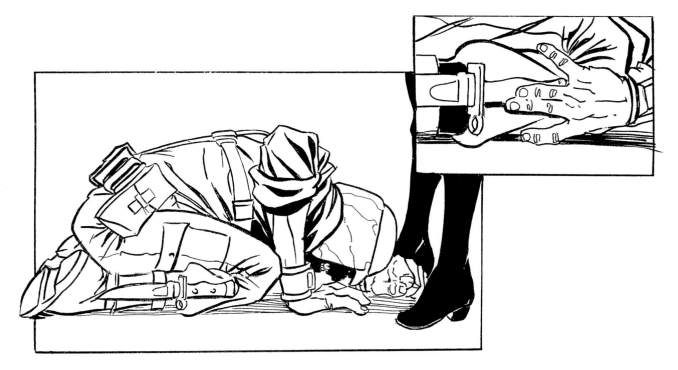

Skroce: The soldier, whom Trinity has just disarmed, reaches to get a knife out of his boot, and in one quick move, Trinity breaks his arm [over].

Skroce: Larry and Andy were going to have a shot where the soldier's knife flips up into the air and we see the handle of the knife up close, showing a compass pointing north. We also drew this out with Neo doing the same thing [see page 164].

The knife drops down into Trinity's hand as she sees a soldier grabbing a grenade from his webbing. So she throws the knife, pinning his wrist to his sternum, making him drop the depinned grenade [facing].

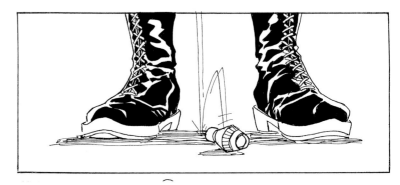

Skroce: The soldier looks down—our "Oh shit!" shot— and then, the big explosion.

Skroce: This is the same idea as in the scene on the Government Roof, but it's Trinity who nails the guy behind Neo's shoulder, rather than vice versa.

Skroce: Here's a shot that wasn't really in the movie, in any form [below]—the two lone warriors standing victorious after they'd taken everybody out.

AFTERWORD

William Gibson
[[[[NEUROMANCER, VIRTUAL LIGHT, IDORU, ALL TOMORROW'S PARTIES]]]]

I was afraid to see this movie. I was afraid because it was very popular, and friends told me it was very similar to my own work, and because it stars Keanu Reeves, who had starred in a film I had written. I was afraid that I would be jealous, or that I would resent the film's creators, or simply be unhappy. I had seen copies of the screenplay, and hadn't thought they promised a great deal, and Hollywood has generally done a very poor job around the theme of virtual reality.

The film had been in release, in America, for several weeks.

When I finally saw it, I only saw it because I found myself alone in an ocean hotel suite, in Santa Monica, and it was dark and cold and raining. My very good friend Roger came and rescued me, and insisted that I would like THE MATRIX. He dragged me out into the rain and his old VW Rabbit.

I knew then I would like THE MATRIX.

I liked it immediately, and liked it even more as the story unfolded. I felt a sense of excite ment that I hadn't felt, watching a science fiction movie, in a very long time. The cynic in me kept waiting to be disappointed, waiting for the wrong move, the shabby explanation, the descent into the mess that Hollywood usually manages to make of a film like this. It never came, and when Neo soars at the end of the film, I went with him, in an innocent delight that I hadn't felt for quite a long time.

When I returned to Vancouver, I immediately took my 15 year old daughter to see THE MATRIX. She had exactly the same misgivings. She loved it.

She loved it, I think, because it's something very special, a big muscular effects movie that's wildly generous with visual thrills, manages never to quit making sense (in the way an sf writer must demand that sf make sense), and, most important of all, has a good heart.

As I interpret it, THE MATRIX is a film about becoming conscious. It tells us that, to become more conscious, to have the courage to seek that which is more real, is its own (and ultimately the greatest) reward. When Morpheus offers Neo the choice of the two pills, and Neo chooses (without knowing where it will take him, as indeed we never do) con sciousness, we embark on a quest more primal than anything offered by STAR WARS.

The ultimate goal in THE MATRIX is not the Force but the Real. When the film's Judas fig ure betrays the heroes, he does so in order to be returned to illusion and denial, the false reality that Neo struggles to escape and overthrow.

American reviewers have interpreted this in Christian terms, seeing Neo as a Christ figure, but I prefer to see in him something more universal, a hero of the Real. I usually have a certain amount of trouble with the very idea of a hero, but in this case no, Keanu's Neo is my favorite ever science fiction hero, absolutely.

William Gibson, 1999

MATRIX

Written and Directed by	LARRY and ANDY WACHOWSKI
Produced by	JOEL SILVER
Executive Producers	BARRIE M OSBORNE
	ANDREW MASON
	ANDY WACHOWSKI
	LARRY WACHOWSKI
	ERWIN STOFF
	BRUCE BERMAN
Director of Photography	BILL POPE
Production Designer	OWEN PATERSON
Editor	ZACH STAENBERG
Costume Designer	KYM BARRETT
Co-Producer	DAN CRACCHIOLO
Casting by	MALI FINN C.S.A
	SHAUNA WOLIFSON
Music Composed, Orchestrated and Conducted by	DON DAVIS
Visual Effects Supervisor	JOHN GAETA

a WARNER BROS. presentation

in association with
VILLAGE ROADSHOW PICTURES -
GROUCHO II FILM PARTNERSHIP

a SILVER PICTURES production

Unit Production Manager	CAROL HUGHES
1st Assistant Directors	COLIN FLETCHER
	JAMES McTEIGUE
2nd Assistant Directors	NONI ROY
	TOM READ
3rd Assistant Director	PAUL SULLIVAN
Kung Fu Choreographer	YUEN WO PING
Sound Designer/Supervising Sound Editor	DANE A. DAVIS, MPSE
Conceptual Designer	GEOFREY DARROW

CAST

Neo	KEANU REEVES
Morpheus	LAURENCE FISHBURNE
Trinity	CARRIE-ANNE MOSS
Agent Smith	HUGO WEAVING
Oracle	GLORIA FOSTER
Cypher	JOE PANTOLIANO
Tank	MARCUS CHONG
Apoc	JULIAN ARAHANGA
Mouse	MATT DORAN
Switch	BELINDA McCLORY
Dozer	ANTHONY RAY PARKER
Agent Brown	PAUL GODDARD
Agent Jones	ROBERT TAYLOR
Rhineheart	DAVID ASTON
Choi	MARC GRAY
Dujour	ADA NICODEMOU
Priestess	DENI GORDON
Spoon Boy	ROWAN WITT
Potentials	ELENOR WITT
	TAMARA BROWN
	JANAYA PENDER
	ADRYN WHITE
	NATALIE TJEN
Lieutenant	BILL YOUNG
FedEx Man	DAVID O'CONNOR
Businessman	JEREMY BALL
Woman in Red	FIONA JOHNSON
Old Man	HARRY LAWRENCE
Blind Man	STEVE DODD
Security Guard	LUKE QUINTON

Guard	LAWRENCE WOODWARD
Cop Who Captures Neo	MICHAEL BUTCHER
Big Cop	BERNIE LEDGER
Cops	ROBERT SIMPER
	CHRIS SCOTT
Parking Cop	NIGEL HARBACH
Helicopter Pilot	MARTIN GRELIS
Stunt Coordinator	GLENN BOSWELL
Assistant Stunt Coordinator	PHIL MEACHAM

Stunt Doubles

Neo	CHAD STAHELSKI
	DARKO TUSKAN
Neo/Agent Smith	PAUL DOYLE
Trinity	ANNETTE VAN MOORSEL
Morpheus	ANDRE CHYNA McCOY
Agent Brown	SHEA ADAMS
Agent Jones	NIGEL HARBACH
Switch	GILLIAN STATHAM
Cypher	BOB BOWLES
Mouse	NASH EDGERTON

Stunts

RAY ANTHONY	GREG BLANDY	RICHARD BOUE
SCOTT BREWER	DAVE BROWN	TODD BRYANT
MICHAEL CORRIGAN	HARRY DAKANALIS	DAR DAVIES
TERRY FLANAGAN	SCOTTY GREGORY	JOHNNY HALLYDAY
BRIAN ELLISON	LOU HORVATH	NIGEL KING
ALEX KISS	ALEX KUZELICIKI	IAN LIND
SCOTT McCLEAN	PHIL MEACHAM	CHRIS MITCHELL
TONY LYNCH	DARREN MITCHELL	STEVE MORRIS
BRETT PRAED	BAIT SOOBY	SOTIRI SOTIROPOULOS
GLENN SUTOR	BERNADETTE VAN GYEN	MARIJKE VAN GYEN
MICK VAN MOORSEL	WARWICK YOUNG	

Hong Kong Kung Fu Team

YUEN Eagle SHUN YI	HUANG Sam KAI SEN	LAM Dion TAT HO
LEE Chew TAT CHIU	CHEN Tiger HU	LEUNG Madye SING HUNG
NILS BENDIX	DAXING ZHANG	

Associate Producers	RICHARD MIRISCH
	CAROL HUGHES
Art Directors	HUGH BATEUP
	MICHELLE McGAHEY
Assistant Art Directors	JULES COOK
	FIONA SCOTT
	TONY WILLIAMS
Miniatures and Models Supervisor	TOM DAVIES
Storyboard Artists	STEVE SKROCE
	TANI KUNITAKE
	COLLIN GRANT
	WARREN MANSER
Art Department Researcher	TARA KAMATH
Art Department Coordinator	TRISH FOREMAN
2D/3D Conceptual Designer	SERGEI CHADILOFF
Graphics	KAREN HARBOROW
Illustrator	PHIL SHEARER
Set Designers	SARAH LIGHT
	JACINTA LEONG
	GODRIC COLE
	JUDITH HARVEY
	ANDREW POWELL
	DEBORAH RILEY
Set Decorators	TIM FERRIER
	LISA 'BLITZ' BRENNAN
	MARTA McELROY
Script Supervisor	VICTORIA SULLIVAN
Camera Operator	DAVID WILLIAMSON
Camera/Steadicam Operator	ROBERT AGGANIS
1st Assistant Camera	DAVIA ELMES
2nd Assistant Camera	ADRIEN SEFFRIN
Stills Photographer	JASON BOLAND
Sound Recordist	DAVID LEE
Boom Operators	JACK FRIEDMAN
	GERRY NUCIFORA
Video Playback Operator	MICHAEL TAYLOR
Property Master	LON LUCINI
Props	MURRAY GOSSON
	ADRIENNE OGLE
	KATIE SHARROCK

Key Armourer	JOHN BOWRING
Action Vehicle Coordinators	JOHN ALLAN
	TAPIO PIITULAINEN
Gaffer	REG GARSIDE
Best Boy	ALAN DUNSTAN
Rigger Gaffers	CRAIG BRYANT
	PAUL CUMMINGS
	PAUL MOYES
	STEVE JOHNSTON
	MILES JONES
	CHRIS LOVEDAY
	KEN TALBOT
	COLIN WYATT
Key Grip	RAY BROWN
Head Grip	IAN BIRD
Dolly Grips	MICK VIVIAN
	MAL BOOTH
	GREG KING
	ARON WALKER
Cam-Remote Operator	PAUL MICALLEF
Rigging Grip	DAVID BIRD
Standby Painters	TONY PILIOTIS
	JON STILES
Special Effects Supervisors	STEVE COURTLEY
	BRIAN COX
Special Effects Coordinator	ROBINA OSBOURNE

Special Effects

RODNEY BURKE	MONTY FEIGUTH	DAVID PRIDE
ARTHUR SPINK JR	DAVE YOUNG	AARAN GORDON
RICHARD ALEXANDER	BRIAN BELCHER	NICK BERYK
JEFFREY BRIGGS	DARREN DE COSTA	PAUL FENN
LLOYD FINNEMORE	RAY FOWLER	BERNARD GOLENKO
DAVID GOLDIE	PAUL GORRIE	PAUL GREBERT
LEO HENRY	DAVID JAMES	JIM LENG
JUDY MAE LEWIS	SHANE MURPHY	JOHN NEAL
BRIGID OULSNAM	PETER OWENS	DANIEL PATMORE
GARRY PHILIPS	PIETER PLOOY	REECE ROBINSON
LOU STEFANEL	EDWIN TREASURE	THOMAS VAN KOEVERDEN
KERRY WILLIAMS	SOPHIE DICK	WALTER VAN VEENANDAAL

Key Makeup Artist	NIKKI GOOLEY
Mr Fishburne's Makeup	DEBORAH TAYLOR
Hairdresser	CHERYL WILLIAMS
Assistant Makeup	SHERRY HUBBARD
Assistant Hairdresser	SIMON ZANKER
Costume Supervisor	LYN ASKEW
Costumers	MARY LOU DA ROZA
	ANDREA HOOD
	ANDREW INFANTI
	PAULINE WALKER
	JENNY IRWIN
	HELEN MATHER
	NICK GODLEE
	FIONA HOLLY
	NICOLE BROWN
Hero Eye Wear Designed by	RICHARD WALKER of BLIND OPTICS
Footwear Designed by	AIRWALK
1st Assistant Editors	PETER SKARRATT
	CATHERINE CHASE (USA)
	NOELLEEN WESTCOMBE (AUS)
Assistant Editors	TOM COSTAIN
	JENNIFER HICKS
	JOHN LEE
	BASIA OZERSKI
Visual Effects Editor	KATE CROSSLEY
Assistant Visual Effects Editors	MARY E. WALTER
	ALLEN CAPPUCCILLI
	ELIZABETH MERCADO
Sound Effects Editors	JULIA EVERSHADE
	BRIC LINDEMANN
	DAVID GRIMALDI
Dialogue Editors	CHARLES RITTER
	SUSAN DUDECK
Supervising Foley Editor	THOM BRENNAN
Foley Editor	VALERIE DAVIDSON
1st Assistant Sound Editor	NANCY BARKER
Assistant Sound Editors	BARBARA DELPUECH
	DAVID McCRELL
	FRANK LONG
ADR Mixer	TOM O'CONNELL
Foley Mixers	MARYJO LANG
	CAROLYN TAPP

Foley Artists	JOHN ROESCH
	HILDA HODGES
Re-Recording Mixers	JOHN REITZ
	GREGG RUDLOFF
	DAVID CAMPBELL
2nd Stage	KEVIN CARPENTER
Music Editors	LORI ESCHLER FRYSTAK
	ZIGMUND GRON
Music Score Recorded by	ARMIN STEINER
Music Score Mixed by	LARRY MAH
Production Accountant	MARGE ROWLAND
Production Accountant - Australia	ALISTAIR JENKINS
1st Assistant Accountant	MANDY BUTLER
Assistant Accountant	MICHELE D'ARCEY
Locations Manager	PETER LAWLESS
Production Coordinator	MEGAN WORTHY
Assistant Production Coordinator	KATHERINE GAMBLE
Production Secretary	JUSTINE VOLLMER
Hong Kong Kung Fu Coordinator	CAROL KIM
Assistant to the Wachowski Brothers	PHIL OOSTERHOUSE
Assistant to Joel Silver	MICHELLE TUELLA
Assistants to Barrie M. Osborne	ANNIE GILHOOLY
	ANGELA PRITCHARD
Assistant to Andrew Mason	EMMA JACOBS
Assistant to Dan Cracchiolo	ROB POLGAR
Assistant to Mr. Reeves	REINALDO PUENTES-TUCKI
Assistant to Mr. Fishburne	SANDRA HODGE
Australian Casting	MULLINARS CASTING
Extras Casting	TIM LITTLETON
Dialect Coach	SUZANNE CELESTE
Physical Trainers	DENISE SNYDER
	MICHELLE ROWE
Cast Sports Masseur	'LONGY' NGUYIN
Medical Advisors	DR. IAN I.T. ARMSTRONG, M.D.
	DR. JOSEPH M. HORRIGAN, D.C.
Publicist	FIONA SEARSON
Safety Coordinator	LAWRENCE WOODWARD
Safety Officers	SPIKE CHERRIE
	KERRY BLAKEMAN
Nurse	JACQUIE ROBERTSON
Unit Manager	WILL MATTHEWS
Assistant Unit Manager	GRAYDEN LE BRETON
Construction Supervisor	PHIL WORTH
Construction Coordinator	MARIANNE EVANS
Scenic Artist	PETER COLLIAS
Construction	JOHN PICKERING
	ANDREW STAIG
	MARCUS SMITH
	TONY BARDOLPH
	BRETT BARTLETT
	MARK GATT
	TERENCE LORD
	WAYNE PORTER
	JOHN REGA
	TREVOR SMITH
Caterers	KEVIN VARNES
	KERRY FETZER
	GUY FIRTH

2nd Unit

Director	BRUCE HUNT
Director of Photography	ROSS EMERY
1st Assistant Director	TOBY PEASE
Production Coordinators	JANE GRIFFIN
	JULIA PETERS
1st Assistant Camera	FRANK FLICK
Gaffer	PAUL JOHNSTONE
Best Boy	ROBBIE BURR
Key Grip	TOBY COPPING
Dolly Grip	BEN HYDE
Script Supervisor	GILLIAN STEINE
Video Operator	ANTHONY TOY
Locations Manager	ROBIN CLIFTON
Props	JAMES COX
	JAKE CLIFTON
	SHANE BENNETT
Makeup Artist	KATHY COURTNEY
Wardrobe	FIONA NICHOLLS
Unit Manager	SIMON LUCAS
Assistant Unit Manager	DICK BECKETT
Production Secretary	LIZZIE EVES
2nd Assistant Director	JEREMY SEDLEY
Production Aide	BELINDA DEAN

454

Titles Designed by   GREENBERG/SCHLUTER
Titles and Optics by   PACIFIC TITLE/MIRAGE

Soundtrack Album on MAVERICK RECORDS

"DISSOLVED GIRL"
Written by
ROBERT DEL NAJA, GRANTLEY MARSHALL,
ANDREW VOWLES, SARA J. AND MATT SCHWARTZ
Performed by MASSIVE ATTACK
Courtesy of VIRGIN RECORDS LTD.
by Arrangement with
VIRGIN RECORDS AMERICA, INC.

"MINDFIELDS"
Written by LIAM HOWLETT
Performed by PRODIGY
Courtesy of
MAVERICK RECORDING COMPANY/
XL RECORDINGS/BEGGAR'S BANQUET
By Arrangement with
WARNER SPECIAL PRODUCTS

"CLUBBED TO DEATH (KURAYAMINO MIX)"
Written by
ROB DOUGAN
Performed by ROB D
Courtesy of
A&M RECORDS LIMITED/
UNIVERSAL-ISLAND RECORDS
Under License from
UNIVERSAL MUSIC SPECIAL MARKETS

"BEGIN THE RUN"
FROM "NIGHT OF THE LEPUS"
Written by JAMIE HASKELL

"I'M BEGINNING TO SEE THE LIGHT"
Written by
DUKE ELLINGTON, DON GEORGE,
JOHNNY HODGES and HARRY JAMES
Performed by
DUKE ELLINGTON
Courtesy of
THE RCA RECORDS
LABEL OF BMG ENTERTAINMENT

"WAKE UP"
Written by
ZACK DE LA ROCHA, BRAD WILK,
TIM COMMERFORED and TOM MORELLO
Performed by
RAGE AGAINST THE MACHINE
Courtesy of EPIC RECORDS
By Arrangement with
SONY MUSIC LICENSING

"DRAGULA (HOT ROD HERMAN MIX)"
Written by
ROB ZOMBIE and SCOTT HUMPHREY
Performed by ROB ZOMBIE
Courtesy of GEFFEN RECORDS
Under License from
UNIVERSAL MUSIC SPECIAL MARKETS

"LEAVE YOU FAR BEHIND
(LUNATICS ROLLER COASTER MIX)"
Written by
SIMON SHACKLETON and HOWARD SAUNDERS
Performed by LUNATIC CALM
Courtesy of
UNIVERSAL MUSIC (UK) LTD.
Under License from
UNIVERSAL MUSIC SPECIAL MARKETS

"PRIME AUDIO SOUP"
Written by
JACK DANGERS and C.DODDPerformed by
Performed by MEAT BEAT MANIFESTO
Courtesy of NOTHING RECORDS
& PLAY IT AGAIN SAM/HEARTBEAT RECORDS
Under License from
UNIVERSAL MUSIC SPECIAL MARKETS

"MINOR SWING"
Written by DJANGO REINHARDT
and STEPHANE GRAPPELLI
Performed by DJANGO REINHARDT
Courtesy of
THE RCA RECORDS
LABEL OF BMG ENTERTAINMENT

"SPYBREAK!"
Written by ALEX GIFFORD
Performed by PROPELLERHEADS
Courtesy of
DREAMWORKS RECORDS/WALL OF SOUND
Under License from
UNIVERSAL MUSIC SPECIAL MARKETS/
PROPELLERHEADS

"ROCK IS DEAD"
Written by MARILYN MANSON,
TWIGGY RAMIREZ and MADONNA WAYNE GACY
Performed by MARILYN MANSON
Courtesy of NOTHING/INTERSCOPE RECORDS
Under License from
UNIVERSAL MUSIC SPECIAL MARKETS

Cinematography by SIMON CAROL ARCHIVE

The Prisoner Clip provided by POLYGRAM FILMED ENTERTAINMENT

The Producers wish to thank the following
THE CITY OF SYDNEY COUNCIL
THE NSW PREMIER'S DEPARTMENT
THE NSW FILM & TELEVISION OFFICE
CASA
THE MARITIME CENTRE, SYDNEY
STREETLIGHTS PROGRAM
AMX

Filmed on location in SYDNEY, AUSTRALIA
and at FOX STUDIOS AUSTRALIA

Filmed with PANAVISION® Camera and Lenses

Color by ATLAB AUSTRALIA

Prints by TECHNICOLOR®

KODAK Motion Picture Products

DOLBY DIGITAL in selected Theatres

DIGITAL DTS SOUND in selected Theatres

SONY DYNAMIC DIGITAL SOUND in selected Theatres

MOTION PICTURE ASSOCIATION OF AMERICA

THIS MOTION PICTURE
©1999 WARNER BROS. - - U.S., CANADA, BAHAMAS & BERMUDA
©1999 VILLAGE ROADSHOW FILMS (BVI) LIMITED - - ALL OTHER TERRITORIES

STORY AND SCREENPLAY
©1999 WARNER BROS. - - U.S., CANADA, BAHAMAS & BERMUDA
©1999 VILLAGE ROADSHOW FILMS (BVI) LIMITED - - ALL OTHER TERRITORIES

THE STORY, ALL NAMES, CHARACTERS AND INCIDENTS PORTRAYED IN THIS PRODUCTION ARE FICTICIOUS. NO IDENTIFICATION WITH ACTUAL PERSONS, PLACES, BUILDINGS AND PRODUCTS IS INTENDED OR SHOULD BE INFERRED.

THE MATRIX

www.whatisthematrix.com
password: steak

WARNER BROS.
A TIME WARNER ENTERTAINMENT COMPANY

SILVER
PICTURES

VILLAGE ROADSHOW PICTURES

THE ACADEMY AWARDS ®
FOUR NOMINATIONS • FOUR WINS

"First, THE MATRIX won the Oscar® for Best Sound. Then it won for best sound-effects editing. Fine, both were technical categories in a movie celebrated for its technical achievements. But then THE MATRIX beat out George Lukas's STAR WARS: EPISODE 1— THE PHANTOM MENACE and its groundbreaking special effects for the evening's best visual effects prize.

And finally it beat out AMERICAN BEAUTY, the eventual winner of the best-picture prize and four other Oscars®, for the film editing award."

— Rick Lyman, The New York Times

SOUND
John Reitz, Gregg Rudloff, David Campbell, and David Lee

Acceptance Speech
"This little guy represents so much hard work by so many people and we're very proud to be able to represent them tonight. There's too many to thank individually, but we do want to thank the Wachowski brothers and Joel Silver for being just a wonderful experience; they're a lot of fun to work with. And Joel, we truly appreciate all your trust and support. Thank you very much."

"This is smart filmmaking... Naive viewers may think THE MATRIX is just a cool way to pass the time while sitting in the PHANTOM MEN-ACE waiting room. They should think again, breathe deep, get strapped in for a brain popping trip. THE MATRIX is a careering cyber-ride without the headset, a virtual masterpiece. The Bible meets Batman; Lewis Carroll collides with William Gibson; Greek and Geek mythology bump and run."

— Richard Corliss, Time Magazine

SOUND EFFECTS EDITOR
Dane A. Davis

Acceptance Speech
"So, this is where the rabbit hole goes. I want to thank Larry and Andy Wachowski and Joel Silver, Zach Staenberg, and everybody at Warner Bros. for trusting me with such a terrific movie. It was a blast from start to finish. I want to thank our mixers, John, Greg, and Dave, con-gratulations. I want to thank my terrific crew, led by Julia Evershade, Bric Lindemann, John Reitz. I want to thank my mother and father, my wife Francine, my sons Jeremy and Ryan, for being there for me when I came back from being in the Matrix. This is a great honor. Thank you everyone in the Academy. Thank you."

FILM EDITOR
Zach Staenberg

Acceptance Speech
"Thank you very much. It's really wild being up here. Thank you, Larry and Andy Wachowski, for your vision, creativity, intelligence, daily inspiration, and most of all your friendship. You accomplished the seemingly impossible. A movie with action, suspense, and an intelligent, provocative message. Take the blue pill and stay where you are. Or take the red pill and see just how deep the rabbit hole goes. We had a great team, quite a few of whom have been honored here tonight. They made my work great. I'd like to thank Lorenzo Di Bonaventura and everybody at Warner Bros. for the creative freedom and support. Joel Silver and Barrie Osborne for fighting some good fights on our behalf. My entire assistant editing team led by Peter Skarratt, you all know who you are. Thanks to my wife Bonnie, my son Robert, I love you. There is no spoon."

MATRIX SETS DVD MARK
"HOLLYWOOD — Warner Bros. has shipped a record-breaking 1.5 million units of its THE MATRIX DVD to retailers in a little over a week."

— Marc Graser, Daily Variety

VISUAL EFFECTS
John Gaeta, Janek Sirrs, Steve Courtley, and Jon Thum

Acceptance Speech
"Andy and Larry Wachowski, this is their vision on the screen. These guys made my decade. They gave my career a path and I am most thankful. And they are great friends of all of ours. They're very by the heart. They're making their films. I'd like to dedicate this to my son Skylar, this is inspiration. I'd like to thank my wife Rose for standing by me through all of this. I'd like to thank the executive producers, Barrie Osborne, Andrew Mason, ultra-producer Joel Silver. I'd like to thank Lorenzo Di Bonaventura of Warner Bros., for standing behind a very risky picture, and really making this film what the filmmakers wanted it to be. I want to point out that there are some great visual effects companies that did this picture. MVFX, Rob Bobo, thank you very much for putting all of your efforts behind innovation, behind the spirit of doing visual effects in service to a story. I'd like to thank Animal Logic and Dfilm for quality work and a great experience. And most of all the artists. WhatIsTheMatrix.com. Go there."

WhatIsTheMatrix.com
"GRADE A. The site absolutely captures the film's futuristic world. Add the cyber-comic book, Shockwave game, and the interview with the boom operator, and you've got THE MATRIX for a winner."

— James Oliver Cury, Entertainment Weekly

KEY ART
+
STILLS

For the most part, this section presents a selection of stills from the finished film, with a smattering of corresponding storyboards.

However, pages 458, 460, and 462 showcase a selection of possible key art (one-sheet theatrical posters) done for the film prior to release.

Page 458 is the version finally selected as the U.S. key art.

Page 460 is the first of two posters almost selected. While not chosen as the theatrical poster, this image, referred to as the Fetus Pod poster, did get seen in the occasional ad.

Page 462 was seen the least. Referred to as The Waterfall poster, prior to this book, its only use was as the back cover of the international press packet.

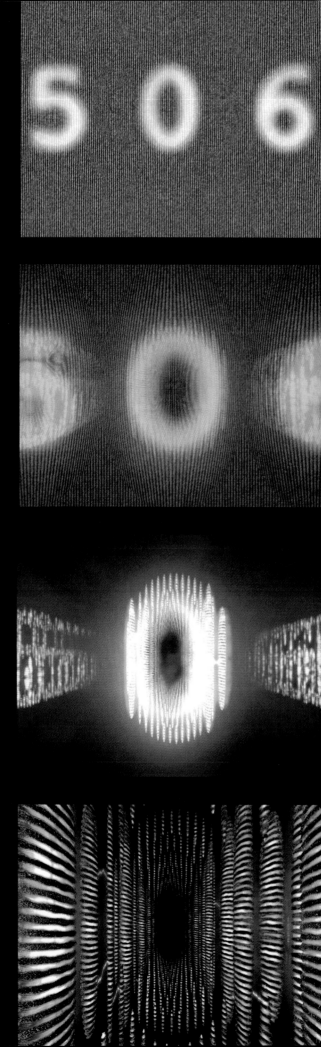

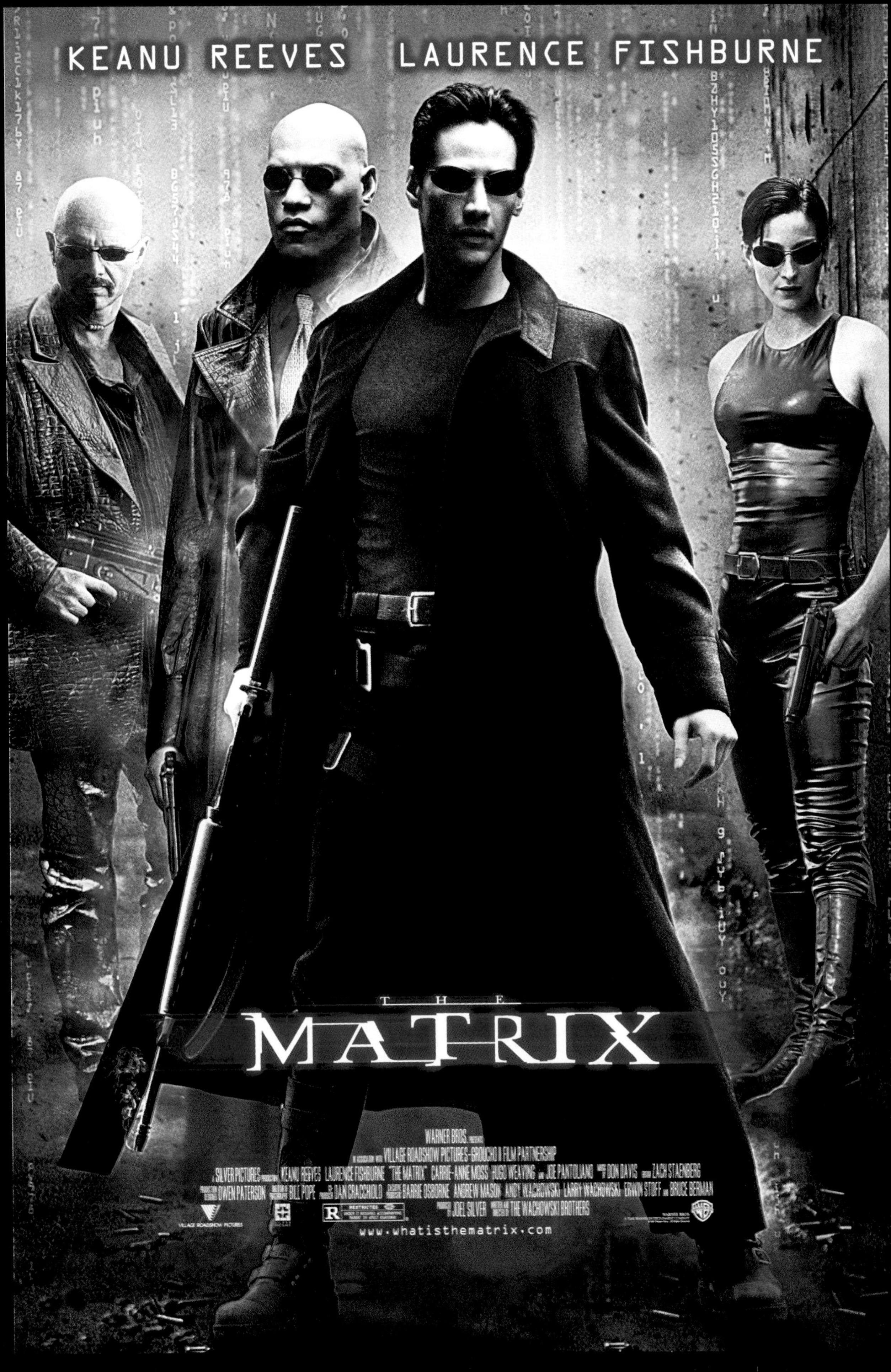
KEANU REEVES
LAURENCE FISHBURNE
THE
MATRIX
WARNER BROS.
VILLAGE ROADSHOW PICTURES-GROUCHO II FILM PARTNERSHIP
SILVER PICTURES
KEANU REEVES LAURENCE FISHBURNE "THE MATRIX" CARRIE-ANNE MOSS HUGO WEAVING JOE PANTOLIANO DON DAVIS ZACH STAENBERG
OWEN PATERSON BILL POPE DAN CRACCHIOLO BARRIE OSBORNE ANDREW MASON ANDY WACHOWSKI LARRY WACHOWSKI ERWIN STOFF BRUCE BERMAN
JOEL SILVER THE WACHOWSKI BROTHERS
VILLAGE ROADSHOW PICTURES
R
RESTRICTED
www.whatisthematrix.com

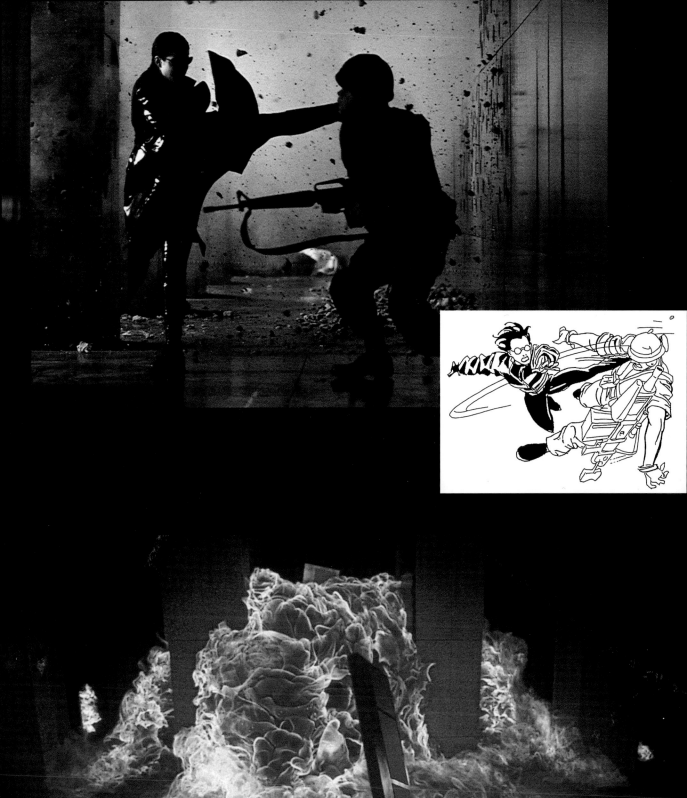

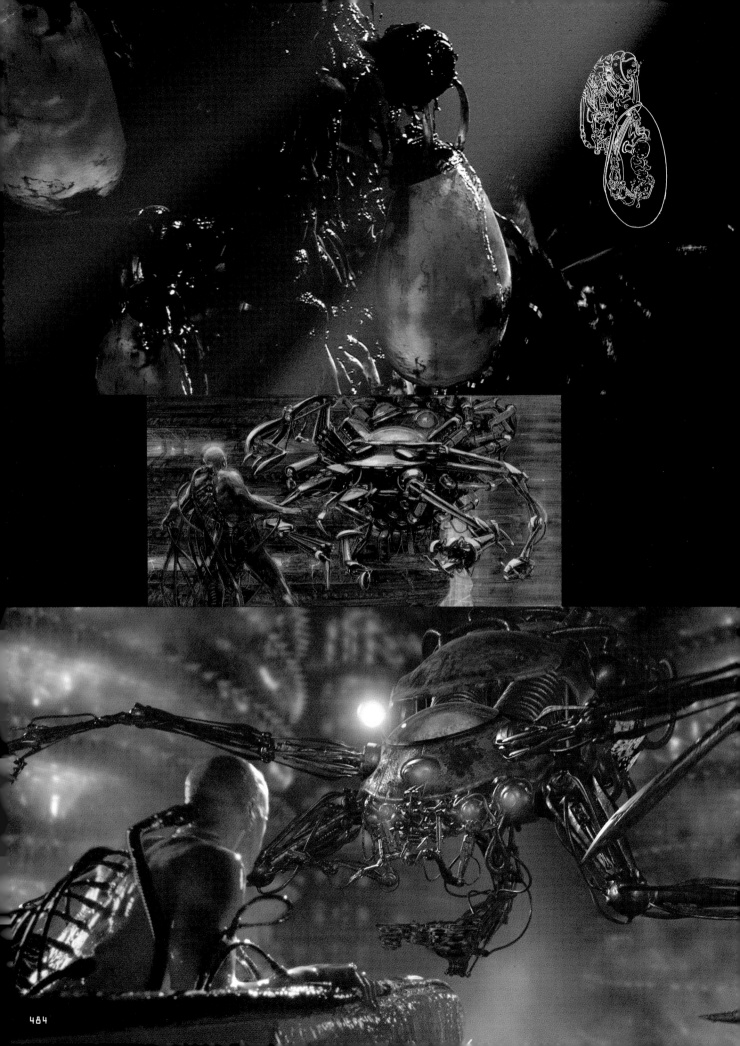

THE MATRIX

Sequels are under way.

There will be two,
filmed backed to back.

At the time of this writing, the production office has been open
for over a month and a half. Officially, the start came with the
toss of a bottle against an outside wall on June 10th, 2000.

However, it should be noted, the script writing and
storyboarding process began months before.

The scripts are done.

Steve Skroce, Geof Darrow, and a slew of new artists continue
to work on the storyboards and conceptuals.

The Oscar® winning team from MVFX, led by John Gaeta, are
already developing new techniques to visualize the FX in the
scripts by Larry and Andy Wachowski.

Keanu Reeves, Laurence Fishburne, Carrie-Anne Moss, and
Hugo Weaving, among others, are returning. Along with a
good many new faces.   °

Physical training begins shortly.

Principal photography begins in 2001.

For breaking news, remain plugged in, via:

WhatIsTheMatrix.com

LARRY AND ANDY WACHOWSKI

Larry and And Wachowski (Writers/Directors) have been working together for 32 years. Little else is known about them.

STEVE SKROCE

Steve Skroce hails from Canada. A long-established comic-book artist, his credits include runs on the books ECTOKID, THE AMAZING SPIDER-MAN, CABLE and X-MEN. THE MATRIX is his first foray into storyboarding. Most recently, he expanded his role as artist to include writing, where he both illustrates and writes a four-issue story arc for Marvel Comics' WOLVERINE. Currently, Steve is storyboarding THE MATRIX sequels. Next up, he plans to write and illustrate a comic series based on characters he creates.

GEOF DARROW

Geof Darrow was born in Iowa, but no longer lives there. His career as a comic-book artist includes such noted titles as HARD BOILED and BIG GUY AND RUSTY THE BOY ROBOT, both by Frank Miller, ANOTHER CHANCE TO GET IT RIGHT by Andrew Vachss, and coming soon from Dark Horse Comics, SHAOLIN COWBOY, where he both illustrates and writes. Recently, Geof began the massive task of conceptual designs for THE MATRIX sequels.

TANI KUNITAKE

Born in Detroit, Michigan, Tani studied industrial design at the Center for Creative Studies in Detroit. From there, he went on to storyboarding for commercials at Industrial Light and Magic. He swiftly moved into storyboarding special effects for film at Digital Domain, establishing himself as a production illustrator through production designer Alex McDowell. Films he has worked on include FIGHT CLUB, FEAR AND LOATHING IN LAS VEGAS, ARMAGEDDON, BLADE, WHAT DREAMS MAY COME, THE ROCK, THE CHAMBER, BATMAN AND ROBIN and THE CROW II.

WARREN MANSER

Originally from Detroit, Warren studied industrial design, majoring in transportation. While working in the auto industry, he designed the Ford SPLASH show car. In 1990, he relocated to Los Angeles, where he has been involved in a wide variety of projects, covering theme parks, animation, video games, and film design. Besides THE MATRIX, Warren has provided conceptual art for films such as THE LOST WORLD, AMISTAD, CASTAWAY, TWELVE MONKEYS, THE PATRIOT, and, one of his personal favorites, EVIL DEAD III: THE ARMY OF DARKNESS. Currently, Warren is back at work on the Warner Bros./DreamWorks co-production A.I., directed by Steven Spielberg, based on Stanley Kubrick's epic tale.

COLLIN GRANT

Collin Grant was born in England. He worked for a number of years in advertising, visualizing products for commercials. In 1994 Collin moved to Los Angeles and began working on storyboards for feature films. The first film he tackled was Luc Besson's THE FIFTH ELEMENT. From there he worked on THE EDGE, BATMAN AND ROBIN, STIGMATA, END OF DAYS, ARMEGEDDON, and INSPECTOR GADGET, among others.

ZACH STAENBERG

Editor Zach Staenberg, a graduate of the University of Wisconsin at Madison, with a degree in communications, began his film career as a production assistant on Brian De Palma's THE FURY. On his next feature, THE OMEN II, he became an apprentice editor and, from that experience, decided to concentrate on editing. Among his film credits are POLICE ACADEMY, THE TENDER, NOWHERE TO RUN, EYES OF AN ANGEL, BLACKOUT, STRIPPED TO KILL, and BOUND. His television credits include the 1997 Robert Harmon feature GOTTI for HBO (for which he was nominated for an Emmy,® a CableACE Award and won an American Cinema Editors' Eddie Award), as well as the films WEAPONS OF MASS DISTRACTION, CISCO KID, CONNAGHER and LA PASTORELA. For THE MATRIX, he has won his second Eddie Award and his first Oscar.®

PHIL OOSTERHOUSE

Phil Oosterhouse was born in Grand Rapids, Michigan. After studying philosophy, English, and photography at Calvin College, he moved to Los Angeles. In LA, he spent some time writing and working until he took a job as Larry and Andy Wachowski's assistant on BOUND. This job continued through production of THE MATRIX. For the sequels, he will be the Associate Producer.

SPENCER LAMM

Born in New York, Spencer studied literature and film at NYU. In 1998 he formed REDPILL PRODUCTIONS (Redpill.com), producing the official websites for Warner Bros.' THE MATRIX (WhatIsTheMatrix.com and HackThe Matrix.com). Currently, he is preparing for the sequels, developing new content for these ever evolving sites. A past editor at Marvel Comics, Spencer also edits THE MATRIX comic-book stories, which includes such talent as Geof Darrow (HARD BOILED), Paul Chadwick (CONCRETE), John Van Fleet (BATMAN: THE ANKH), Neil Gaiman (SANDMAN) and Dave Gibbons (WATCHMEN). The stories, set in the world of THE MATRIX, are free to download and can be found at...

WhatIsTheMatrix.com

...oes Neo die at the end or does Morpheus? unhappy battery Wednesday, April 14, 1999 at 10:33 AM PDT I got two F's on my Report card! I cant see the Matrix for a Week! NOOOOO! OOoTrinity Wednesday, April 14, 1999 at 10:33 AM PDT HEY! this site put Matrix over the matrix!! OOoTrinity I need to see the movie again... Dadealer Wednesday, April 14, 1999 at 10:30 AM PDT When is the sequel coming out? Great movie. I want to see the sequel, if th Dadealer Wednesday, April 14, 1999 at 10:29 AM PDT Nebuchadnezzar was the king of Babylon who took the Jews into captivity. In the 2nd chapter of Daniel, he has a dream that really, really bugs him, and he has to find out what it me 10:28 AM PDT The matrix has found you. Hello, Andy! Andy B Wednesday, April 14, 1999 at 10:28 AM PDT I NEED A SEQUEL!! ZZaT Wednesday, April 14, 1999 at 10:27 AM PDT anyone have any clue to what's on the disks neo is c M PDT I don't understand alive... who is Nebuchadnezzar? unhappy battery Wednesday, April 14, 1999 at 10:26 AM PDT dyla: Watch the movie again and stay through the end of the credits. Also, poke around this website, including pas pril 14, 1999 at 10:25 AM PDT battery: And Nebuchadnezzar, in the Bible, was desperate to find the meaning of his dream. ALiVE Wednesday, April 14, 1999 at 10:24 AM PDT Here are the codes: Steak deja vu Neo Morpheus Trinity g 4, 1999 at 10:23 AM PDT anyone know what the button in the corner looking for a code email is about? dyla Wednesday, April 14, 1999 at 10:22 AM PDT Who knows when the sequel will come out? mia Wednesday, April 14, 1999 at xtraordinary movie. Amir Wednesday, April 14, 1999 at 10:19 AM PDT battery: How about prophecies? (And the matrix itself.) ALiVE Wednesday, April 14, 1999 at 10:17 AM PDT I SAW THE MOVIE!!! IT WAS INCREDIBLY MIND-BOGG ne by Paul Chadwick. Gave it away at movie theaters... It's pretty amazing. The thing has pin-ups by other guys, Bill Sienkiewicz and some others. I hear the directors are writing one for the site... Bring'em on... comic fan Wednesday, A or purchase? Where can i get em? Neo Wednesday, April 14, 1999 at 10:14 AM PDT There are going to be comic book stories??!!! Yeah, baby!! Great friggin movie! Want more. Comics at the site, very cool!!! Are they going to be printed ead, their on the soundtrack. enzo Wednesday, April 14, 1999 at 10:12 AM PDT What is the song that Neo is listening to on his headphones when Trinity first contacts him over his computer? MrMiz Wednesday, April 14, 1999 at 10:0 :12-17. ALiVE Wednesday, April 14, 1999 at 10:02 AM PDT your movie kicked ass!! chris day Wednesday, April 14, 1999 at 10:01 AM PDT Awesome movie...when is the sequel? Keith K Wednesday, April 14, 1999 at 10:00 AM PDT omething is wrong and there must be more than this), let's talk. ALiVE Wednesday, April 14, 1999 at 9:55 AM PDT Hi I am a big fan of The Matrix, I know I probably not the first person who has said this. Great Movie! I saw it last nigh 999 at 9:53 AM PDT The Matrix kicks ass! And is or is not Keanu FINE in this movie, or what? Valerie Wednesday, April 14, 1999 at 9:53 AM PDT The Matrix is finger licken good234235569785374808768509687085924057437 ok like neo. could you please give me the mark of all the clothes that he wears ryo Wednesday, April 14, 1999 at 9:49 AM PDT One would like to remind you that the rules are all in your mind, for one to hack the matrix it is required that plendor Sanction Wednesday, April 14, 1999 at 9:45 AM PDT The Matrix is a network of humans connected to a central computer that feeds them information, making them believe that they are actually living the program being download o Power. By favouring strength over religious qualities, asceticism over loving thy neighbour'. This is the world we should be in, and now the dream can be realised, subconsciously; The weak shall perish, as they should. Wowbagger Wedne masterpiece! Daniel Wednesday, April 14, 1999 at 9:41 AM PDT The Matrix? Only the most ass kicking movie ever!!! Keep it real and how about a sequel? Maxim Wednesday, April 14, 1999 at 9:41 AM PDT Sorry, Mia. Don't get all of omething my whole life, perhaps the matrix is the best explanation for what I have felt. please help if you're out there, help me Wednesday, April 14, 1999 at 9:41 AM PDT Is the world a computer program which keeps humans from the t pril 14, 1999 at 9:40 AM PDT Not quite, try agentbullettime ALiVE Wednesday, April 14, 1999 at 9:38 AM PDT When is someone gonna come here and get me out of this matrixing Matrix?? Ryan C Wednesday, April 14, 1999 at 9:3 ur own subconscious, our imagination and our dreams. Our lives are separate, but our mind is trapped inside the Matrix. believer Wednesday, April 14, 1999 at 9:33 AM PDT THE MATRIX IS HOW YOU PERCEIVE THE WORLD AROUND Wednesday, April 14, 1999 at 9:31 AM PDT Whatever you want it to be... Tripper Wednesday, April 14, 1999 at 9:29 AM PDT Magus, there are probably far too many messages for people connected to the movie to read them all. But t 9:28 AM PDT code: mirrormirror ALiVE Wednesday, April 14, 1999 at 9:27 AM PDT Hi, I was wondering what the cell phones they use in the movie are? Nokia? Motorola? What model? Thanks! Mageus Protagonist Wednesday, April 1 999 at 9:24 AM PDT steak jeff Wednesday, April 14, 1999 at 9:23 AM PDT Are these messages read by someone in the "real world"? Magus Wednesday, April 14, 1999 at 9:22 AM PDT To ALiVE: The Biblical equivalent to the Matrix pril 14, 1999 at 9:22 AM PDT So... are we just jacked in somewhere virtually discussing the "MATRIX", or are we jacked in somewhere virtually being jacked in somewhere else virtually discussing the "MATRIX", or... The Matrix is WHAT we pril 14, 1999 at 9:18 AM PDT The Matrix was a kick ass movie. The camera angles were very creative. The martial arts in this movie were done incredibly well. And the plot of the whole movie makes you wonder. Laurence Fishburne red AI (artificial intelligence) computers, the computers began to 'take over' The best that the humans of this era could come up w/ to save humanity was to 'block out' the sun. The AIC's (<- see above) should have stopped working. How help? D'Hero Wednesday, April 14, 1999 at 9:11 AM PDT The Matrix is all around us all the time. Reality is not what is given to you...its what you make of reality XdevilBearX Wednesday, April 14, 1999 at 9:11 AM PDT Explore the v bdes to "enter the matrix"? Just Wondering Wednesday, April 14, 1999 at 9:05 AM PDT whiteghosts: Click around until you're asked to enter a code. (You can do it right on this screen.) ALiVE Wednesday, April 14, 1999 at 9:04 AM PD ne W brothers did that was so ground-breaking was to use the style of Japanese animation, except with live actors. ALiVE Wednesday, April 14, 1999 at 9:01 AM PDT THE MATRIX is the thing that we all perceive and accept as the tru eems to stop. AliVE Wednesday, April 14, 1999 at 8:58 AM PDT One of the best sci-fi movies I have ever seen. The special effects are like nothing you have ever seen before. Be prepared for the movie experience of your life. I told some rove it. Imagine a design for a new car. Imagine a design totally new and original, something not based on stuff that you have seen, heard, or been told about. It's impossible. No matter what you picture in your head, it'll probably have a ti lea come from' Haven't you seen this before somewhere? Maybe you saw it in a movie or perhaps read about it in a book. The truth is that we are all programmed into believing in originality, an originality that cannot and does not exist. O Wednesday, April 14, 1999 at 7:14 AM PDT Note that NEO is an anagram for the ONE. ALiVE Wednesday, April 14, 1999 at 8:54 AM PDT well i guess i'd still be more satisfied with the movie by thinking of neo as the superman who bking as well as fun and aesthetically pleasing. A must see. Claire Wednesday, April 14, 1999 at 8:53 AM PDT pshyco, one of the great things about the movie is that it has so many different layers. You can enjoy it on many levels. But an I get a pair? Joe Wednesday, April 14, 1999 at 8:50 AM PDT Oh yes, the ship... As the W brothers noted in this week's TIME magazine, Nebuchadnezzar had a dream that disturbed him, and he desperately wanted to know what it me ersations with friends after watching the movie that I started to realize the similarities. Alice Wednesday, April 14, 1999 at 8:46 AM PDT So the list now stands at The holy TRINITY, the betrayal of Jesus by Judas, The resurrection, Zion 4, 1999 at 8:46 AM PDT ALive, I agree with you, but I didn't really notice them while watching the movie. missa Wednesday, April 14, 1999 at 8:45 AM PDT Ah yes, coming back to life, I forgot about that one.unhappy battery Wednes :44 AM PDT why wouldn't she be in the credits? Even small parts get into them, don't they? I'm sure you could find the name if you watched it again. Missa Wednesday, April 14, 1999 at 8:43 AM PDT This is one of the best sites I hav aradox Wednesday, April 14, 1999 at 8:42 AM PDT Best movie in a very long time. Very interesting Jesus reference with his coming to save mankind, and the death and ressurection. The wire stunts made me gape open mouthed. When pril 14, 1999 at 8:40 AM PDT i loved the movie, especially when keanu was learning all of those martial arts. Also, the end scene when the sentinels are coming and Neo kills the agents. cool movie altogether Ksilebo Wednesday, April 1 2 or say 3 hundred years or more Artificial intelligence has been created and we are in the Matrix right now. Plausible? I say yes. Or imagine that it is supreme Extraterrestrials that are watching us and controlling us taking a few poor s ell into paranoid delusions. Mote Wednesday, April 14, 1999 at 8:30 AM PDT how does this code stuff work? do they give out a new code everyday or once a week or random? richie Wednesday, April 14, 1999 at 8:26 AM PDT The m lightest consideration or if there is no scientific proof that it is so. Ouch. unhappy battery Wednesday, April 14, 1999 at 8:24 AM PDT can the matrix survive without agents peter Wednesday, April 14, 1999 at 8:23 AM PDT Matrix rot :11 AM PDT This movie simply rocks hard core!! Scales Wednesday, April 14, 1999 at 8:08 AM PDT I haven't gone to see the movie yet, but I'm going this weekend and I've heard it was pretty good!! By the looks of all these people, it r M PDT Great movie!!! Really worth the dough! I had high expectations and was not disappointed at all! Great SFX and awesome fight scenes! Hope you guys come up with another soon! Mr. D Wednesday, April 14, 1999 at 7:57 AM PDT alent with all the distractions of everyday life. Hopefully, like in the movie, I can find the inspiration that I need to come out on top. The movie was great! mikal Wednesday, April 14, 1999 at 7:53 AM PDT the hippest movie of the year, w hree times now and I could watch it over and over and over and over and over... you get the point. Strange thing - last night I had a dream that I thought was real, I was trying to figure out if I had dreamt something that was happening. :50 AM PDT This movie is the type that never makes me tired. COOL STUFF Bong Wednesday, April 14, 1999 at 7:49 AM PDT I've seen this movie 4 times now. That movie is the Bomb. I loved it. Me and my friend got so hyped after th ot be gleaned from this website. darwin Wednesday, April 14, 1999 at 7:48 AM PDT One thing I think is that most people fail to see the underlying issues in this movie. 1. We as a human race created AI. And therefore created our ow end me anything and everything you can on it. I want a copy of the story and wallpaper and the works! Thanks! Patrick Wednesday, April 14, 1999 at 7:44 AM PDT COOL Dan Wednesday, April 14, 1999 at 7:42 AM PDT He'd operated on he world you want to be in. Cho Wednesday, April 14, 1999 at 7:37 AM PDT The Matrix is a highly advanced ever expanding computer program designed by robots to deceive the human race. The humans in the Matrix actually think it i 4, 1999 at 7:34 AM PDT The Matrix is a good movie, there should be more movies like that. I think there is a review about the Matrix on Dateline NBC @ 10pm @ Wednesday, April 14, 1999 at 7:34 AM PDT Our entire existence pete bly beautiful K Wednesday, April 14, 1999 at 7:33 AM PDT This movie kicked ass! Curtis Wednesday, April 14, 1999 at 7:32 AM PDT I believe the movie Matrix has a lot of meaning for today's world. For instance, there is no doubt th haracter was Trinity....Joanna Wednesday, April 14, 1999 at 7:29 AM PDT Isn't matrix the surround sound on tv's anyways, its a super computer in the future, that has experiments with people's minds when they are in that goop. it is rs'...there IS a hacker named Trinity who DID hack into the IRS...i wanna find more info about these people...I reckon it'd be cool to contact them. Morgant Wednesday, April 14, 1999 at 7:25 AM PDT steak Dave P. Jr. Wednesday, April 999 at 7:24 AM PDT Morgant I can fly! Can you? I left the matrix the other night and it was a blast. Anyone can do it if they first give themselves permission to, then just FREE YOURSELF!! gotta fly.now it's so much fun!!! freedreamer W :21 AM PDT anyone have a url of the real "Trinity" not carrie-anne moss _-= Morgant =-_ Wednesday, April 14, 1999 at 7:21 AM PDT This movie kicked ass and made me think. Very well done movie. Looking forward to seeing it on DV Wednesday, April 14, 1999 at 7:20 AM PDT what kind of glasses does reeves wear in the movie? Duh Wednesday, April 14, 1999 at 7:19 AM PDT The Matrix is what you make it to be, the Matrix is the ultimate prison for your mind Wednesday, April 14, 1999 at 7:17 AM PDT The Matrix is the ultimate battery charger. Duracel Wednesday, April 14, 1999 at 7:16 AM PDT The Matrix is the place where anything we can imagine can come true. I bet in the Matrix every artial arts. Not bad at all for only 4 months of training. I hope he uses it again in the future! This is a movie I didn't want to end. halo 4 Wednesday, April 14, 1999 at 7:15 AM PDT how old is the girl that played trinity marc Wednesday, eally part of the matrix too?? all is possible. Daggie Wednesday, April 14, 1999 at 7:14 AM PDT I have seen the movie and loved it. Boy does it raise questions about what 'big brother' could get up to! Well done & thanks... kym Wednes ttime,and lobby Thats all I know. For now anyway... darwin Wednesday, April 14, 1999 at 7:07 AM PDT the matrix is a computer that creates a reality by reading the human mind and display by stimulating the neurons of the brain to cre appened to?? Acid Burn Wednesday, April 14, 1999 at 7:02 AM PDT Great special effects!!! Great story!!! BUT...the ending wasn't what I was hoping for. I was expecting to see him fight all the droids and save the world from the matrix. azMan Wednesday, April 14, 1999 at 6:58 AM PDT is anyone as addicted to this movie as i am? one addicted fan Wednesday, April 14, 1999 at 6:57 AM PDT Does anyone online this morning have any insight into the significance of t :54 AM PDT Loved the matrix. Saw it three times. Make sure your movie theater has Digital Surround Sound! It's the only way to see it!! kim Wednesday, April 14, 1999 at 6:54 AM PDT The Matrix is the world that has been pulled over ame "banner" at the top. THAT's your secret entry portal. That's where you type "steak". Also, type in your email address to get a different password that does something else. Asmodeus Wednesday, April 14, 1999 at 6:51 AM PDT click c pril 14, 1999 at 6:43 AM PDT Follow the white rabbit, and stay in wonderland and i'll show you how far the rabbit hole goes- it's Wonderland Laadidaaians Wednesday, April 14, 1999 at 6:40 AM PDT what's going on with this Password ad to concentrate alot on it to to get the plot, so not one to bring your gf/bf to. The actors were brilliant, Keanu played the part very well (as well as the other actors). Great movie. Kags Wednesday, April 14, 1999 at 6:39 AM PDT Yo E 4, 1999 at 6:36 AM PDT i thought Trinity acted her part the best...Morpheus was pretty good too. Tammie, where in the credits was this password? _-= Morgant =-_ Wednesday, April 14, 1999 at 6:33 AM PDT It's like a cool computer econd (or less). I hope they make a sequel or something where they wipe out the machines. Even so, this show ROCKS!!! Steve Wednesday, April 14, 1999 at 6:29 AM PDT An alternate reality Grant Wednesday, April 14, 1999 at 6:2 rama, and a little comedy. WillZ™ Wednesday, April 14, 1999 at 6:15 AM PDT i thought the movie rocked by the way...seen it twice so far and wanna keep going _-= Morgant =-_ Wednesday, April 14, 1999 at 6:13 AM PDT The first nd i loved it but it's a bit unbelievable but what movie isn't 10/10 Azzer Wednesday, April 14, 1999 at 6:09 AM PDT steak...machan Wednesday, April 14, 1999 at 6:06 AM PDT A consensual hallucination experienced by millions daily. he film is concerned, is a Virtual Reality World which imprisons the minds of humanity, leading them to believe they are living in a real world. MAGUS Wednesday, April 14, 1999 at 5:50 AM PDT I think if you only saw it once, you should idn't cost me anything. It was an awesome movie, I loved the martial arts scene. DW Wednesday, April 14, 1999 at 5:41 AM PDT If you are just about to eat some pizza, you are not tasting it yourself, the matrix sends waves to your m that you smell. It is what you see when you look out of the window, when you wake up in the morning, when you come home at the end of the day. The matrix is a false world the world you are in now. The world we are living in is just a falsi 999 at 5:29 AM PDT How's life. Is it really life. Am I really typing this message to you??? Who knows?? Hey send some cool stuff for me to look at. Talk to you later. Will I?? See ya'. monkey Wednesday, April 14, 1999 at 5:29 AM PDT M omes up, type 'steak' instead of an e mail. Wednesday, April 14, 1999 at 4:57 AM PDT Nope, I haven't got the password, I was too busy being thrilled by trailing thoughts of the movie to pay attention, and I had to pee real bad! alonda W Wednesday, April 14, 1999 at 4:46 AM PDT I don't know what the password is for kate alonda Wednesday, April 14, 1999 at 4:46 AM PDT At the end of the credits it says the webpage address then gave a password - what's it for? Vednesday, April 14, 1999 at 3:59 AM PDT Certainly the reason this movie is so unpredictably successful is not from the individuals that see The Matrix...It is from those individuals that see it repeatedly. But am I going to throw the fir inking about this movie, it is by far the BEST I'VE EVER SEEN! It combines a captivating plot with a hot) well known actor, excellent special fx, and an awesome soundtrack all in one! i'll never forget it (or stop thinking about it) and can't w how the truth out there: of 'what is the Matrix'...Princess Wednesday, April 14, 1999 at 3:50 AM PDT If you don't get it the first time you see it, try seeing it again! You will understand "everything² right from the very start!! redpilz Wed omething we cannot tell u, it is something u have to see for urselves!!! hehehehe Wednesday, April 14, 1999 at 3:40 AM PDT My Life Was Changed After This Film Ven Wednesday, April 14, 1999 at 3:31 AM PDT The Matrix is the Best just has a nose clip. Thanx! Dan Wednesday, April 14, 1999 at 2:38 AM PDT THE MATRIX IS CLOSER TO REALITY THAN YOU THINK. I KNOW! BLUEPILL Wednesday, April 14, 1999 at 2:35 AM PDT The matrix is everywhere Nox W MOVIE The Matrix Wednesday, April 14, 1999 at 1:57 AM PDT WOW!!! Dark Schneider Wednesday, April 14, 1999 at 1:54 AM PDT Drew If I could I would, but nowhere in the known universe that I can reach in my own lifetime is safe fr ave D.K Wednesday, April 14, 1999 at 1:49 AM PDT An awesome well thought out movie. Plot twists and effects were super. It was an absolutely great movie! See it again Putain Wednesday, April 14, 1999 at 1:47 AM PDT And for thos would be a living Hell. So just stop making out that you are experts on something which you have not experienced, especially since there is no indication it exists. If there is a Matrix, you are already linked to it, for if anything fits the defin ee! It's an uncontrollable world which can be changed easily and drastically. The reason for this is due to the fact it's a computer program... a program for our minds. Our bodies are in one place and our minds are set off in The Matrix. Thi ink. Cupid Wednesday, April 14, 1999 at 1:16 AM PDT Love the site! Terry D Wednesday, April 14, 1999 at 1:14 AM PDT the matrix is a computer generated reality that is the coolest thing in the world i know from experience. matrix ttempt to inform us about reality. All roads in Matrix point to an Invisible agenda - each member of Morpheus' group being a member of an Invisible cell, the awakening that each person must go through, the general conspiracy and alte Vednesday, April 14, 1999 at 1:03 AM PDT There is a Matrix comic series? Cool! Solshade Wednesday, April 14, 1999 at 12:59 AM PDT Wow, I Love Keanu Reeves, he's so matrixy... i love him, i love him–kiss! Angela Wednesday ocked I've seen it three times already. Jon Wednesday, April 14, 1999 at 12:54 AM PDT We all are presently living in our own self created matrix and should be "conscious" to this fact, we all live in our own prison ('ruts') by what we con unds us whilst knowing when to have blind faith and the belief to trust, (esp. in what we know and feel is right) share and grow to reach all we can become. Only at the individual level will the war be won to break free of the matrix we ex LEASURE TO EXPERIENCE. I'VE SEEN IT FOUR TIMES AND I'M STILL DYING TO SEE IT AGAIN. THE STORY, SPECIAL EFFECTS, CAMERA PHOTOGRAPHY NOT TO MENTION THE ACTING OF THIS MOTION PICTURE WAS WELL CREATED the whole entire web. Hey a great web page for the greatest movie ever, who could ask for any thing more. I come here every day to play your game or just fiddle. Thanks Kyle Wednesday, April 14, 1999 at 12:40 AM PDT the matrix is a r s as a power source. The problem was that humans can't survive without purpose and consciousness, so it created a world for our minds in which we would live without ever knowing that this was not the real world but just a computer pri y. When in truth, it is a device of enslavement by the machine to extract from us the energy it needs to sustain itself. This is the truth that we have been blinded from since birth. The memories we have and senses we believe tell us of o d by the machines. Created in order to pacify and control the human mind and the "human crops", so that their bodies can be used for sweet energy. matrixeus Wednesday, April 14, 1999 at 12:29 AM PDT This is without doubt. THE BE 4, 1999 at 12:25 AM PDT Everyone that is coming to this site should have seen the movie by now, cause its really great...(don't read this if you haven't seen it, and are planning to) The Matrix is a 'virtual reality', in which people just live ondered that at times? What you saw in the movie is just a small part of what really is going on. Look at the big picture, The Matrix is what we all see in every day life, what we touch/smell/see/hear it's all a lie. "Trust No One" if you thi how who had seen the film. In my opinion, the Agents had to be cold and detached for them to be an effective force. No love and sentiments for them. As for the women being butch, please, people! They just cut their hair short for the part eseen several times. There has got to be a sequel! Karl Wednesday, April 14, 1999 at 12:18 AM PDT The Matrix is an illusion, an illusion all people live under James H Wednesday, April 14, 1999 at 12:15 AM PDT The Matrix is the 07 Wednesday, April 14, 1999 at 12:13 AM PDT This site rules Jordan Wednesday, April 14, 1999 at 12:06 AM PDT The Movie rocks!!! I'm curently making a review for the Matrix. I've found several great sites for info. This is arson all you have to do is BELIVE. The Matrix Wednesday, April 14, 1999 at 12:06 AM PDT Geof skroce darrow wrong number guns morpheus trinity deja vu steak agentbullettime crash lobby mirrormirror neobullettime sentinel nebucha st impact of any I have EVER seen. I came out thinking, what if it's real? We could be surrounded by exactly that, reality right now, and we'll never know it. Escape the boundaries of your mind. Wake up and smell the revolution. You are on 3, 1999 at 11:55 PM PDT I think that this website rocks. SKOot Tuesday, April 13, 1999 at 11:55 PM PDT The Matrix is an excellent movie! It not only challenges the mind, but makes you wonder about what we perceive as reality. Qua 3, 1999 at 11:51 PM Hi there. I just saw The Matrix and I must say it was excellent. I liked the special effects. Thanks for filming it in australia, Sydney. If you haven't guessed I am an Aussie. The movie has been a great sucess here. I wesome. The Matrix had the best special effects I have seen. I would say it is a movie I could watch over and over again. Robert Tuesday, April 13, 1999 at 11:41 PM PDT Keep these movies' coming, I love them and they aren't that far from reality. san l 13, 1999 at 11:40 PM This